Modern Political Regimes

Patterns and Institutions

Roy C. Macridis
Brandeis University

Little, Brown and Company Boston Toronto

Library of Congress Cataloging in Publication Data

Macridis, Roy C.
Modern political regimes.

Bibliography
Includes index.
1. Comparative government. I. Title.
JF51.M325 1985 320.3 85-12892
ISBN 0-316-54285-7

Library of Congress Catalog Card No. 85-12892

9 8 7 6 5 4 3 2

ALP

Published simultaneously in Canada by Little, Brown & Company (Canada) Limited

Printed in the United States of America

To Daniel and Alexi

Preface

Men and women in society live a "structured" and "patterned" life. They have "roles" to play and "functions" to perform — things that they are expected to do not when whim and fancy strike but as a matter of "obligation." There are "norms" — expected, learned, and valued obligations, things that have to be done — and "forms" — crystalized formal procedures of how to do them. "Norms" and "forms" make up the institutions in which we live. Life in society is highly "institutionalized" — a veritable hell of impositions of things that we must or must not do that dry up creativity and volition. Every institution seems to limit our freedom — our free will and the free expression of our own Self. But there is also another way to look at it. "Institutionalized" behavior gives a direction and a predictability to our lives that guarantees in turn the freedom to act, work, and play that we would not otherwise have. Life would be even a greater nightmare than it now appears to some because of so many constraints if freedoms, property, communication, transportation, family life, the working day and the holidays, the police and the banks were not structured and institutionalized to provide for assured and predictable behavior — assured ways of doing things and planning our lives. Institutions provide the means for the realization of common endeavors.

This is a book about political institutions — about political regimes, political structures, and political patterns. It is written to counter the emphasis that has been put recently on what may be called the "demand side" of politics, e.g., the study of orientations, attitudes, demands and interests, that constantly pressure decision-making units. Political institutions and structures pattern and fashion the "demand side"; they are just as important as socioeconomic, cultural, ideological, psychological, economic, and attitudinal factors. People act and organize differently in different institutional contexts. Interests, consent, participation, the organization of political parties, individual freedoms and compliance, limitations upon and the accountability of governments — all depend very much on the institutional setting and vary accordingly. Knowing a political regime — its structure and organization and the relationships it establishes between the governors and the governed — is knowing a great deal about individual and group actors. The purpose of this book is to tell the student something about the organization of the contemporary state. The state and its organization delineate the contours within which associations and individuals operate and sets the parameters of their actions, freedom, and obligations.

Many colleagues and friends have helped me with this manuscript. I wish to thank Professors Howard Wiarda of the University of Massachusetts (Amherst) and Michael Rochon of Princeton University for reading the manuscript at least twice and offering me invaluable advice. My colleague Donald Hindley read the last two chapters on Authoritarian Regimes and his careful comments and suggestions helped me eliminate innumerable errors. Professor James R. Townsend read Chapters 6, 7, and 8 and I followed many of his suggestions, especially with regard to my brief section on China. My colleague Steven Burg read the parts on the Soviet Union, Poland, and Yugoslavia and offered many suggestions. Two graduate students at Brandeis, John Wooding and Bertha Zimba helped me with some research chores and I thank them both. What I appreciated most, however, was the involvement and interest of all those who helped me with the manuscript even when some of their reactions were critical. I hope this will also be the case with colleagues who read or use this book. It is at times intentionally argumentative. I often exaggerate to make a point and to invite a rebuttal. I try to raise more questions than I can answer and some of the vignettes I give of tyranny, military regimes, coporatism, Cuban totalitarianism, the institutional flux in China, the breakdown of Communist totalitarianism in Yugoslavia, Soviet Communism, Nazism, Fascism, and Iranian traditional totalitarianism are meant only to be suggestive and illustrative — they *all* call for further study.

Finally, I wish to thank Brandeis University and Little, Brown and Company for the help and support they gave me. I am particularly grateful for a travel grant I received from Brandeis, through the Mazer Fund for Faculty Research in the spring of 1984. Both the Political Science Editor and the Book Editor at Little, Brown, John Covell and Billie Ingram, were a constant source of support in the preparation and production of the book. Anne Fulchino did a remarkably careful job with the copyediting of the final version of the manuscript, and Geri Spaulding typed a number of versions at short notice.

This book is dedicated to Daniel and Alexi, six and three years old, and their peers, with the hope that as the years go by institutions and structures will loosen their grip on the individual in many parts of the world and provide a better setting for the good life in others.

Roy C. Macridis
Waltham, Mass.

Contents

And when many villages . . . join themselves together . . . to form but one society, that society is a city (i.e., state) . . . first founded that we might live, but continued that we might live happily.

ARISTOTLE Politics

1 The Study of Political Regimes: A Frame of Reference

Ours is a world of nation-states. People are grouped together into separate geographic boundaries, living under their own political regimes. There are about 175 states — the term *state* is often used synonymously with *political regime.* A political regime embodies the set of rules, procedures, and understandings that formulate the relationship between the governors and the governed. In every political regime there are a variety of political institutions — the legislature, the political party or parties, the bureaucracy, to mention a few — that perform the allotted tasks and roles involved in governance.

There are many types of political regimes. Even when institutions carry the same label we find great variations in their roles and their performance; political parties or legislatures, for instance, play different roles in different regimes. Each political regime obeys different historical, cultural, economic, social, and international determinants that shape the political behavior and attitude, both of the governors and the governed. Regimes vary notably in stability and legitimacy, degree of institutionalization, development, and above all, in the substance of the rules that structure the relations between the governors and the governed. They vary in the organization of political power, the forms of political participation, the organization and articulation of interests, and the configuration of political rights.

Our political world is one of great variety. It is a source of pleasure and wonder to the traveler and the historian, as Herodotus found out so many centuries ago, but a virtual nightmare for those who try to put some order in the profusion of regimes and the confusion their differences entail. As we look at the world around us from Nicaragua to Argentina, China and the Soviet Union, and some of the "solid" or "established" democracies in England, the United States, or Switzerland, and as we watch military dictatorships succeeding each other in many countries, is it possible to find general patterns — common characteristics and styles — that will enable us to separate some regimes from others?

Our first job in making a comparative study is to develop some general concepts that will help us find the fundamental similarities and differences that are necessary to arrive at some descriptive generalizations. But descriptive generalizations do not come easily. We must first set up our basic criteria; that is, we must develop a general theory of a political regime. Only then can we ask the proper questions about political organization and political behavior. Unless we establish a framework in terms of which we can identify similarities and differences, classify political regimes, and generalize about them, we will not succeed in trying to understand our political universe.

Political Regimes: General Characteristics

Introduction

Let us begin at the abstract level of system theory. A political system consists of functions and structures. *Functions* relate to the things that have to be done. *Structures* relate to the institutions, the mechanisms, the arrangements, and the procedures through which these things are done. System theory suggests the major functions of a political system and of their interrelationships and interdependence, but only in general terms. *A political regime, on the other hand, denotes the particular ways and means in which these functions are structured and patterned into institutions and procedures and of their specific relationships.* What, then, are the major functions of a political system and what are the institutions corresponding to them?

A regime must:

1. Generate commonly shared goals and to do so it must provide for socialization, for a common acceptance of the goals and the institutions through which these goals are to be realized. This concept underlines the importance of commonly shared ideas, that is, the prevailing ideology.
2. Provide the mechanisms for decision making.
3. Establish mechanisms for the articulation of interests and the aggregation of interests that determine policy.
4. Provide for the ways and means whereby decision makers are selected, together with the rules for their succession.
5. Maintain order by providing for effective controls against disruptive behavior.
6. Be capable of self-preservation.

All political regimes attempt in varying degrees to perform these functions through the institutions they establish, and it is in terms of their ability to perform them that they are generally judged.[1]

There are four major interacting processes, each one associated with different institutions, that characterize the functioning of a political regime:

The *organization of command* — in essence the state and its agencies — what we often refer to as "the government"
The *organization of consent*
The *configuration of interests*
The *organization of rights*

The Organization of Command

Politics and a study of a political regime is concerned primarily with power and its exercise, regardless of why or how that power is used. Command, imperium (what the Greeks called "kyrion"), souverain, and sovereignty are the terms we most frequently come across to denote the existence of political power within a given territory. When we use the term *state,* we are referring to an organization that can make decisions and make them stick. As a noted British author wrote more than a half century ago, "The state consists of a relatively small number of persons who issue and execute orders which affect a larger number in whom they are themselves included; it is of the essence of its character that, within its allotted territory, all citizens are legally bound by those orders."[2]

The state differs from all other associations in a great number of ways: First of all it is all-inclusive. Some of us may be members of the Catholic or the Unitarian church; some of us may belong to a trade union or the American Medical Association or to the Chamber of Commerce; others are proud members of the Elks or the Lions. *But all of us are in the state.*

Second, the purposes of the Elks, the Lions, the Catholics, the Unitarians, or the American Medical Association are special purposes and usually narrow in scope. The purposes of the state, however, are far more encompassing in scope, wider than those of all other associations combined. The state rules on matters such as defense, order, and social justice. Harry Eckstein waxes enthusiastic, very much in the spirit of Aristotle, when he writes that in the last analysis the state represents the principle of justice. "It is the only awesome power we have"![3]

1. For a discussion of the structural-functional approach that has mesmerized teachers and students for the last thirty years, see David Apter, *Introduction to Political Analysis* (Boston: Little, Brown, 1982). Unit VI, pp. 377–451; also Gabriel Almond and G. Brigham Powell, Jr., *Comparative Politics: A Developmental Approach* (Boston: Little, Brown, 1981).
2. Harold Laski, *The Grammar of Politics* (London: George Allen and Unwin, 1925), p. 295.
3. Harry Eckstein, "On the Science of the State," *Daedalus* (Fall 1979), 18; also Eric Nordlinger, *On the Autonomy of the Democratic State* (Cambridge, Mass.: Harvard University Press, 1981). According to Nordlinger, however, there is nothing awesome in the state. It is but another actor that manipulates the political forces. It is not the embodiment of justice!

Third, we can move from one association to another or get out of all or any of them, but it is extremely difficult to move out of the state you are born in.

Fourth, you can disobey the rules and regulations of an association and nobody will bother you except your friends or your conscience. You are free to comply or not. But you do not have the same freedom when it comes to the tax collector, the judge, or the traffic light. The state possesses what no other association has: the right to use force to secure compliance. It sanctions its decisions with force.

Finally, while the state can use force (it has "the monopoly of force"), it also must rely on emotional supports and loyalty. The modern state, except in some extreme and usually short-lived cases, requires consent and supports in order to have its decisions obeyed without the need for force. Force is usually but an insurance against the few who refuse to comply. As long as the majority of its citizens comply, the state can function with a minimum use of force, but if the majority do not comply, then the state cannot even exist.

Major Organs of Command Despite the many differences, the formal organs most commonly associated with the command structure appear to be similar in virtually all political regimes: the executive branch is at the top, and subordinate to it is the administration, or bureaucracy; the legislature makes laws; and the judiciary applies the law and settles disputes about the law. In almost all regimes, there is a functional division of judicial, legislative, and executive power and separate structures corresponding to these functions. Another similarity is that their relationships are arranged by a *constitution* — a written (but occasionally unwritten) set of rules that sets forth the limits of power, the manner in which power will be used, and the responsibilities and freedoms of the citizens.

Governing Elites In studying the command structure and the institutions and agencies operating within it, we do not limit ourselves to those officially elected or appointed. In most political regimes the decision makers, generally the officials who hold responsible positions (they issue and execute orders), are part of what may be loosely called the *governing elite.* The governing elite in general consists of people with greater income or knowledge and skills, or status and political influence, including those who occupy decision-making positions. Industrial leaders, managers, intellectuals, political leaders, religious leaders, representatives of major interests and other groups and associations, doctors, lawyers, engineers — they all make up the elite. The government officials and even the political leaders who make decisions, the *political elite,* are only a part of the elite and in some regimes it is but the tip (not the top) of the elite iceberg. In this case, however, what is not visible often counts more.

While the study of the command structure always tells us what the formal arrangements are, the study of the elite will almost always provide us with the missing (and sometimes the most important) links in the organization, namely, the distribution and limits of power. When the late Secretary-General of the Soviet Politburo, Nikita Krushchev, visited this country, he should have been given high grades in politics for asking Averell Harriman, a political man, but one who had the best possible connections with American industrialists, bankers, and financiers, to give him the opportunity to meet "the elite" in the United States. Mr. Harriman obliged by arranging a gathering to which only a few political leaders were invited. Thus, while Mr. Kruschchev met only a handful of Americans, they were the ones whose preferences about major policy issues generally prevail. Similarly in our study of political regimes, we will always try to connect the command structure — the government — with the elite — those who have a great deal of influence.

The Organization of Consent

A medieval French writer wrote that oxen are bound by their horns and people by their words and wills. The structure of command is fundamentally a matter of fashioning relationships that will allow some to command with the expectation that they will be obeyed. It is more a matter of values, myths, symbols, and habits rather than force.

A political regime needs supports in order to maintain itself and to survive over a given period of time. Supports consist of the positive orientations and attitudes of the citizenry with regard to their political regime. They are addressed toward the political regime itself (the constitution, we might say), the government in power (any given government), or a given policy at a given time. Supports are usually broken into two major types: affective and instrumental.

Affective and Instrumental Supports[4] *Affective* supports are the attachments the citizenry has for the political regime. Those who sing the national anthem during their morning shower obviously have a deep affective orientation for their country and its political regime. The opposite is the case of those who dream and plot to destroy it. It takes many years to develop deep emotional attachments to the point where they have crystallized or hardened into a behavior pattern, but when these values and beliefs do develop they open up such deep emotional grooves that the individual feels compelled to follow them.

In contrast to affective supports, *instrumental* supports are primarily generated by utilitarian considerations. They relate to the satisfaction of personal interests and to the realization of personal goals and demands. A regime that has maintained order, provided important services, kept the people out of war or did not lose one, preserved individual security and rights, and allocated resources evenly and generously will be accepted

4. I am following David Easton's seminal analysis, "An Approach to the Analysis of Political Systems," *World Politics*, 9 (April 1957), 383–400.

and respected and supported by most. The people give support in return for what they are getting. It is a quid pro quo arrangement. It is a case of "help me and I'll help you." "I'll do all for my country if my country does enough for me!" Support will be given provided services are rendered. In other words, acceptance of the regime, its *legitimacy*, is conditional.

When both affective and instrumental supports go hand in hand the extent and intensity of consent to and acceptance of the regime is likely to be very wide and very deep. The opposite is equally true. If the regime is not valued and does not provide for services, its legitimacy is very uncertain. More intriguing are the cases where there is tension between instrumental and affective supports: when the system performs well but is not valued, or when the system is highly valued but begins to perform inadequately. In the first case there may be gradual acceptance — legitimization. Prosperity and well-being will satisfy all except perhaps groups that share deep-felt loyalties for another regime or who may want to secede from the existing one for historic or ethnic or racial reasons (in fact, the latter is quite likely to occur in multiethnic states). In virtually all other cases, instrumental supports, with the help of socialization, will increasingly become affective supports.

The reverse is the case of a regime that enjoys deep affective supports but begins to fall down on performance. Take the 1929 depression in the United States. Can such a failure impair affective supports? How fast? We frankly cannot answer this in the abstract. It all depends on how deep and time-honored the affective supports have been and on how serious and lasting the crisis facing a regime is. In societies where legitimacy is not deep and a regime has shown only marginal performance, a crisis, such as war or an economic depression, may unhinge the regime. Conversely, in societies where both legitimacy and performance (in other words, both affective and instrumental supports) have been strong for a long time, nonperformance and the resulting waning of instrumental supports may not affect legitimacy even if the problem continues for a fairly long time. In 1929 and throughout the economic depression, few Americans turned against their government or the Constitution. However, in Germany, in 1933, three years after an equally severe economic depression, the Germans had toppled their democratic constitution. The American political regime had a thick cushion of legitimacy and managed to withstand the crisis; not so with the German democratic constitution that was replaced by the Nazi dictatorship. Some regimes can afford mistakes and even prolonged periods of nonperformance; in others, the cushion of legitimacy is but thin ice on which they skate at their own peril. Even for political regimes that have enjoyed legitimacy for a long time there is a point of crisis. The war in Vietnam (1964–1973) and widespread resistance to it accounted for the first serious political crisis in the United States since the Civil War; many people turned not only against their government but against the political institutions — against the political regime and the Constitution.

When people accept the regime they live in even though they do not agree with some specific policy decisions, we call this regime *consensual*, or *legitimate*. It is based on shared wills and shared values. It links the command structures — those who make decisions or who "authoritatively allocate values"[5] — with the citizenry at large: those who obey. The people consent (rather than obey) and those who make decisions have authority (rather than power).

There are four processes associated with the organization of consent: socialization, representation, participation, and mobilization.

Socialization comprises the various processes through which loyalties and attachments to a political regime and its institutions are developed. It plays a crucial role in the development of support. The family, the school, and various associations propagate values consistent with the goals and the institutions of the given regime.[6] Ideology is often the instrument used to rationalize the existing political regime. By the time most children become adults, they have imbued the prevailing ideology and are ready to give their supports. Habit is equally important: the sheer imitation of the elders; the doing of things the way they are done by others; the tendency to follow peer groups or to act in accord with neighbors and friends or other reference groups; all these factors shape and crystallize orientations and loyalties vis-à-vis the political regime. Specifically how different regimes socialize the young and the citizens, or how they fail to do so, is a matter we will examine when we discuss individual cases. The socialization process in general, however, is necessary for the maintenance of any political regime, regardless of the specific methods used.

Representation, at least in theory, puts elected representatives in charge of the command structure. Representative assemblies speak for the whole and are beholden to the whole. In obeying, therefore, we but obey decisions made by delegates we ourselves chose.

Participation provides an active communication and interaction between the citizenry and those in command positions. We organize and agitate and talk about everything from garbage collections to a nuclear freeze. Associations promote various points of view on domestic and foreign policy questions. And through a political party or even without one, we exert all sorts of efforts (and often expenditures) to ensure that the people who reach a position of command are the people we want elected. Of all these agencies that provide for such participation, however, the political party is still the most powerful one.

Mobilization is often used to denote the awakening of political involvement of people who had remained disenfranchised or alienated. For instance, nationalism and national independence movements mobilized the masses in Europe in the nineteenth century and in many colonies after World War II — it brought them into politics. But the word can also be used, and I use it in this sense, to denote intensive participation: a great

5. The expression is used by David Easton, ibid.
6. Kenneth Langton, *Political Socialization* (New York: Oxford University Press, 1969); Richard E. Dawson and Kenneth Prewitt, *Political Socialization* (Boston: Little, Brown, 1969).

commitment and sustained activity, a deep involvement. In this sense one might say that the proabortion or antiabortion movements mobilize groups into action in the United States. They spur intensive political activity among participating citizens; so did the war in Vietnam; so did the legislation prepared by the French socialist government that appeared to interfere with the autonomy of Catholic schools. It is in this sense that we use the term mobilization to denote intensive participation.

The Configuration of Interests

Within a political regime various actors, both groups and individuals, seek to articulate their various interests. They have certain expectations, they make certain demands, and they seek the realization of their needs and desires. The term *interests* should be defined in the broadest possible sense: material interests; family interests; professional interests; religious convictions; and heartfelt values such as honor, patriotism, rights, and humanitarian considerations. There is nothing static about interests. They shift and change depending on a great number of factors. At times law and order (i.e., security) may be even more important than equality or freedom; sometimes freedom is such an overwhelming interest that even equality and welfare considerations yield to it; sometimes it is equality, both material equality and equality of opportunities, that take precedence.

Specific interests speak through specific organizations, usually associations and groups. *Groups* are generally identified and defined in terms of some objective traits shared in common by individuals: tribal groups; occupational groups; age-cohorts: teenagers, the elderly, etc.; religious and ethnic groups: Protestants, Catholics, Jews, Greeks, Italians, Irish, etc. *Associations* are formally constituted and organized by individuals in order to protect their common interests: the Association of Retired Persons, the NAACP, the NAM, the AMA, the AFL-CIO, etc.[7] *Political parties* are associations that bring many interests together into a general purposive activity; that is, the party expresses various interests, reconciles them, and synthesizes them into one policy statement. The party platform embodies the goals to be pursued by its leader if that party assumes control of the command structure.

The Organization of Rights

Individual rights have traditionally been defined as individual claims *against* the state. Originally they were the claims against absolutist monarchies; freedom to think, to worship, to form associations, to be immune from arrests, to have the right to a fair trial, to be presumed innocent until

7. For interest group analysis, especially with reference to American politics, one should consult the pioneering works of Pendleton Herring, especially his *Group Representation Before Congress* (1929; rpt. New York: Russell & Russell, 1967). See also Arthur F. Bentley, *The Process of Government* (New Brunswick, N.J.: Transaction Books, 1983) and David Truman, *The Governmental Process* (New York: Alfred A. Knopf, 1947).

found guilty, etc. Rights, however, are also viewed, especially since World War II, as claims *for* services — in health, welfare, education, employment, security, etc. In this case, the people expect these services to be provided by the government. They feel that they are *entitled* to them. The first are, strictly speaking, referred to as *individual rights* or civil rights; the second, inasmuch as they involve groups and material and economic services for them, are *social rights.* Finally there are *political rights:* to vote, to run for office, or organize political associations and political parties.

Political regimes vary in their emphasis on civil rights, social rights, and political rights. Some emphasize all three; others, one or two. But few are the regimes that do not pay attention to any. The way they do it, the particular protection they provide, the values that are attached to them is a matter for empirical study of particular political regimes.

In all political regimes there is a constant dynamic in the relationship between command, consent, interests, and rights. There is a constant interaction and tension between the various groupings and associations and the command structure. Relationships between the executive, the administrative, the legislative, and the judiciary branches also shift and change. "Presidential government" and "congressional government" may alternate over time. In a given period the "party is king," and in another, "the party is over." Legislative supremacy may give place to cabinet supremacy; political leaders may be replaced by the experts. Political institutions gain or lose autonomy in their relationships with social, economic, or other organizations: the army, the party, the state, trade unions, the clergy. They all play musical chairs at one time or another. Likewise political associations and groupings — lobbies; single-issue associations; political action committees, whose major task is to influence the decision makers in the command structure — constantly seesaw with respect to the influence they can muster while new ones try to get into the playground. All we can do, therefore, is to identify in various political regimes the major institutional patterns and relationships and indicate current trends. We shall do so in terms of the four basic categories we set forth: *command, consent, interest, and rights.*

Political Regimes: Major Patterns

Introduction

While the term *system* is used to identify major concepts, functions, and structures, the term *political regime* denotes the particular institutional arrangements: the manner in which political relationships are structured, patterned, and organized in a given country. System represents an analytical concept; regime represents an empirical and descriptive category. We will discuss here three major "patterns," three types of political regimes: democratic, totalitarian, and authoritarian. They correspond to major descriptive generalizations based on the criteria we set forth, that

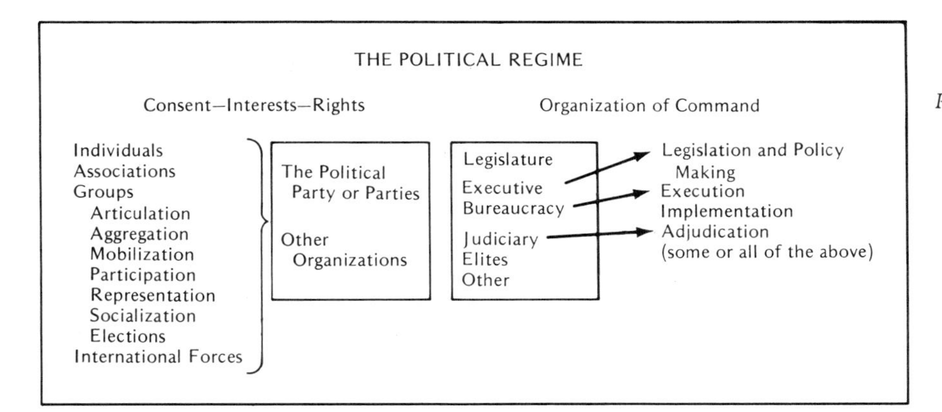

is, the different ways in which command, consent, interests, and rights are organized. We shall also pay particular attention to how the relationships between the state and the society are structured.

Our descriptive generalizations reach out to identify only general characteristics, because drawing detailed profiles would require careful and in-depth study of individual political regimes. As we will see, there are significant variations from one democratic regime to another and there are a great variety of authoritarian and even totalitarian forms.

The Democratic Model

In democratic theory (and in varying degrees in democratic regimes) there is a sharp distinction made between state and society. The basic assumption is that in society the individuals are free, rational, independent entities, born with inalienable rights: life, liberty, and property. Individuals seek fulfillment in religious, artistic, economic, and many other forms of expression, and society provides the outlets for achieving these aspirations. Relations among individuals and the associations they form are based on equality: there is no subordination of one to another. Since associations and groups are freely formed and they remain free and independent of each other, they denote a pluralistic pattern, allowing a great variety of forms of expression. Morality and the "good life" is what the individuals decide. People seek their own interests. They are all armed with a little pocket calculator, so to speak, figuring out what is pleasurable and good (in the most material but also the loftiest sense of the words) and what is painful or bad, pursuing the one and avoiding the other without any outside interference.

According to this liberal *democratic model,* the state — the command structure — has one single and narrow function: to preserve order. It has the right to use force but only to prevent violence and to provide the opportunity to each and all of us to do "our thing." The state has no overriding ethical purpose: it cannot decide what is true and false, moral or immoral. The individuals, as members of the society, consent to form a state when they agree to set up a constitution that spells out the organization of the state, the limits of its power, and the rights to be preserved. After they have set up a constitution that defines the organization of individual rights and consent that sets the limits of state action, they return to their pursuits in the society with the knowledge and the guarantees that they will be able to live in peace and tranquility.

This democratic model stacks the cards on one side: the side of the individuals and the associations they voluntarily form, which represent the creative forces of progress and change. The state is their creature, dependent upon society for its existence and limited by the established rules. Thus, while society is *independent* of the state, the state is *dependent* upon society. The individual is sacred; the state is a necessary evil, like an insurance policy we take against the many hazards that confront us.

Despite many profound and radical social and economic changes that have accounted for drastic reconsiderations of this model, it still remains the true one for most liberal and democratic regimes. Institutional arrangements continue to safeguard individual rights and pluralism and to distinguish sharply between what belongs to the state (and comes under the purview of its activities) and what belongs to the individuals, including their free and spontaneous world of social life. Democracy, from liberalism to socialism, continues to emphasize, despite growing interdependencies between the state and society and the growing scope of state action (especially in the economy), the *separateness* between the state and the society.

Limitations and Accountability A democracy limits the power of its decision makers. First of all, the command structure is ordered in such a way that the decision makers cannot make arbitrary decisions because they are bound by the established legal order. The element of separateness that we just mentioned ensures that the political power given to the decision makers will be a *limited* power. Second, those who occupy the command structure are held responsible for their decisions. They can tax and they can drop an atom bomb but they will be held *accountable* for what they do. Periodic and free, at least in theory, elections as well as many other mechanisms institutionalize this responsibility (which will be discussed more fully in Chapters 3 and 4).

It is in terms of the institutionalization of accountability and limitations that democracy differs from all regimes that do not limit the scope of political power and do not establish clear-cut principles and institutions to make the holders of political power ultimately responsible to the people. But again the student must bear in mind that we must think not in absolute but in relative terms. There is no political society where a ruler can be totally unlimited and totally irresponsible. Nor can there be one where the government is both limited and totally responsible for each and every one of its acts. It is always a matter of degree, but it has to be measured carefully because even a few degrees count a great deal!

The Totalitarian Model

The *totalitarian model,* as opposed to the democratic one, advances a diametrically different view of the relationship between society (associations and individuals) and the state. The command structure — and all the means through which it is organized and through which it manifests itself — is controlled by a well-organized political elite, to the exclusion of all others. There is, in varying degrees, a domination over the society. Initiative and inspiration; the distinction between what is true and what is false; all social activities: economic, cultural, religious, even family; all come under the official and direct control of the dominant political organization, sometimes the state and sometimes the political party. One and only one ideology, the "official ideology," is propounded and the individual and all social groups must conform to it.

Totalitarian regimes establish or attempt to establish the subordination of everything to a political organization and advance a "total" ideology to manipulate and determine the organization of interest, the organization of consent, and the organization of rights. The individual and the various social groups are made to march in unison for the attainment of a prearranged purpose.[8] Totalitarian regimes of course vary in their ability to integrate society into one mold. Very often some social groups show great survival capabilities — religious groups and churches, for instance. Others may have special skills or develop a certain degree of autonomy, for example, the military or the scientists. The monopoly of the political elite may be undermined.

Authoritarianism[9]

Authoritarianism and the various forms of authoritarian regimes continue to be but an expression of the oldest and some would say the most corrupt aspect of political life: rule by force. In fact, authoritarianism is a catchall name for political regimes that we are more or less familiar with: autocracy, tyranny, satrapy, dictatorship, absolutism, bonapartism, despotism, military rule, junta, oligarchy, a "political boss," theocracy, and even outright gangsterism. They all provide for command arrangements that concentrate power and force in the hands of one or few leaders who rule without much regard for the organization of consent, the organization of interests, and needless to say, without any respect for individual rights. Authoritarianism in its naked form is almost always associated with instruments of coercion and their pervasive use. The army, the police, and the jails or concentration camps — even outright assassination of dissenters — are ever present and constantly used.

This is of course a highly simplified account of the authoritarian

8. For an admirable account of a totalitarian regime, see Karl D. Bracher, *The German Dictatorship: The Origin, Structure and Effects of National Socialism* (London: Weidenfeld & Nicholson, 1970).
9. For authoritarian regimes, see Amos Perlmutter, *Modern Authoritarianism* (New Haven, Conn.: Yale University Press, 1980).

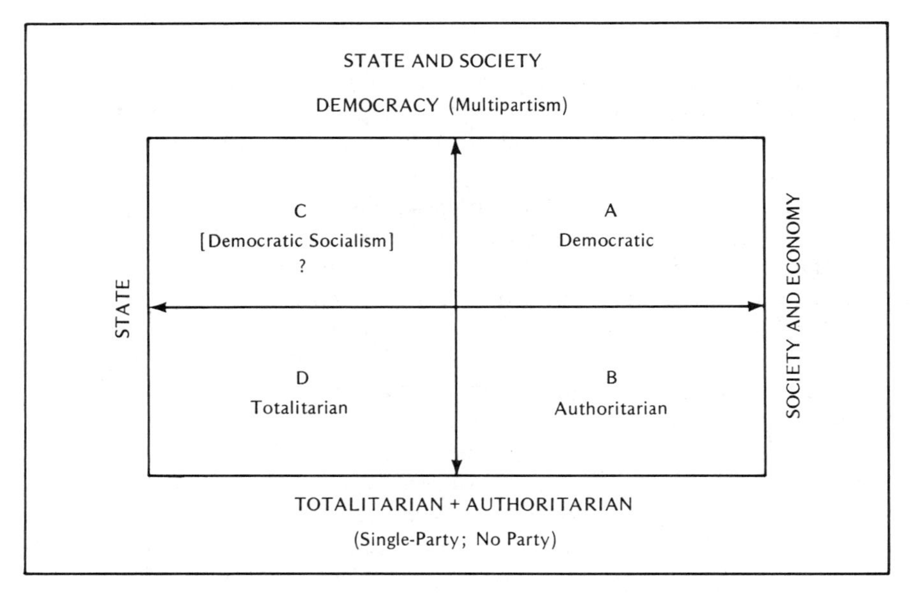

model. It tells us that in authoritarian regime the command structure is emphasized. Obedience rather than participation is the rule; the organization of consent and individual rights yield to the imperative of force.

The diagram above helps us visualize the relationship between the state and the society in authoritarian, democratic, and totalitarian regimes. In the top right-hand square societal life is free and spontaneous (but always to a degree) with regard to economic, social, cultural, and educational pursuits and rights. It corresponds by and large to contemporary liberal democracies, including the United States. At the bottom right-hand corner the state is the dominant force, but considerable autonomy is given to certain societal forces (especially the economy and property rights) and also to certain associations (particularly the church). Political freedoms, especially a multiparty system, prevalent in A do not exist or are very narrowly circumscribed. The bottom left corner D corresponds to a situation where all societal forces including the economy are under the complete (or virtually complete) control and direction of the state or political agencies like the single party. The regimes that fall in this square are totalitarian. Finally the most intriguing (and difficult to find in our world) pattern is that of the left top square, C. It represents control of some societal forces by the state (mainly the economy) but also a great deal of autonomy and spontaneity for other societal forces (associations, education, competing ideologies, etc.), including political dissent and a multiparty system. This square corresponds to democratic socialism. Some of the totalitarian regimes that show signs of allowing a certain amount of economic and political freedoms, like Yugoslavia and perhaps China, may be moving from D to C. Some democracies like France have moved from A in the direction of C. It is not always easy, however, to fit regimes into the four squares given; there are always qualifications to be made and we will discuss some of them.

Table 1-1 Authoritarian, Totalitarian, and Democratic Regimes Similarities and Differences: A Checklist

	Authoritarian	Totalitarian	Democratic
1. Limitation on command structure	None	None	Yes — many
2. Effective responsibility	None	Some (political party)	Considerable/great
3. Organization of command structure			
State	Yes	yes	State and state agencies
Bureaucracy/military	Yes	Under the party	Subordinate
Individual leader	Yes	Yes (collective leadership)	Elective
4. Penetration of society by political organs	Weak	Comprehensive	Limited
5. Mobilization for supports	Weak	Strong	Variable
6. Official ideology	Weak	Strong	Weak
7. Parties	Weak, if any	Single	Many
8. Police, force, intimidation	Yes	Yes	
9. Individual rights (protection)			
In form	?	Yes	Yes
In substance	None	None	Generally yes

Political Regimes: The Governing Elite

All discussions about elites begin with the pithy statement of the Italian sociologist Gaetano Mosca. There is "a class that rules and a class that is ruled." It is a universal phenomenon. The ruling class is . . . "always the less numerous, performs all political functions, monopolizes power and enjoys the advantages that power brings."[10] It is unnecessary to add that the "other" class — the majority — are under the control of the first.

To many people, this statement is unduly cynical. It is difficult to reconcile it with democracy where the majority are supposed to govern and where egalitarianism is the dominant concept. Nonetheless, if we study the structural organization of contemporary societies, we find that they are all stratified in terms of status, power, and income, with the few at the top and the many at the base. Also, there are oligarchic tendencies in all organizations: the few invariably assume positions of authority and command: in business organizations, educational institutions, trade unions, political parties, and fraternal associations. In all organizations and especially in political ones, including the political party and the state, there is, what another author called in a famous phrase, an "iron law of oligarchy."[11]

As stated earlier in this chapter, an elite is a group of people with the power to make others conform to its preferences or to prevent others from following their preferences if contrary to its own. It can do so in two ways: *directly*, by occupying the decision-making organs and shaping policy and policy outcomes (it is strictly speaking the political elite), or *indirectly*, by influencing the political elite that makes policy. In the past, powerful industrialists were reputed to have operated behind the scenes of government and it has been said that they pulled the strings: J. P. Morgan or the Rockefellers, for instance; or the "two hundred families" that ruled France; or Krupp, the German industrial magnate who exclaimed gleefully in 1932: "We have hired Herr Hitler." Today, in many democracies, big corporations and multinationals are supposed to be exercising the same influence. There are also other elites to be reckoned with: the high clergy, university presidents, the military, managerial groups, labor union leaders, owners and directors of the media, leaders of mass organizations. Similarly, in Communist regimes there is a governing elite that comprises not only policymakers but also other important elites: the bureaucracy, the military, the scientists, the managerial groups. Djilas spoke of the political, administrative, and managerial leaders of the Soviet Union as a "new class": a new oligarchy, a group of a few who ruled over the many — the "powerful" and the "powerless."[12]

As we examine various types of regimes we will try to locate the

10. Gaetano Mosca, *The Ruling Class* (New York: McGraw-Hill, 1939).
11. Robert Michels, *Political Parties: A Sociological Study of the Oligarchical Tendencies of Modern Democracy* (London: Collier Books, 1962).
12. Milovan Djilas, *The New Class* (New York: Praeger, 1957).

elite: the officials in the government and the most powerful elite groups that operate within the government or behind the government. We will try to find out what distinguishes one elite from another and what institutional devices different elites use to organize their respective powers. We suggest the following criteria.

CRITERIA FOR DISTINGUISHING ELITES

Dimensionality Does the elite consist of one identifiable group with similar traits (i.e., wealth, organizational skills, education, status, etc.) or is it multidimensional, consisting in effect of different groups with different (and often competing) skills and resources in the society? How unified and homogeneous is the elite as opposed to being diversified and heterogeneous?

Monopoly of Power How exclusive is the elite's power over decision making or how much sharing is there? The implication is that the more sharing of power there is, the less likely it is for a political elite to have the monopoly of power.

Self-perpetuation All elites try to maintain themselves in power and influence and to pass on their advantages to their heirs. Some succeed better than others. What specifically are the instrumentalities used by various elites in different political regimes to perpetuate themselves?

Closed or Open Some elites are closed to outsiders — they develop intricate and difficult "entrance exams" and the examiners are themselves carefully screened if not self-appointed to stop newcomers. Mobility from non-elite to elite status is controlled by the criteria of birth, wealth, education, religion or political affiliation, status, and family position. Elites intermarry, pool their property, and make education and training in new skills so difficult for the many that they are destined to remain outside. Closed elites often develop a high level of experience in government, and eventually they put experience above innovation and stability above change. Open elites, on the other hand, are much more amenable to change. They put a premium on innovation even if they lack the experience to implement their goals.

Recruitment The techniques used by an elite to recruit new members is another indication of its closeness or openness. Does recruitment take place only from a small and exclusive segment of the society or is it open to a relatively large part of the population? Can the qualifications for recruitment be easily learned and assimilated so that people without family background or wealth can master them? Clearly a regime that requires Latin and Greek exams for entry into the civil service doesn't facilitate the recruitment of the many!

Transformation of Elites Even closed elites cannot stop change and block newcomers. Socioeconomic changes and new forms of wealth invariably create new groups that represent new forms of influence, wealth, and power. The aristocracy gave place to the upper bourgeoise. Then the middle classes emerged to give place in turn to new groups: managerial, technical, and scientific people. Finally a third new class surfaced: the workers. All political regimes go through elite transformation even though the tempo of change varies.

Constraints What limitations does a regime establish and effectively implement vis-à-vis a governing elite? There is an apparent contradiction in this question. What characterizes an elite is its ability to make its preferences stick. Constraints imply the existence of external forces that impose themselves on the elite. The implication, however, is, as with power sharing, that when such constraints exist and are operational, the elitist phenomenon is considerably qualified and perhaps even diminished. All elites have to be sure, at least to some degree, that their own preferences will be acceptable to the people in the society. Awareness by elites of possible reactions and the very anticipation that some reactions can be unfavorable may amount to a restraint. Similarly, noninstitutionalized forms of popular or mass reaction — strikes, demonstrations, riots, etc. — may constitute another restraint. There are regimes where elites operate under a manifold set of institutionalized restraints and others where constraints are less institutionalized and effective. The existence and institutionalization of constraints through courts, elections, and the legislature make a good deal of difference — for the elite and for all others!

Guarantees for the Governed Everybody will agree that the position of a late nineteenth-century Russian or Mexican farmer who lived under the shadow of the landlord's chateau was a far cry from what their respective positions are today! And again there will be no argument that between the time of Dickens and the present-day world the position of the average worker has greatly improved not only in England but also everywhere. Guarantees — social, economic, and political —

MAJOR CRITERIA TO STUDY ELITE CONFIGURATION

1. Dimensionality
2. Monopoly of Power
3. Self-perpetuation
4. Closed or Open Group
5. Recruitment
6. Transformation of Elites
7. Constraints
8. Guarantees for the Governed
9. Ideology

of the governed against the elite have been developed and have gained strength. As we examine the various political regimes we will look into these guarantees. They consist not only of things that the elite cannot do but also of what the governed can do and what sanctions the people can impose upon the elites, both the political elite and all others. We will also discuss the institutionalized procedures through which members of the elite can be sanctioned.

Ideology Elites propagate ideas that allow them to maintain their position as well as legitimize it. They are the ones who guide all of us in what we think and in what we do. They make the maps and we travel by following their signs.

For an elite to maintain its position, it must have a common ideology. Differences, cracks, and splits in the ideology invariably suggest lack of cohesiveness and multidimensionality. Therefore, the first step we should take in any comparative study of elites is to find out if there is an ideology, a common map. Its existence is prima facie evidence of unity and power. Where it cannot be found, we may infer that the elite is divided, in conflict, or in the process of rapid internal transformation. Its power is declining and it is writing different maps with conflicting and confusing instructions. It would not be difficult to detect disunity in the elite in France before the French Revolution or within the Catholic Church before the Reformation. And it would not be difficult to detect a high level of divisiveness about some crucial policy issues, namely slavery, in the United States before the Civil War and more recently during the Vietnam war. Today there are significant differences about foreign policy, economic policy, and the role of the government within the French, British, and American elites. Similar differences may exist in the totalitarian regimes, but they cannot be so easily detected. The elite appears to be united and differences, if they exist, do not spill beyond its confines. The public is given only one map to read!

If the existence of an elite is a universal phenomenon, the degree of elitism, the way membership in the elite can be secured and maintained, the constraints that exist, and the guarantees available to the governed to protect them against the elite become crucial variables in any comparative survey.[13] The arguments that some regimes are elitist and others are democratic, that in some the people govern while in others it is the bosses who rule miss the point. Let us repeat: *In all regimes there is an elite that is a little more equal than all others!* But regimes differ, and often fundamentally, in how inequality is perceived, how it is maintained, what privileges are bestowed on some, and what deprivations others suffer. In sum, if there are elites everywhere, some are more powerful than others and some regimes are more elitist than others. Likewise while the many are ruled everywhere, in some regimes they are a little more powerful than in others.

We will review the composition and the ideology of elites in democratic, totalitarian (particularly the communist), and authoritarian regimes including military dictatorships. The structure, composition, and ideology of the elite profoundly affects the organization of consent, the distribution of power, the organization of interests, and the configuration of individual rights.

We are now ready to turn to the major political regimes. In studying them we will continue to use the major criteria we set forth: organization of command, organization of consent, configuration of interests, and organization of rights. In each case we will try to identify the political relationship between state and society and the characteristics of the governing elite.

Bibliography

Almond, Gabriel, and Sidney Verba. *The Civic Culture.* Princeton, N.J.: Princeton University Press, 1963.

Almond, Gabriel, and G. Bingham Powell. *Comparative Politics: System, Process and Policy.* Boston: Little, Brown, 1981.

Apter, David. *Introduction to Political Analysis.* Cambridge, Mass.: Winthrop/Boston: Little, Brown, 1982.

Bill, James A., and Robert L. Hardgrave, Jr. *Comparative Politics: The Quest for Theory.* Lanham, Md.: University Press of America, 1982.

Blondel, Jean. *Comparative Political Institutions.* New York: Praeger, 1973.

Davis, Morton R., and Vaughan A. Lewis. *Model of Political System.* New York: Praeger, 1971.

Easton, David. *A Framework for Political Analysis.* Chicago: University of Chicago Press, 1979.

13. The best overview on political elites is Robert D. Putnam, *The Comparative Study of Political Elites* (Englewood Cliffs, N.J.: Prentice-Hall, 1976).

Eckstein, Harry. *The Evaluation of Political Performance: Problems and Dimensions.* Beverly Hills, Calif.: Sage Publications, 1971.

Eckstein, Harry, and David Apter. *Comparative Politics: A Reader.* Glencoe, Ill.: The Free Press, 1963.

Ehrmann, Henry. *Comparative Legal Cultures.* Englewood Cliffs, N.J.: Prentice-Hall, 1976.

Finer, Samuel H. *Comparative Government.* London: Penguin Books, 1970.

Friedrich, Carl J. *Man and His Government: An Empirical Theory of Politics.* New York: McGraw-Hill, 1963.

Holt, Robert T., and John E. Turner. *The Methodology of Comparative Research.* New York: The Free Press, 1970.

Macridis, Roy, and Bernard Brown (eds.). *Comparative Politics: Notes and Readings.* 6th ed. Homewood, Ill.: Dorsey Press, 1986.

Mahler, Gregory S. *Comparative Politics: An Institutional and Cross-National Approach.* Cambridge, Mass.: Shenkman Publishers, 1983.

Taylor, C. C., and O. A. Jodich. *World Handbook of Politics and Social Indicators.* New Haven, Conn.: Yale University Press, 1983.

Tilly, Charles, ed. *The Formation of Nation States in Western Europe.* Princeton, N.J.: Princeton University Press, 1975.

On Governing Elites

Blondel, Jean. *World Leaders: Heads of Government in the Post-War Period.* Beverly Hills, Calif.: Sage Publications, 1980.

Michels, Robert. *Political Parties: A Sociological Study of Oligarchical Tendencies in Modern Democracies.* 1911; rpt. London: Macmillan, 1962.

Mosca, Gaetano. *The Ruling Class.* Trans. by Hannah Kahn. Westport, Conn.: Greenwood Press, 1980.

Putnam, Robert D. *The Comparative Study of Political Elites.* Englewood Cliffs, N.J.: Prentice-Hall, 1976.

Part One
Democratic Regimes

I can conceive of a society in which all men would feel an equal love and respect for the laws of which they consider themselves the authors; in which the authority of the government would be respected as necessary . . . and in which the loyalty of the subject to the chief magistrate would not be a passion, but a quiet and rational persuasion. With every individual in the possession of rights which he is sure to retain, a kind of manly and reciprocal courtesy would arise between all classes . . . The people, well acquainted with their own true interests, would understand that, in order to profit from the advantages of the state, it is necessary to satisfy its requirements . . .

ALEXIS DE TOCQUEVILLE Democracy in America

Introduction Contrary to past hopes and expectations that democracy was the "natural form of government"[1] and that human progress was associated with its diffusion, there are only a small number of genuine democratic regimes today. They exist in Western Europe and Scandinavia and, since the early 1970s, in the countries of Southern Mediterranean: Spain, Greece, and Portugal. In other parts of the world democratic regimes of long standing are also few in number: Great Britain, Canada, the United States, Australia, and New Zealand. India is maintaining a democratic regime and in Japan democracy has been accepted since World War II. Almost everywhere else democracy has failed to gain any roots. Of the 175 nation-states in our world today not more than thirty-five are genuine democracies.* It seems that democracy is the exception rather than the rule.

Constitutional Order The two basic premises of democracy are: *limitations* on the state and its agencies and *responsibility* of those government officials to the people at large. Limitations are procedural or substantive and often both. *Procedural* limitations relate to the manner in which the powers of the state are exercised, that is, how certain things are done. *Substantive* limitations relate to substantive matters, individual or associational rights that are considered beyond the jurisdiction of the state.

1. In James Bryce, *Modern Democracies,* 2 vols. (London: Macmillan, 1924).
*See Appendix A.

They are "things that the state cannot do." Responsibility is a far more elastic concept. It holds officials accountable, politically or legally, for their acts. It is associated with an independent judiciary, representative government, *and* elections.

In democratic regimes both limitations and responsibility are set forth in broad outlines in a constitution. All democracies operate under a set of rules agreed upon and generally accepted by the people. Constitutions define the ends of government (and its limits) and the means — the processes and procedures — through which they will be attained. A constitution is the fundamental law in the sense that its violation will be sanctioned by courts or by other means.[2]

In virtually all democracies constitutions are written documents,[3] but they are always qualified or altered by conventions, understandings, and judicial interpretations. Thus the United States Constitution can hardly be understood without going over the interpretations and reinterpretations of the Supreme Court. England, on the other hand, has no formal written document that we can call a constitution, except for some basic enactments of Parliament that provide for individual rights and the organization of governmental powers. France, in contrast, has had many written constitutions. The last one is the constitution of 1958, which established the Fifth Republic. Most of the democracies established in the Mediterranean and the Third World have promulgated constitutional documents.

In every constitution there is a statement about rights, individual rights. The first ten amendments to the U.S. Constitution that form part of the original document and also the thirteenth, fourteenth, and fifteenth amendments list rights, that is, areas of individual or associational life that cannot be impaired or invaded by government. The same is the case with the French Declaration of the Rights of Man, which dates back to 1789 and which was reproduced in all subsequent French republican constitutions (First, Second, Third, Fourth, and Fifth Republics) and virtually in all European democratic constitutions. Today most political regimes have endorsed the United Nations Universal Declaration of Human Rights, which we will discuss in Chapter 5.

Organization of Power If constitutions spell out individual rights, they also organize and structure the political regime. Aristotle defined a constitution (the supreme law) as the "ordering of the commonwealth" — the command structure — and linked it with the organization of supports and consent. All democratic constitutions assign *specific roles* and *powers* to various organs and define them with regard to the powers and

2. On representation, limitations, and responsibility, see Carl J. Friedrich, *Constitutional Government and Democracy*, 4th ed. (New York: Ginn & Blaisdell, 1968).
3. Samuel H. Finer, *Five Constitutions: Contrasts and Comparisons* (London: Penguin Books, 1981), includes the texts of the constitutions of the Soviet Union (1936 and 1977) (not a democracy), of the Federal Republic of Germany (1949), of the French Fifth Republic (1958), and of the United States. There is a good introduction that spells out some of the characteristics of the English constitutional arrangements.

the roles of the others. The major roles, functions, and powers are allotted to three organs: the executive branch, the legislature, and the courts. There are some democratic constitutions where political parties or the army or functional and economic representative or consultative councils are given a share of the power to make decisions or to deliberate in the making of decisions.

Generally speaking, a constitution implicitly or explicitly establishes a hierarchy of powers. In most democratic regimes the people hold sovereign power, delegating it to their elected representatives under specific conditions. In Britain, for instance, the Parliament is supreme and all other powers are subordinate to it. In France the situation is less clear; for some matters the National Assembly is supreme; for others it is the president of the Republic. There are some matters that can be decided authoritatively by the people in a referendum. In the United States the three organs, legislative, executive, and judiciary, are equal and separate, with one checking the other even at the risk of a stalemate. But there is only one power, one branch of government, that can ultimately and authoritatively resolve all conflicts as well as interpret the Constitution: the Supreme Court. Nowhere else has the judicial power such authority and power as in the United States.

Responsibility It is not enough to organize the governmental powers and divide work among them and structure their relations. It still is necessary to make sure that the people who occupy the roles assigned to them will play them according to the rules and will perform their tasks in the manner the constitution sets forth. Since the beginning of the nineteenth century, those who had legislative or executive power — presidents or prime ministers and their subordinates — have been held responsible to the elected representative assemblies and to the people. In presidential regimes the president must answer directly to the people through the process of periodic elections. It is only under very special circumstances, for breaking the law or treason, that the president is judged by the legislature or special courts. In all parliamentary regimes, which include most of the contemporary democracies, the prime minister is held directly responsible to the legislature and at election time to the people.

In summary, a constitution defines rights, organizes the structure of command linking it with specific limitations on the major organs of government, and establishes in various ways the responsibility and accountability of officeholders to freely elected representative assemblies (whose members are themselves responsible to their constituents), and ultimately to the people.

In this part we will address ourselves to the institution of democratic regimes. In Chapter 2 we will discuss the organization of the command structure: the executive, the bureaucracy, the configuration of elites, and the limitations imposed on them. In Chapters 3 and 4 we will examine the organization of consent: representative assemblies, political parties, and elections. In Chapter 5 we will deal with the organization of interests and individual rights.

2 *The Command Structure: Governing*

Introduction

The command structure comprises numerous officials, elected or appointed, organized in numerous agencies, who have the power to make decisions and to implement them. They issue commands in the form of laws, executive orders, rules, and regulations. They have the power to send the army abroad, to use force at home, to tax, and to spend money. These are awesome powers, which appear to be antithetical to individual and associational freedoms. In order to preserve the latter, we must not only develop ironclad rules of responsibility and accountability but also, and especially, we must weaken the command structure as a whole: we must build dams and fences and obstacles to its exercise. "Liberty," wrote Thomas Hobbes, is "power cut up in pieces."

In democracies, as in no other political regimes, the command structure is so carefully circumscribed and so meticulously surrounded by so many booby traps that explode in the face of those who trespass into areas of decision making outside their allotted field or who attempt to use short cuts in making decisions. This is what makes our discussion of the command structure in democratic regimes both difficult and fascinating. It is almost as if the combined ingenuity of every person writing about democracy or living in a democracy or preparing a democratic constitution was applied to avert the possibility that some officeholders would abuse the office and the powers associated with it. "If men were angels no government would be necessary" wrote Madison.[1] And because we are not angels and because we do need a government, every effort should be made to keep the devils out or if they sneak in, to make it impossible for them to prevail! An impossible task, perhaps, but nonetheless one worth trying.

The Organization of the Executive Branch

In almost all democratic regimes, there are two basic ways of organizing the executive branch: the presidential form and the parliamentary, often referred to as the cabinet, form. A few democratic regimes combine some of the characteristics of a presidential system with those of a parliamentary system, as is particularly the case with the French constitution of the Fifth Republic. (See Table 2-1.) The prototypes we will use (because they are the oldest form of presidential and parliamentary governments) are the United States and England.

TABLE 2-1 Democratic Regimes*

PRESIDENTIAL OR LEANING TOWARD PRESIDENTIALISM	PARLIAMENTARY	
United States	England	Ireland
France	Australia	Israel
Colombia	Austria	Italy
Costa Rica	Belgium	Netherlands
Mexico	Finland	Japan
Senegal	Canada	New Zealand
Venezuela	Denmark	Norway
Argentina	West Germany	Spain
Brazil	Greece	Portugal
Sri Lanka	India	Sweden
Cyprus		

*Actually Mexico, Argentina, and Brazil do not, properly speaking, belong among democracies. Virtually all regimes in Latin America and Africa are presidential or semipresidential, but they are not democratic. Finland, and Portugal give to their president some independent personal powers. In all other parliamentary systems the chief executive — a monarch or an elected official — is a figurehead. France has a strong parliamentary component.

Cabinet Government[2]

In parliamentary regimes the legislature makes the laws, controls the finances, appoints and dismisses the prime minister and his fellow

1. James Madison in the *Federalist Papers*, no. 51, para. 4.
2. The classic statement on cabinet government is Walter Bagehot, *The English Constitution* (1867; rpt. Oxford: Oxford University Press, 1936); *see also* Ivor Jennings, *Cabinet Government* (London: Macmillan, 1940).

ministers (the cabinet), and debates public issues. Parliament is supreme. Yet because of the development of strong and disciplined parties and the support they give to their leadership, the relationship between executive and legislative has changed. It is the cabinet that now initiates legislation and makes policy. Government measures (government bills) have precedence over any other business and their passage is virtually a formality. The majority party in the legislature votes for the measure proposed by its leadership — the prime minister and the cabinet. The opposition party or parties are given time to criticize but after the allotted time for debate has been spent, only a few days at most, a vote in favor of the government bill invariably follows. The majority party votes for its leadership — the prime minister and the cabinet. It is only when the party majority in Parliament is very tenuous or when the majority consists of a coalition of parties that support for the government is uncertain.

Thus the parliamentary regime has in fact become transformed into a cabinet government whereby the leadership of the majority party and its leader, who is prime minister, control the command structure. The supremacy of the legislature has become transformed into the supremacy of the executive in a manner that even an American president would covet.

The cabinet has the totality of executive power. This concentration of power, however, is qualified by responsibility, since the cabinet is at all times responsible to the Parliament and is constantly scrutinized by the Parliament and, through the Parliament, by the people. As Walter Bagehot wrote, "The . . . secret of the English constitution may be described as the close union, the nearly complete fusion, of the executive and the legislative powers. . . .*The connecting link is the Cabinet.*"[3] But in order for this type of command structure to exist, some conditions have to be met and must continue to obtain:

1. The political parties must be well disciplined; their members in Parliament must vote as one. Cross-voting should be the exception.
2. The parties must be few in number, ideally only two. Parliamentary regimes with more than two political parties cannot provide for a strong and stable cabinet government since there will be no clear majority to support it.
3. The right of dissolution of the Parliament and holding a new election is explicitly and unequivocally given to the prime minister with no strings attached.
4. It is generally expected that the winning party will have a majority and not a mere plurality of the popular vote. If over a period of time a mere voters' plurality is translated into a comfortable parliamentary majority, the strength of the command structure may become weakened. People will dispute its right to act as if it represented the majority. This has been the case, increasingly, both in England and in the Federal Republic of Germany.

3. Bagehot, p. 67.

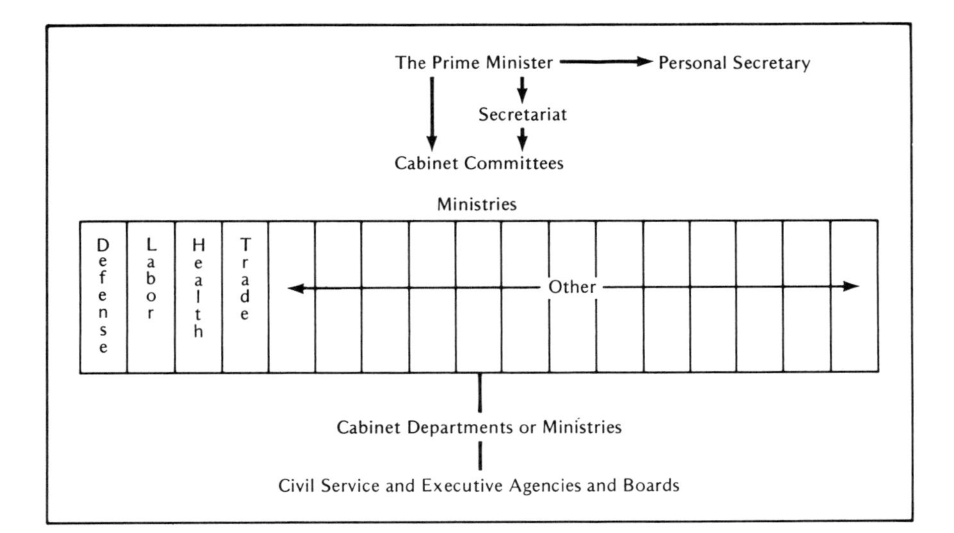

5. Finally it is expected that neither one of the major parties will retain a majority over a long period of time. In most parliamentary regimes the major parties, or party blocs, alternate in office.

The Organization of the Cabinet

Over time the cabinet and the prime minister have emerged as quasi-independent policy-making institutions. Furthermore, the prime minister's role has become institutionalized: it has become an *office* with bureaucratic agencies that give to it a structure with an identity separate from the cabinet. In this regard, the following specific trends should be noted:

1. The development of the office of the prime minister.
2. The development of cabinet committees.
3. The development of a number of specialized agencies for the purpose of assisting the prime minister and the cabinet in the formulation and the determination of policy.
4. The development of coordinative, information, and research agencies.
5. The power of the prime minister to determine the agenda of the cabinet meetings and cabinet committees. Some of the most important cabinet committees in Great Britain have been the Legislative Committee, the Overseas Policy and Defense Committee, the Social Services Committee, the Home Affairs Committee, the Economic Policy Committee, the Public Expenditure Scrutiny Committee, the Production Committee, and the Legislation Committee.
6. The development of a cabinet secretariat.[4]

4. Samuel H. Beer, *The British Political System* (New York: Random House, 1974), Chap. 2, especially pp. 39–40.

The secretariat is an office composed of a group of high-ranking civil servants, attached to the cabinet, whose duties are to keep minutes of the cabinet meetings and coordinate the work of the cabinet committees, record and communicate the decisions taken, help the prime minister prepare the agenda for the cabinet meetings, and circulate the agenda to the cabinet members in advance of the meetings. Also it provides the prime minister and the cabinet members with information to assist the prime minister in supervising the implementation of policy.

Under the constitution of the Federal Republic of Germany the chancellor — the equivalent of the British prime minister — has seen his powers grow so much so that the regime has been referred to as a "Chancellor's democracy" *(Kanzeldemokratie).* Today the chancellor's office has assumed, in addition to defense and foreign policy, the task of policy coordination. The chart on page 31 shows that the chancellor's office — as with the American or French presidents, and perhaps even more than the British prime minister — has developed the structure and the services that enable him to develop policy guidelines and coordinate the cabinet and the civil service accordingly.

Presidential Regimes: The United States

In all presidential regimes the president is at the top of a vast and sprawling executive network with special and personal powers. In the United States these powers derive directly from the Constitution and directly from the president's election by the people. According to the Constitution, the president is:

1. *Commander-in-Chief.* He is responsible for the preparedness of the armed forces, their equipment, their strategy, and their offensive or defensive posture.
2. *Foreign Policy Negotiator.* He actually lays out the broad objectives of the nation's policies in time of war or peace.
3. *Manager-in-Chief.* His duty to see to it that the laws are faithfully executed makes him the head of the administrative apparatus of the federal government. It is for the president to make certain that everything in the executive branch is being done efficiently and expeditiously.
4. *Party Leader.* Since his direct election by the people provides him with the tools for political leadership, he is the leader of the political party under whose label he has run for election. He is, therefore, a partisan figure, responsible for the party program and concerned with the party's political welfare and electoral strength.
5. *Spokesman of the Public Interest.* The president, more than any other government figure, speaks on behalf of the nation, and is presumed to act in accordance with what he considers the national interest. Given the manner in which he is elected, he represents a national constituency, whereas both the House and the Senate are often presumed to represent local and state interests.

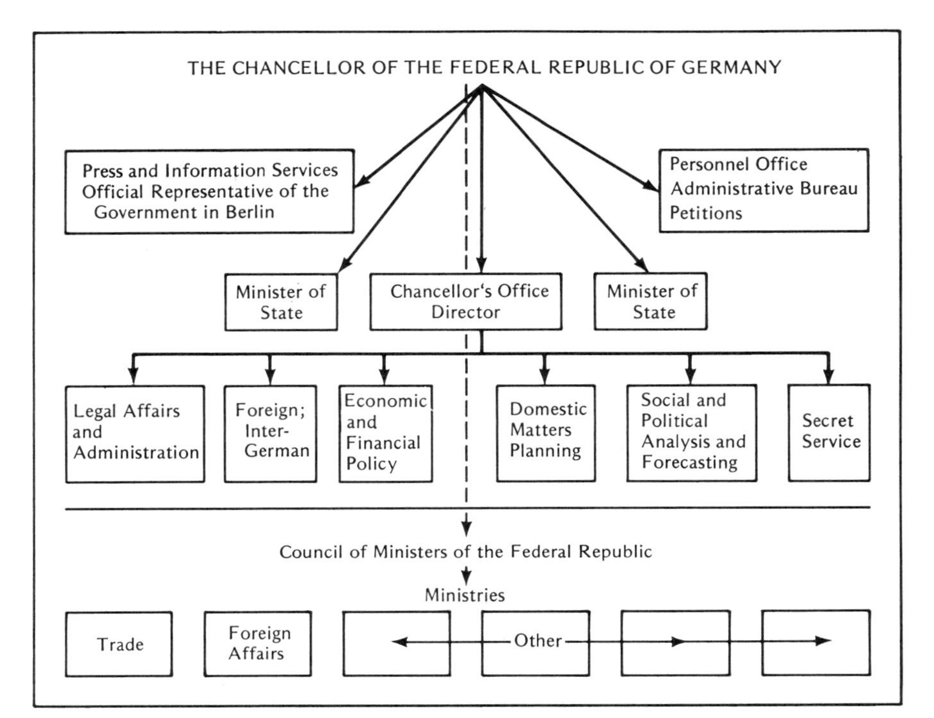

Note: Preparation of this chart was made possible through the courtesy of the Chancellor's Office in Bonn.

6. *Broker of Ideas and Policies.* Presidential pronouncements and policies attract public attention. Through a number of media at his disposal — press conferences, radio, and television — the president focuses the attention of the nation on certain issues. He marshals opinion in one direction or another, organizes consent, and mobilizes the public.[5]

The Organization of the Presidency

In the last fifty years or so the presidential structure has grown as rapidly as the policy-making functions of the presidency. The chart on page 32 speaks for itself. The president is at the very top of the executive branch with his own office, the executive office of the president. He is assisted by a personal staff, the White House office. The executive office consists of a number of agencies and committees that guide, regulate, and supervise the various departments or act directly on his behalf. Some provide research and information, others coordinate and decide on major policies and provide the major policy guidelines. They all speak to the president but more frequently they speak for him. They have become semi-autonomous executive bodies, a division of labor and of tasks, that no

5. The classic statement on the powers of the presidency is Edward S. Corwin, *The President: Office and Powers*, 5th rev. ed. (New York: New York University Press, 1984).

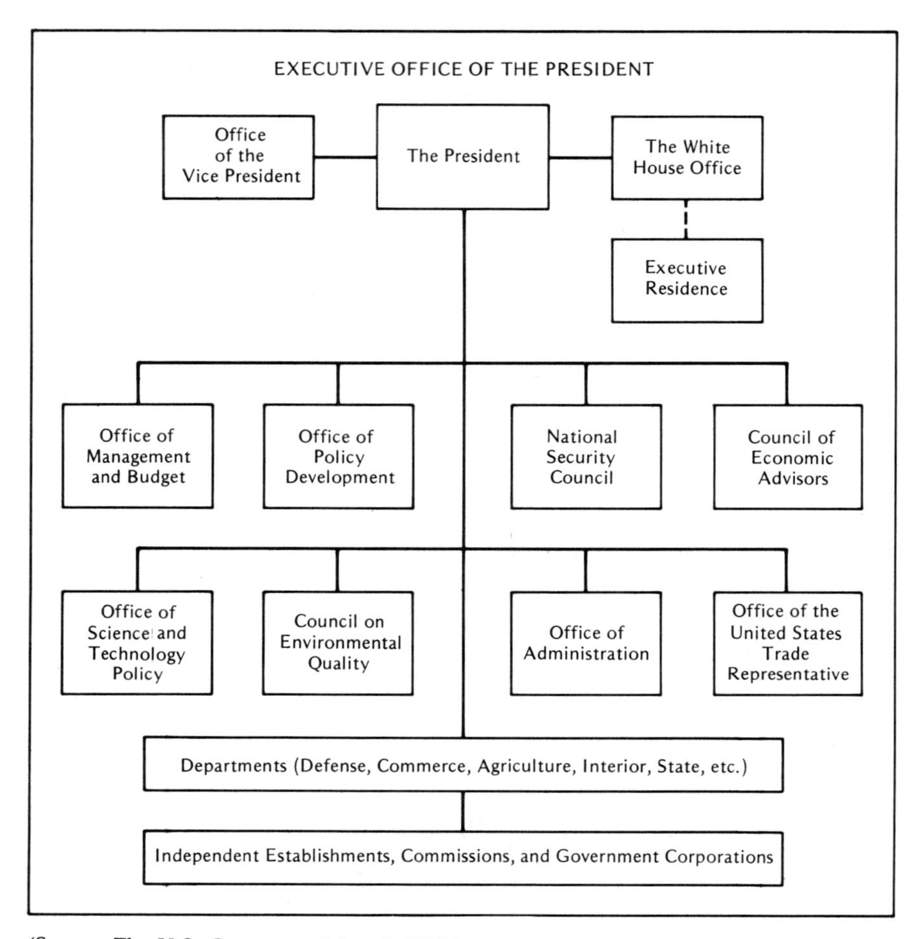

(Source: The U.S. *Government Manual,* 1984.)

president could ever fully coordinate. An enormous delegation of decision making is therefore implicit in the structure of the presidency and the offices it comprises.

SEMIPRESIDENTIAL AND SEMIPARLIAMENTARY REGIMES: THE CASE OF FRANCE

The framers of the constitution of the Fifth Republic (endorsed on September 28, 1958) reacted against the two major problems that had afflicted French republican regimes: an all-powerful legislature and an executive (the prime minister and the cabinet) that lacked stability and autonomous powers — in fact, the executive was dominated by the legislature. In order to eliminate these two problems, the French introduced an independent and strong presidential component, reinforced the powers of the prime minister and the cabinet, and reduced those of Parliament. The constitution is both presidential and parliamentary.[6]

The Presidential Sector The French president today holds the supreme executive power. He is no longer the symbolic head of the state — he is its real head. He is given personal and discretionary powers that no other president holds in any presidential system, even in the United States. He can dissolve the legislature at any time for any reason and call for an election; he can submit proposals to a referendum and if the proposal is accepted by the electorate, it supersedes existing legislation; he can appoint and remove the prime minister and he also has broad appointive and dismissal powers over all cabinet ministers and top officials in the army and the top civil service; he formulates the broad policy guidelines that the prime minister and the cabinet follow; he is in charge of foreign policy and defense, and conducts negotiations himself; he presides over the meetings of the council of ministers. Under certain circumstances he has the power to declare a state of siege and to govern by executive orders. He is elected directly by the people for a seven-year term and is reeligible for another seven years. Direct popular elections entitle him to speak on behalf of a national constituency, as is the case with the American president. Finally, again like the American president, he cannot be overthrown by the legislature and cannot even be impeached. He can be tried by a special tribunal only if he has committed treason or criminal acts as defined by the Criminal Code.

The Prime Minister and the Cabinet In addition to the presidential sector there is also a cabinet led by a prime minister. The prime minister "determines and conducts the policy of the Nation and is responsible before the Parliament." Special recognition is accorded to the prime minister. He directs the action of the government. He "assures the execution of the laws and exercises the rule-making power" (Articles 20 and 21). He determines the composition of his cabinet, presides over its meetings, and directs the administrative services. He defends his policy before the Parliament, answers questions addressed to him by the members of Parliament, states the overall program of the government in special programmatic

6. The best and most up-to-date discussion of the French constitution of the Fifth Republic is Jean-Louis Quermonne, *Le Gouvernment de la France sous la 5ième Republique,* 2d ed. (Paris: Dalloz, 1983).

declarations, and in general governs as long as he and the cabinet enjoy the confidence of a majority in the National Assembly (the lower house of the legislature).

What is worth noting is that the executive has been divided into two parts: the major part is the president, while the lesser one is the cabinet. The cabinet is the creature of the president, executing his major policy guidelines: financial, economic, social, strategic, and in foreign policy. Any disagreement between the prime minister and the president is resolved quickly, as has been the case a number of times, with the resignation of the prime minister and the nomination of his successor by the President.

Presidential Dominance The French regime has evolved increasingly in the direction of presidential dominance. The president decides on policy issues without consulting his prime minister and cabinet; he has an office of the presidency, which is staffed with experts who elaborate and make policy and through which he directs the activities of the ministries; he meets with the cabinet, not to reach collective decisions but to hear views before deciding himself. The president has also assumed an increasingly larger political role: he has intervened actively in the legislative elections by asking the people to vote for his supporters, in order to gain a majority.

The dominance of the presidency has been translated into the growing institutionalization of the office (similar to that of the American presidency). The chart on page 35 indicates that in the Elysé (the equivalent of the White House), the French president disposes of personal staff, of technical advisers, of his own cabinet, and a large number of people in the general secretariat through which the ministries, the agencies of economic planning, the nationalized industries, welfare and social security services, employment, and of course defense and foreign affairs come under presidential control. Policy originates at the Elysé and the president has the authority and the means to check that his policy is implemented by the prime minister, the cabinet, and all subordinate governmental agencies.

While helped by the constitutional provision, presidential dominance has come about primarily because of extraconstitutional and political reasons. Since the inception of the 1958 constitution, coherent comprehensive, and disciplined political parties have developed in France. Ultimately the Gaullists and their allies stood on one side and the Socialists and their allies on the other to form a two-party bloc system. For almost twenty-five years the Gaullists dominated the legislature and supported the prime minister and the cabinet appointed by *their* president. "His" government in

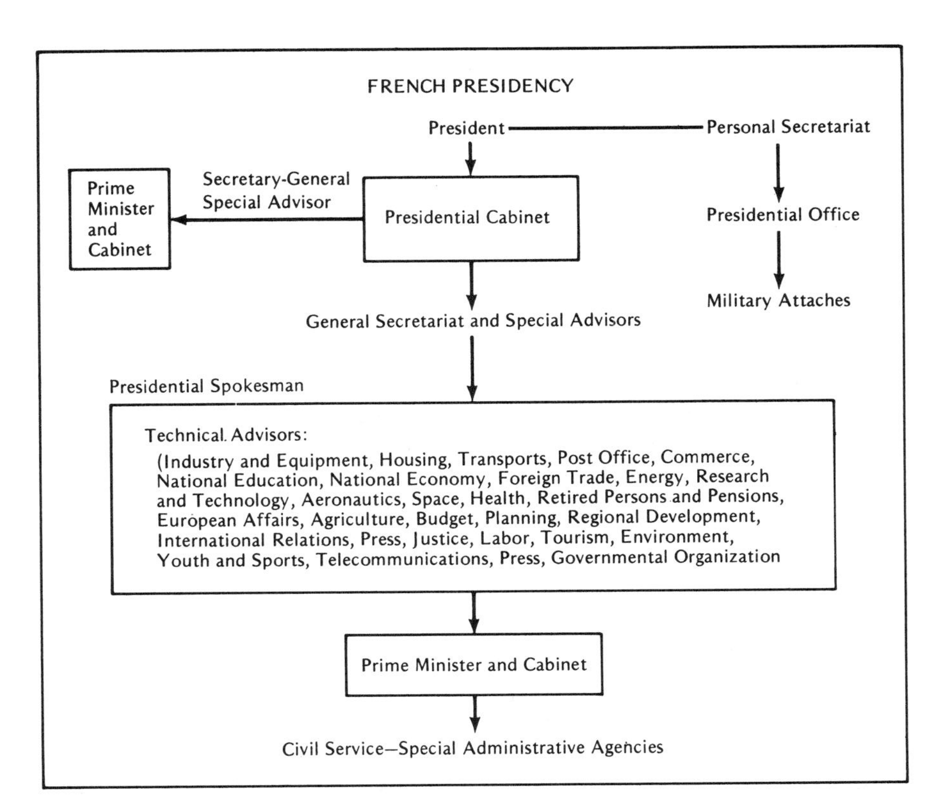

Note: I am grateful to my French colleagues Jean-Claude Colliard, chief of the cabinet of the French presidency, and Professor Jean-Louis Quermonne for the information they sent me in order to prepare this chart.

the National Assembly enjoyed majority support. In 1981 the political winds shifted, but the powers of the presidency remained. The Socialist candidate won the presidency in the national election in April–May 1981. He immediately dissolved the National Assembly and called for an election by which an all-Socialist majority was returned in the National Assembly to support the new president and his prime minister and cabinet. A deadlock was averted through the mechanism of dissolution.

Although the French system appears more flexible than the American one and more responsive to the majority of the electorate, what if a majority is elected in the legislature that is *against* the president of the French Republic? Will the president be able to defy it or will he submit to it? Will the regime be able to overcome and survive a deadlock as the American regime has learned to do? Is it possible to envisage a "cohabitation" between an incumbent President and a hostile majority in the legislature — so common in the United States — or is a "confrontation" between the two unavoidable?

Presidentialism: Diffusion and Distortion: A Note

Presidential regimes outnumber parliamentary ones. Many Latin American regimes have adopted at least in form the American presidential system, while most African countries have adopted some of the measures of the French semipresidential system. In many parliamentary regimes, the powers of the presidency have been reinforced. In Portugal and Finland the president is granted independent powers. In Portugal, Finland, and Sri Lanka, as in France, the president is elected directly by the people.

The diffusion of the presidential form amounts also to its distortion. Conceived in the United States and in France to operate in the context of democracy and a multiparty system, it has been only too frequently used to accentuate the concentration of political power, often absolute power, at the expense of democratic institutions and individual liberties. For example, in Latin America "presidentialism," has been used by military dictatorships: the military leader who takes power proclaims himself a "president." This has often been the case in Brazil, Argentina, Paraguay, Chile, and elsewhere. Similarly, presidential government has been used in single-party regimes. Mexico is the best illustration of a presidential single-party regime: it has been in operation for over fifty years.

The strengthening of the presidential sector in the French constitution of 1958, together with the need to establish a centralized political authority, account for the adoption of presidential government in many of the new African states (which were part of French Africa). Virtually all the former French colonies copied the French constitution of 1958. But as with Latin America, in many of these countries the president is a military ruler or the leader of a single party. Presidential power has amounted to the concentration of power and arbitrary rule in the hands of one individual or, at best, a small group. In such cases, presidentialism has been used as a device to control the centrifugal forces, to mitigate fragmentation, and to provide for unifying symbols. It has functioned as an instrument of authoritarian governance rather than in the democratic context envisioned in the United States and in France.

The Bureaucracy

Today, the bureaucracy is an essential part of the command structure in all advanced societies whatever the political regime. It has become institutionalized into well-organized, permanent organs that relate the activities and services of the modern state — from defense to welfare and education. It comprises departments, regulatory agencies, commissions, bureaus, public corporations, and nationalized industries, and it employs a sizable portion of the work force. Contrary to the traditional view that policy making is the job of elected and responsible officials and that the bureaucracy only implements and executes, the bureaucracy is an integral part of policy making, deliberation, and legislation. It straddles the major functions of government: legislative, executive, and judicial, and often serves as the buckle that binds them into a functioning entity. The bureaucracy deliberates and legislates, organizes and represents interests, adjudicates conflicts, and has wide discretionary powers in the provision of services without which our rights would be seriously undermined. In terms of sheer presence and numbers it overshadows all other organs of the state.

Policy Making

According to one long-standing view, there is a distinction between those who prepare the groundwork for policy (the bureaucrats) and those who make it (the political leaders in the executive branch or the legislature). However, this distinction is no longer tenable in any democratic society, or for that matter in any other contemporary political regime. Bureaucrats directly influence policy not only because of the information and advice they give but also because the bureaucratic organizations and the civil servants manning them are explicitly empowered to make policy. They in fact legislate.

Legislation Bureaucracies are the most important lawmaking organizations of the modern state. They fix prices and wages, decide on social security adjustments, determine the rules on labeling products, allow or disallow the sale of drugs, regulate transportation and fix its rates, determine unemployment compensation benefits, and establish environmental rules and restrictions. In short, they set rules and standards that affect our everyday lives. This indeed covers a vast area of delegated or administrative legislation, and it involves discretion, judgment, initiative, and knowledge.

But that is not all. Quite frequently legislation enacted by the legislature is itself initiated and/or prepared by the relevant bureaucratic organizations. It may include: major legislative reforms, the reorganization of the civil service, the development of institutions and policies for economic planning, the reorganization of branches of the executive, the establishment of new ministries and departments, the development of national health insurance plans, the initiation of major energy policies, the reorganization of the foreign service, the setting of subsidies for industries and agriculture, and even the preparation of the budget. The expertise and training of the bureaucrats entitles them to receive special attention from the political leaders. In reality, the lines between policy making entrusted to the latter and policy implementation for which the former are responsible are very much blurred. As a result, there is one question that is constantly being raised about the nature of the bureaucracy: Is it *representative?*

Representativeness Bureaucrats are not elected; they are appointed; they have no constituency — they serve their political masters; they have no policy commitments — they execute policy; they seek no supports beyond those that the recognition of loyal service (merit promotions and a good salary) entitles them to. They are supposed to be men and women without passions and political preferences. These generalizations hardly apply to contemporary democracies.

The distinction between what is *public* and what is *private* is no longer clear. Bureaucracies and private interests both have the same areas of concern. They have, in the words of Charles Merriam, common areas of "cooperation and cohesion in the common cause and on a common basis in many fields of common action."[7] This cooperation, what may be called "osmosis," is nowhere seen more clearly than in the areas of economic and social policy that bring the bureaucracy and a host of private interests together, both in the drafting and implementation of policy. Public officials and private interests that may be affected by decisions meet to discuss them. Advisory bodies is the order of the day. The French Economic Plan, for example, is staffed literally by thousands of such committees both on a territorial basis and on a functional basis. Here in the United States, there are 1,500 advisory committees in the federal government. In the various departments or ministries discussions on every policy issue will include representatives of private groups so that they can express their views on taxation, imports policy, investment, etc. There is an institutionalized dialogue in which either the civil service or the private sector takes the initiative. Multinationals and big corporations are linked with the bureaucracy when it comes to energy, foreign policy, economic aid, and the like. It is all these advisory committees that give the bureaucracy a representative character.

Constituency Building A constituency is the territorial unit from which a representative (that is, an *individual*) is elected. But bureaucratic *organizations* have their own constituencies as well; they consist of the interests a particular bureaucratic organization relates to, regulates, and affects. Bureaucratic organizations go out of their way to establish direct links with these interests (advisory committees are but one form). In fact, the strength of a given public service and its effectiveness depends on the relations it establishes with its interest constituency and, equally to the point, the welfare of the interests involved depends in turn on the relationships they have established with a given bureaucratic organization. Bureaucracies, therefore, represent and often organize interests. They speak for a given public and can claim a representative function just as legitimate and powerful as that of the legislature.

Thus the bureaucracy overlaps with the legislature, the executive, and the judiciary. It initiates and makes policy; it represents and speaks for a great variety of interests; it integrates interests and makes policy *with*

7. Quoted in Mark Nadel and Francis E. Rourke, "Bureaucracies," in *Handbook of Political Science*, Vol. V, p. 407.

them and *for* them; it is given a wide discretion in implementing policy; and it adjudicates conflicts between individuals and the state or among competing parties and interests. It is therefore not an adjunct to the state or subordinate to the state; it is an integral part of the command structure. Its size and organization correspond to the authoritarian component that exists in all democracies. It is a component that may grow beyond control, and one of the most important problems facing democracies is to reconcile its power with individual rights and freedoms.

The Configuration of the Elite[8]

The elite comprises individuals and groups that are close to the command structure. They directly and indirectly influence the policy makers: the executive branch, the administration, the lawmakers, and even the judges. Elites are the social matrix within which the government officials operate, and in democratic regimes they have the following characteristics:

Multidimensionality

There are many reasons why the elite attain their position: economic resources; education; and communication, professional, technical, and organizational skills. There are also many groups that comprise the elite: journalists, columnists, TV commentators and news analysts, trade union organizers, political organizers, the scientific community, the military establishment, the churches, the government officials themselves (especially those who have held high civil service positions in the foreign service or in technical, economic, and social services), businessmen, and certain professionals such as doctors and lawyers.

In advanced industrial societies there are millions of people who constitute the elite. Not only do they have access to policy makers, they are deferred to by the policy makers. They also directly influence the attitudes of people who are not members of any elite group but who defer and listen to them because of their social standing. Such an elite could be exceedingly powerful if it were unified and if it functioned on behalf of one single purpose. But the *multidimensionality* of the elites in democratic regimes is characterized by the many attitudes and the many positions different groups within it take, that is, *its heterogeneity.*

Heterogeneity

The elite is divided and holds different positions on the same issues. Sometimes the differences are between just two groups: this is typically

8. Two contrasting points of view about the elite in democracies are presented in Robert A. Dahl, *Who Governs: Democracy and Power in an American City* (New Haven, Conn.: Yale University Press, 1961), and in C. Wright Mills, *The Power Elite* (New York: Oxford University Press, 1956).

the situation of trade union leaders and the managers of a company. Sometimes the differences cluster: some groups are for a given policy, others are against it. For instance, groups favoring more defense spending and less welfare cluster against those who favor more welfare and less defense spending. Sometimes the differences are sharp and pit a given elite against government officials: for instance, the business and industrial groups who oppose higher income taxes. Ideologies can splinter the elite into many groups as, for example, in the case of groups who have strong feelings about particular issues, such as peace, nuclear weapons, environmental policies, economic controls and planning, socialization of the productive resources, and so on. Occasionally, especially in times of national danger or war, there may be a convergence of the most influential elite groups and they may manage to silence or to neutralize the others. Heterogeneity leads to the third characteristic of democratic elites: *competitiveness*.

Competitiveness

In democracies there is a genuine competition for influence, resources, and power among elite groups. It often amounts to a political contest that pits a given array of elite groups against another or that cuts across the elites themselves. The rules of competition, however, also determine its limits. Competition is almost always about increments, it is not about wholes; it is about something, not everything. It relates to policy shifts and policy outputs that by and large do not affect the existing status quo. Even when a cluster of elite groups is united on one side of an issue and is pitted against a cluster that opposes it, competition does not involve the destruction of one; it is at most a confrontation, more often an accommodation, but hardly ever a war! Even when the differences that separate groups appear to be irreconcilable, they hold each other at bay, which leads to the fourth characteristic of democratic elites: *multivalence*.

Multivalence

Each elite has a certain weight. Some are heavier than others. But shifts and combinations, shufflings and reshufflings of elite groups with regard to electoral choice, policy making, and allocation of resources very often amount to a situation where various combinations *counter* others. The idea of countervaling power — for example, trade unions against management or the church against the state — is the societal equivalent of checks and balances. No single dominant group within the elite can gain a monopolistic position. The situation is oligopolistic (a few). We noted that a convergence might occasionally develop, but it is a convergence that amounts to a temporary agreement of some groups and it always carries the seeds of divergences. In other words, even if a power elite consisting of the most important groups is dominant over a period of time, it constantly faces the prospects of dislocation. It is at best only a coalition.

Whatever consensus it might be able to fashion and impose is in the long run no more than tentative, which leads to a fifth characteristic: *circulation.*

Circulation

Some elite groups disappear and new ones come upon the scene. The immigrant, the technician, the corporate managers replace the native-born families, the property owner, or the family firm. New techniques create new social groups and new skills replace the old. New technology spawns a brand new class of managers and officers in the defense establishment to replace the old. Deference for elite groups shifts and changes as their respective position changes in terms of status, income, and skills. Also, even within a single elite group, the door remains open for outsiders. Ethnic minorities move up into important political positions; disfranchised segments of the population gain political power; the children of workers go on to higher education, which moves them up to professional elite groups and the status that goes with them. With all these changes the elites are always in a state of flux and while their dominant position may appear to be solid, in reality it is never secure. There was a time when only the sons of the nobility could occupy positions in the British Foreign Office, which was once referred to as the "outdoor relief department of the British aristocracy." There was a time when the Lowells and the Cabots controlled the economy and the politics of New England. Not anymore. The senator from Massachusetts during the 1978–1984 term was the son of a Greek immigrant and the incumbent he defeated in 1978 was a black.

The argument is often made that the elites coopt people from non-elite groups and that by so doing they maintain and propagate their position and point of view. This is true, but there can never be assurance, and in fact there never is, that the individuals coopted will not become renegades. Very often they do! No elite has ever developed foolproof screening devices, not even the Catholic church. Only in totalitarian regimes, as we will see, where the political elite is dominant, can the screening of newcomers be thorough. In democratic regimes, where there are many competing and different elite groups, it is easier for newcomers to move in. All they need is shrewdness and talent, not orthodoxy.

The argument cannot be pushed too far, however, because there are limits to accessibility and circulation. There are rigidities and entrance requirements that many cannot satisfy or overcome. Even in the most open democratic regimes elites set up barriers to prevent new entrants, and they establish their own codes and standards to bind their members. Newcomers who have educational and social disabilities, for example, cannot easily compete with the advantages of those with wealth, status, and power.

Interchangeability

With open circulation there is also a great deal of interchangeability in elite positions among different groups. A person belonging to one elite group may move to another. A general may seek the Presidency; a lawyer may become a politician and in turn may shift to corporate management; ecclesiastics have joined political parties and have been elected to office only to relinquish it to become university presidents; army officers have moved to managerial positions and one astronaut gave up the search for the stars to seek the presidency. There are, however, limits to interchangeability. It is difficult to see an army general becoming a bishop (even though the Born-Again Christians may find a way) and rather unlikely for a corporate manager to lead a trade union. But at the very top of each elite group the interchangeability remains great and much in evidence in many democracies.

Limitations on the Command Structure

As we have seen, the executive and the bureaucracy and the elite within which they operate are the major forces, organs, and instrument of decision making. They govern. But they do so under a set of limitations. As previously noted, all democratic regimes impose limitations on the command structure: the executive, the bureaucracy, and even the lawmakers. In all democracies we find clearly spelled out limitations — "no trespass" signals. There are two types. One deals with the substance of power, what those in command can or cannot do. The second deals with the procedures for the exercise of power, the manner in which decisions are made. Limitations, substantive and procedural, are many and varied, and once established they develop their own dynamic, like all other institutions, and undergo changes to adapt to new needs and conditions. Whatever the limitations, they are not worth much unless those who ignore them can be sanctioned and unless the decisions they make can be set aside. The existence of an independent body (in democracies it is the judiciary) remains one of the most important vehicles for enforcing the limitations imposed upon those who are in command. We note here some of the most prevalent limitations.

Federalism

A federal system is generally one where the power to command is divided between two separate and independent governmental units operating within the same territory. The federal government is allotted a set of powers to be exercised over all citizens. Other powers are given to individual units, the states. These powers are residual or specific and are determined by the constitution. They involve actions that the states can take through their own governments within their own separate territorial jurisdictions. The federal government is usually empowered to act for defense, foreign affairs, currency and banking, postal services, and commerce and trade between the states. The states are usually granted most other powers. Often some of the powers of the federal government and of the states can be exercised concurrently with those of the states, and there can be overlap, conflict, or cooperation.

Besides the United States and Switzerland we find federal arrangements in many democracies, including the Federal Republic of Germany, Canada, India, and Australia. In some federal systems the jurisdiction of the federal government is clearly circumscribed and the residual powers that belong to the individual states — the cantons as they are called in Switzerland — are extensive and exclusive. In the United States judicial interpretation has widened the scope of the power of the federal government. A new concept of federalism has developed, which stresses cooperation between the states and the national government with the former acting to implement policies that are decided upon and financed by the latter.

In all federal systems there is a second chamber — an upper house: the Senate in the United States, the Bundesrat in West Germany, the Council of States in Switzerland. These bodies represent the individual units that comprise the federation. Each individual state in turn has its own legislature and executive to deal with all matters under its jurisdiction. Legislation or constitutional amendments that affect the powers or the representation of the states must be approved by the second, or federal, chamber.

Decentralization

Decentralization is the process whereby the central government delegates a number of functions and duties to local units and to their elected representatives, for example, running the schools, taking care of city and municipal roads, providing fire services, raising revenue and spending it, promoting tourism, establishing health clinics, and so forth. Though these powers are delegated by the legislature and technically can be revoked at will by the legislature, local government and its agencies become institutionalized and cannot be easily dismantled. These local powers in turn become limitations on the central authority. They correspond to powerful enclaves that once erected cannot be easily invaded. Decentralization — local, city, or regional — is closely associated with the ideas of self-government, with the rights of people to take care of their own affairs in matters that directly concern their community. It has been very much in evidence in many European states: in West Germany, Italy, England and even France where in 1982 there was a radical overhaul of the territorial arrangements, and genuine self-government in departments and regions with local and regional representative councils with some autonomous powers and some independent financial resources.

Functional Federalism

In contrast to decentralization, functional federalism is not related to the territorial delegation of powers. It involves the delegation by the state of independent powers and functions (television; universities; urban transportation; industrial production in coal, steel, electricity, gas, nuclear energy; banking, etc.) to certain public agencies or corporations. Special agencies are set up to run these activities, sometimes only under the overall supervision of the central authority and sometimes under a charter that allows them the broadest autonomy in managing the activities entrusted to them. Public corporations, many nationalized industries, and supervisory and regulatory boards, all of which abound in modern industrialized democracies, carry on the activities and responsibilities delegated to them — independently of the legislature and the executive. They produce and distribute coal or electricity; they run the national radio and television networks; they control the supply of money. Such functional units gradually develop into institutions; they become legitimized. They gain enough autonomy to limit the powers of the central government.

Separation of Powers: Checks and Balances

Federalism divides power within the same territory between the federal government and the individual states that comprise the federation. Separation of powers divides the command structure at the top. It allots the power to command to different and competing units: the legislature, the executive, and the judiciary. Whether the division is suggested for functional reasons — to attribute distinct and different tasks to separate organs or whether it is simply to split power into distinct and separate organs in order to weaken it — the result is the same: a concentration of political power is avoided.

The checks-and-balances system is inherently associated with the separation of powers. It is a mechanical notion whereby power is institutionalized in the various organs that can block each other in the making of a decision. Checks allow one power to directly make its weight felt upon another. The legislature may impeach the president, members of the executive, or the judiciary; the executive may dissolve or adjourn the legislature in parliamentary regimes and the legislature may vote the government out of office; the president may veto legislation and his veto can in turn be overridden by a reinforced majority in the legislature; one legislative assembly can veto the decisions of the other. Checks are spelled out in detail by Madison in the *Federalist Papers* to show, however, that there is enough cooperation and interaction among the major organs of government for a "balance" to result without paralyzing policy making.[9]

9. Madison, *Federalist Papers,* No. 51.

Bicameralism

Not only in federal but also in unitary democratic regimes a way of limiting legislative power, and hence to contain a given majority, is to establish two legislative bodies and require their concurrence in legislation. One body, referred to as the lower house, is elected directly by the people; the second, the upper chamber, is hereditary or else appointed or elected indirectly on the basis of special qualifications and arrangements.

In most parliamentary regimes the roles and powers of the upper chamber have been sharply reduced. In Great Britain, for instance, the House of Lords has lost all powers over the budget and fiscal matters and cannot block legislation passed by the House of Commons for more than nine months. In West Germany it is only when the powers of the states are involved in any given legislation that the Bundesrat's agreement is needed. In France the lower house (the National Assembly) can override the upper chamber (the Senate) only if it votes on three separate occasions, and at the request of the Prime Minister, on the bill vetoed by the Senate. Many modern democracies have dispensed altogether with an upper chamber, as for example in Spain and Greece. It is only in the United States that the upper chamber (the Senate) maintains powers equal to and in certain matters greater than the House. The House and the Senate are equal partners in lawmaking.

Referendums

The practice of referendums is common for the states in America and for both the national government and the cantons in Switzerland. In France, however, it has been used only occasionally (five times) since 1958 and only on one occasion in Great Britain. It is provided for in a number of democratic constitutions, including some of the most recently drafted, for example, in Portugal, Greece, and Spain. Referendums provide another limitation on both the legislature and the executive. They allow the people to decide, by a majority vote, on certain important issues such as constitutional amendments, nuclear energy, treaties, and so on. The constraint becomes even more powerful when a referendum can be initiated by the people, something that can be done in the United States (but only in the states) and in Switzerland, where a number of cantons or a percentage of voters can initiate a referendum.

Ineligibility

Ineligibility is a provision that prevents an incumbent — president, governor, or mayor, occasionally even legislators — from running for office after serving a given period of time. The usual period of time is one or two terms (seven, five, six, or four years each). Extreme cases of ineligibility can be found in Mexico, where the same president cannot run after his six-year term expires. A spectacular case was that of the Second French

Republic in 1848. The president, like the Mexican president today, was ineligible after his first term. Louis Napoleon Bonaparte, who was elected in 1848, could not run again, but he did not wait long. In 1851 he became an emperor! At times ineligibility may tempt powerholders rather than restrain them.

Amending the Constitution

Officials both in legislature and the executive often frèt about the limitations that are imposed by a constitution, and they may wish to amend it so as to lift the restrictions. All democratic regimes, therefore, make amendments difficult by establishing special procedures and requiring special majorities. Sometimes a referendum is needed; sometimes two-thirds of both chambers must agree; in federal systems the concurrence of more than a majority of the states is required. There may even be some provisions that cannot be amended at all as with individual freedoms in the constitution of the Federal Republic of Germany (Articles 1–18) or with the democratic form of government, as in France and elsewhere. In all cases the requirement of reinforced majorities and special procedures to amend a constitution dampen the temptation of officeholders to bend it to their own will.

Judicial Review[10]

In almost all democratic regimes the courts are the guardians of the constitution against any violations by anybody in the command structure. They maintain the limitations the constitution imposes both with regard to the exercise of power and to its substance. But judicial review varies from one country to another (see Table 2-2).

In the United States any and every act of the command structure — by the President, the Congress, the bureaucracy, the states and their own legislatures or governors — can be challenged before any court as unconstitutional, and the courts, any court, can decide whether it conforms to the Constitution or not. The courts monitor the federal system and protect individual rights.

In most other democracies only special courts can hear cases involving the constitution and can do so only about special provisions of the constitution. Some deal with the federal structure, as in Switzerland, others with both the federal structure and the individual freedoms, as in West Germany. Judicial review is compartmentalized and special courts, as opposed to any court (as in the United States), are established to pass judgment on questions of constitutionality. In France, review for constitutionality is limited and is undertaken by a special body, the Con-

10. The best argument for comprehensive judicial review remains the decision of Chief Justice Marshall in *Marbury* v. *Madison* (1803), in Robert Cushman, *Leading Constitutional Decisions*, 14th ed. (New York: Appleton-Century-Crofts, 1971), pp. 1–11. See also Mauro Cappelletti, *Judicial Review in the Contemporary World* (Indianapolis, Ind.: Bobbs-Merrill, 1971) and Martin Shapiro, "Courts," in *Handbook of Political Science*, Vol. V, pp. 321–372.

stitutional Council, which was established by the constitution of 1958. Originally its major role was to supervise the relations between executive and legislature in order to prevent the encroachment of the legislature on the powers of the executive: the prime minister, the cabinet, and the presidency.

Judicial review of the constitutionality of laws or executive decisions is comprehensive when anybody and everybody can raise it, and for any reason. This is the case in the United States. In other democratic regimes a challenge can be raised only by special bodies: in France by the president of the Republic, the presidents of the National Assembly and the Senate, the prime minister, and by any sixty members of either the National Assembly or the Senate.

In finding an act of the legislature or the executive to be unconstitutional the courts in some democracies are empowered to declare such acts null and void. Their decision not only suspends the application of a law but destroys it. The effect of the decision is to nullify the law, as if it never existed. In other regimes, however, the decision simply suspends the law or invites the legislature to reconsider and redraft it.

Table 2-2 shows the major variations in judicial review, both comprehensive and partial. But we should note that there are democracies, England for instance, where judicial review for constitutionality is not permitted. The courts must enforce all legislative enactments, given the principle of the supremacy of Parliament.

TABLE 2-2 Judicial Review: Variations

	COMPREHENSIVE	PARTIAL
Who can challenge?	Anybody and everybody	Special organs; individuals but only under restrictive conditions
For what reasons?	Any alleged violation of the constitution	Injury/damage/cause
To which court?	Any court	Special courts
At what time?	Any time	Last appeal
Scope of judicial review?	Constitution and constitutional order	Specific parts of the constitution
Impact of decision	Nullification	Suspensive/advisory/nullification

Bibliography

On Democratic Institutions

Andrews, William G. *Presidential Government in Gaullist France.* Albany, N.Y.: State University of New York Press, 1982.

Berkeley, Humphrey. *The Power of the Prime Minister.* London: George Allen & Unwin, 1968.

Blondel, Jean. *The Organization of Government: A Comparative Study of Governmental Structures*. Beverly Hills, Calif.: Sage Publications, 1982.

Corwin, Edward S. *The President: Office and Powers*. 5th rev. ed. New York: New York University Press, 1984.

Dahl, Robert. *A Preface to Democratic Theory*. Chicago: University of Chicago Press, 1970.

Friedrich, Carl J. *Constitutional Government and Democracy: Theory and Practice in Europe and America*. 4th ed. New York: Ginn & Blaisdell, 1968.

Hamilton, Alexander, James Madison, and John Jay. *The Federalist*. New York: New American Library, 1961.

Handbook of Political Science, Vol. V, "Executives," pp. 173–243.

Jennings, Ivor. *Cabinet Government*. Cambridge: Cambridge University Press, 1959.

King, Anthony, (ed.). *The British Prime Minister: A Reader*. London: Macmillan, 1969.

Lindsay, A. D. *The Modern Democratic State*. Oxford: Oxford University Press, 1941.

Lipset, Seymour Martin. *Political Man: The Social Bases of Politics*. New York: Doubleday/Anchor, 1963.

Lowi, Theodore. *The End of Liberalism: The Second Republic of the United States*. 2d ed. New York: N. W. Norton, 1979.

Macridis, Roy C., and Bernard E. Brown. *The De Gaulle Republic: Quest for Unity*. 1962; rpt. Westport, Conn.: Greenwood Press, 1980.

Neustadt, Richard. *Presidential Power: The Politics of Leadership*. New York: John Wiley & Sons, 1960.

Nordlinger, Eric A. *On the Autonomy of the Democratic State*. Cambridge, Mass.: Harvard University Press, 1981.

Powell, G. Bingham, Jr. *Contemporary Democracies: Participation, Stability and Violence*. Cambridge, Mass.: Harvard University Press, 1984.

Quermonne, Jean-Louis. *Le Gouvernment de la France sous la Ve République*. 2d ed. Paris: Dalloz, 1983.

Rose, Richard, and Ezra Suleiman. *Presidents and Prime Ministers*. Washington, D.C.: American Enterprise Institute, 1980.

Rossiter, Clinton. *The American Presidency*. New York: Harcourt Brace, 1956.

Sartori, Giovanni. *Democratic Theory*. 1962; rpt. Westport, Conn.: Greenwood Press, 1973.

Schweitzer, C. C., D. Karsten et al. (eds.). *Politics and Government in the Federal Republic of Germany: Basic Documents*. Frankfurt: Berg Publishers, 1984.

Smith, Gordon. *Politics in Western Europe: A Comparative Analysis*. New York: Holmes & Meier, 1972.

Bureaucracy

Aberbach, Joel D., Robert D. Putnam, and Bert A. Rockman. *Bureaucrats and Politicians in Western Democracies*. Cambridge, Mass.: Harvard University Press, 1981.

Crozier, Michel. *The Bureaucratic Phenomenon.* Chicago: University of Chicago Press, 1964.
Dogan, Mattei (ed.). *The Mandarins of Western Europe: The Political Role of Top Civil Servants.* New York: John Wiley & Sons, 1975.
Ferrel, Heady. *Public Administration: A Comparative Perspective.* Englewood Cliffs, N.J.: Prentice-Hall, 1966.
Galbraith, John Kenneth. *The New Industrial State.* Boston: Houghton Mifflin, 1967.
Gross, Bertram. *The Management of Organization.* New York: The Free Press, 1964.
Heclo, Hugh. *A Government of Strangers: Executive Policy in Washington.* Washington, D.C.: The Brookings Institution, 1977.
La Palombara, Joseph (ed.). *Bureaucracy and Political Development.* Princeton, N.J.: Princeton University Press, 1963.
Nadel, Mark V., and Francis Rourke. "Bureaucracies," in *Handbook of Political Science,* Vol. V, pp. 373–429.

On the Constitutional Order

Andrews, William G. *Constitutions and Constitutionalism.* Princeton, N.J.: Van Nostrand, 1961.
Bagehot, Walter. *The English Constitution.* 1867; rpt. Oxford: Oxford University Press, 1936.
Finer, Samuel E. *Five Constitutions: Contrasts and Comparisons.* London: Penguin Books, 1979.
Friedrich, Carl J. *Constitutional Government and Democracy: Theory and Practice in Europe and America.* 4th ed. New York: Ginn & Blaisdell, 1968.
McIlwain, Charles. *Constitutionalism: Ancient and Modern.* Ithaca, N.Y.: Cornell University Press, 1947.
Spiro, Herbert. *Government by Constitution: The Political Systems of Democracy.* New York: Random House, 1959.
Wheare, Kenneth. *Modern Constitutions.* Oxford: Oxford University Press, 1966.

Federalism

Beer, Samuel, et al. *Federalism: Making the System Work.* Washington, D.C.: Center for National Policy, 1982.
Duchek, Ivo. *Comparative Federalism.* New York: Holt, Rinehart and Winston, 1970.
Friedrich, Carl J. *Trends of Federalism in Theory and Practice.* New York: Praeger, 1967.
King, Preston T. *Federalism and Federation.* Baltimore, Md.: Johns Hopkins University Press, 1983.
Riker, William. *Federalism: Origins, Operation, Significance.* Boston: Little, Brown, 1964.
Wheare, Kenneth. *Federal Governments.* Oxford: Oxford University Press, 1955.

On Judicial Review

Cappelletti, Mauro. *Judicial Review in the Contemporary World.* Indianapolis, Ind.: Bobbs-Merrill, 1971.

Chopper, Jesse H. *Judicial Review and the National Political Process.* Chicago: University of Chicago Press, 1980.

Levy, Leonard W. *Judicial Review and the Supreme Court.* New York: Harper & Row, 1967.

Shapiro, Martin. "Courts," in *Handbook of Political Science,* Vol. V, pp. 321–372.

3 *Organization of Consent: Representative Assemblies and Political Parties*

Introduction

The government — the command structure — consists of the executive, the bureaucracy, and the vast array of commissions, boards, regulatory agencies, and public corporations. In democratic regimes, the government acts on behalf of the people. It is a creature of the society; it represents the various societal forces and groups and is ultimately responsible to the source from which it derives its power: the people. This concept presupposes that the elites and the people organize in one form or another in order to elect their representatives in the command structure. They participate or are asked to participate. Democratic regimes require not only good judgment and restraint on the part of the people, as John Stuart Mill suggested; they also require an active and interested public.

Political participation is not limited only to elections, when people choose the legislature or the executive or both. It requires constant attention and involvement that can be realized only when there are permanent organizations to channel demands and interests. The major vehicle for ensuring participation is the political party. In order to satisfy the minimal requirements of choice, however, there must be more than one party. No regime is genuinely democratic if it consists of only one party, unless that single party includes many factions that are free to organize independently of one another and to present their own views and candidates in a primary election.

Participation and election have a twofold function: first, they give the people at large the instruments to determine the major policy guidelines and choose their representatives accordingly; second, they enable the people to pass judgment on the performance of the representatives they elected, and to hold them responsible for what they did, and quite often for what they did not do, and decide whether or not they deserve reelection. In this chapter we will examine the major instruments of participation and representation: the legislative assemblies and the political parties.

Participation

Politics is not the major concern of citizens, not even in democratic regimes. Most people give priority to major societal concerns: family life, work and business, sports, entertainment and leisure, and most of all the satisfaction of everyday needs.

What is political participation? Simply the various manifestations and activities through which citizens communicate their demands, interests, and expectations for the purpose of influencing the selection or the decisions of government officials, those who are theoretically our representatives. Although there are many specific facets and dimensions to participation, they can be grouped into four general types of activities.[1]

1. Individual citizen activity, initiated by the citizen (e.g., letter writing)
2. Cooperative or group activity (political clubs or associations)
3. Campaign activity
4. Voting

With all four of these activities we can measure the extent of participation easily. Obviously men or women who usually vote and also write two or three letters a year to their representative do not participate to the same extent as those who are constantly on the phone promoting candidates and issues and who are in constant communication with their representatives.

The most common method for measuring participation is to conduct a survey. We ask the critical questions, equate the positive answers to a scale of participation, and come up with aggregate figures. A small sample of the population, if it is carefully selected and if it is truly representative, can faithfully reproduce the nation at large. The questions we ask are based on the major criteria of participation. They relate to the following:

1. Efforts to persuade others how to vote
2. Active work for candidates

1. I follow the excellent analysis given in Sidney Verba, Norman H. Nie, and Jae-On-Kim, *The Modes of Political Participation: A Cross-National Comparison* (Beverly Hills, Calif.: Sage Publications, 1971). See also Norman Nie and Sidney Verba, "Political Participation," in *Handbook of Political Science*, Vol. IV, pp. 1–74 (Reading, Mass.: Addison-Wesley, 1975).

3. Attending political meetings or rallies
4. Contribution of money to candidates or the political party
5. Membership in political clubs
6. Past voting record, usually for the last two national elections
7. Past voting record in local elections
8. Working with others on local policy matters
9. Forming a group to work on local problems
10. Activity and membership in political organizations
11. Communications with local and national officials[2]

Survey findings indicate that except for voting (which ranges from as low as 50 percent to as high as 95 percent), the percentage of participants is very low with regard to all other criteria: it ranges from as low as 8 percent to as high as 30 percent. There is also no uniformity in participation and no clear correlation between one type of participatory activity or another. Some people write to their representatives every other week but they do not belong to a political club and sometimes they even forget to vote! The profile of the participant citizen is lopsided and the conclusion one draws is that participation is sporadic and unstructured even for the small percentage of those who actively participate in politics.

Many authors have drawn gloomy conclusions from this situation. The people appear uninterested, uninformed, apathetic, or alienated. They do not seem to be interested in public affairs and put their private problems before public ones. They accept the regime out of habit, inertia, apathy, or ignorance. Some people get aroused at election time, but this happens only once every two or four or five years; thereafter they lapse back into apathy. How can there be democracy without massive participation? If only few participate, then the foundations of democracies must indeed be frail.[3]

I don't think there is room for such gloomy forebodings. A more cheerful view emerges if we consider participation in terms of two dimensions that are not frequently taken into account: that of *intensiveness* (as opposed to extensiveness) and that of *latency* as opposed to actual participation. If we take this viewpoint, we will find that democratic regimes provide all the requirements for participation and often show a degree of participation that is not matched by any other political regime.

Intensiveness

Intensive participation, often used synonymously with mobilization, refers to concentrated political activities initiated for the purpose of bringing about certain goals. They are related to issues considered very important by some people, even a small minority, even if for a relatively short

2. Nie and Verba, op. cit.
3. In V. O. Key, *The Responsible Electorate* (Cambridge, Mass.: Harvard University Press, 1966) and E. E. Schattschneider, *The Semi-Sovereign People* (New York: Holt, Rinehart and Winston, 1960).

period of time: nuclear energy, pollution and environmental issues, nuclear freeze, the deployment of American missiles in West Germany (for the Germans), the position of England in the Common Market (for the British), unemployment (for almost all in Western Europe or the United States in the eighties), abortion versus the right to life, and so forth. Such activities are spontaneous. Organizers reach out to mobilize sympathizers or make converts. They often bypass the normal channels of political expression: the political parties or their representatives. The impact of such political activities may be far greater than numbers or even voting. It is like a flash in the darkness but it is a flash that lights up and transforms the landscape of inertia and apathy.

Democratic regimes constantly experience such flashes of intense political activity and commitment for or against an issue. The war in Algeria spurred the French into intensive participation for or against, just as Americans were aroused by the Vietnam war. If we review the years since World War II, we will see a series of periodic flashes of intensive participation or mobilization in democratic regimes. Take the United States, for instance: the civil rights movement, the registration of blacks, the student demonstrations in the late sixties, the anti-Vietnam war demonstrations and the antidraft movement, the environmentalist and more recently the nuclear freeze movements, and the antiabortion movement. They are all landmarks of intensive activity about politics and political issues, mobilizing people for one particular purpose and inevitably inviting countermobilization.

Latency

The argument about intensiveness suggests that there is always a potential for political participation and involvement in democratic regimes. The public *may* show no interest and *may* appear apathetic but it *can* show interest and *can* become active, because democracy provides the structures and the institutions whereby what is dormant can come to life. On the surface, democracies appear to leave the citizens alone to their problems and pursuits. Potentially, however, these same citizens may explode into activists, organizers, demonstrators, patriots, or revolutionaries. It is this *latency,* this potential participation, that constitutes a powerful restraint on officeholders lest they take decisions that will arouse citizens. This potential must be taken (and usually is) just as seriously as election returns. The very possibility that the public will be aroused becomes a powerful check, so much so that policy makers may refuse to make some decisions for fear that the support they enjoy will dissolve or turn into active opposition. Thus the anticipated reactions of the public to a given measure serve as guidelines and restraints on policy makers.

Can we measure intensiveness and latency? Only in terms of case studies that show how intensive participation is generated, how it spreads, how mobilizing it becomes, and how effective it turns out to be.

Enough such cases over a relatively short period of time — twenty or thirty years — may show a degree and intensity of public involvement that neither voting nor surveys nor party membership show. Also, as noted above, the very prospect of participation — intensive or latent — is a consideration that officeholders must take into account. Their political survival may depend on it.

Consent and Participation

Is participation a necessary condition of consent? Is nonparticipation or low levels of participation an indication of dissent and hostility toward the regime? Those who consider democratic regimes in terms of the participatory model of ancient Athens will answer both questions affirmatively. In ancient Athens direct participation in the affairs of the city was deemed to be the essence of democracy. The people themselves made policy decisions and had a direct hand in running the government. For modern democracies, however, with tens and even hundreds of millions of citizens involved, the answer to both questions may well have to be negative.

Democratic regimes are based on the acceptance of (1) rules that maintain a set of values and (2) the institutions through which the government makes policy in the context of these fundamental values. Nonparticipation is not always an indication of dissatisfaction or alienation as often argued. It may also indicate satisfaction. It may not be a sign of indifference or hostility but on the contrary it may mean satisfaction and agreement. If those in command, elected and held responsible in periodic elections respect the basic rules and act within them, the political regime is doing precisely what it is supposed to do: defend and protect the values its citizens hold dear. In this case, silence means consent. The fact that intensive participation emerges only when there are sharp differences about policy in a way favors our hypothesis that low levels of political participation may be a sign of satisfaction. In other words, everyday participation and involvement, even if desirable, is not a necessary condition in democracy.

Representation and Legislatures

In all modern democracies the notion of direct government by the people has been replaced by representative government: elected officials who run the government "on our behalf."[4] Representative government exists at virtually all levels of decision making — from the local level to the national government — from the mayor, the town councillors, the state or state representatives in a federal system, and all the way up to the national representatives in the legislature or the executive. As long as the

4. The classic statement is John Stuart Mill, *Considerations on Representative Government* (1867; rpt. New York: E. P. Dutton, 1970).

representatives have been freely chosen and can be held accountable for their actions within a given period of time (two, four, five, six, or seven years), the minimum conditions of representative government are fulfilled.

The hallmark of modern democracies, the institution that is viewed as preeminent, is the legislature — a freely and openly elected body of men and women who make the laws. Legislatures, however, do much more than make laws. They play, in varying degrees, a comprehensive role in virtually all affairs of state. They are multifunctional bodies.

Political and Legislative Functions[5]

The many functions performed by legislatures may be grouped into two categories: those that are literally legislative, such as the making of the laws, and those that are political, and deal with power relations and fundamental policy issues that do not always require legislation.

Legislative Functions *Deliberation and Lawmaking.* In theory, this is an all-important function of the legislature. But as we noted with the British Parliament (and the same is true for virtually all legislatures today), initiating legislation has become increasingly the prerogative of the executive, including the civil service, and deliberation has been reduced to a confrontation of the political parties and their leaders on general policy issues. The legislature does not have the time or the expertise to discuss highly complex measures involving technical, economic, social, and military problems. In virtually all legislative bodies, including even the U.S. Congress, few measures are initiated by the legislators and among them only a small fraction become laws. It is the Cabinet or presidential initiatives that account for the great majority.

Revenue and Expenses. The "power of the purse," the power to tax and to spend, lies at the heart of the origin and development of legislative assemblies not only in England but almost everywhere. Legislative assemblies deliberated and drafted the budget throughout the nineteenth century. But that was a period when the role of the state was limited to some essential services: defense, foreign policy, the police, the post office. The budget today encompasses far more. It has become a complex instrument of economic policy involving investment, modernization, industrialization, reallocation of resources, health, education, transportation, and above all defense and social welfare.

In theory, all legislative assemblies still have the last word on the budget because they are the ones who are empowered to enact a budget. In practice, it is the executive branch (the President or the Prime Minister and the Cabinet) that develops the annual budget, which is then sub-

5. On contemporary legislatures see Jean Blondel, *Comparative Legislatures* (Englewood Cliffs, N.J.: Prentice-Hall, 1973) and Gerhard Lowenberg and Samuel C. Patterson, *Comparing Legislatures* (Boston: Little, Brown, 1979).

mitted to the legislative assemblies for passage. It is only in the U.S. Congress that the budget can be extensively amended. In most other democracies restrictive rules prohibit the legislators from introducing amendments or initiating new taxes and new expenditures.

Investigations. Legislatures are free, within the limits and constraints deriving from the constitution or the internal distribution of political forces, to investigate every aspect of the polity or of policy. The French National Assembly right after the end of World War II produced a monumental series of reports on the causes of the French military defeat. In Great Britain, Royal Commissions, initiated by the Parliament, produced reports that changed policies with regard to welfare, health, the civil service, the organization and recruitment of the armed forces, and other matters. In the United States, investigation is almost "the name of the game" and there has been hardly any aspect of policy that has not been thoroughly investigated and reported on. But investigation, aside from being a necessary condition for deliberation and legislation, is often used as a downright political instrument for control. How funds have been used by a given agency, how funds have been raised for electoral purposes by certain candidates, the efficiency of the Defense Department, the awarding of defense contracts — all give the opportunity to the legislature to oversee the executive branch and interfere in policy making and policy decisions even where no legislation is required.

Subordinate Legislation. With the coming of the welfare state, and the intervention of the state in the economy, legislation has to increasingly deal with specific and technical problems and with discrete social and occupational categories. As a result, in almost all legislative assemblies there has been a tendency to draft laws that provide for a general statement of purpose, often referred to as a "framework law," and to allow the administrative agencies to put legislation in the form of ordinances, executive orders, orders in council, or decrees within the guidelines of the framework law. This has produced a new body of law: "administrative law," or "subordinate legislation." If you consider the framework law to be the parent and subordinate legislation its children, you will find that there has been a legislative population explosion whereby the parent has completely lost sight and control of the children while the children no longer even recognize the parent! The legislature, in other words, has lost cognizance and control of what it has initiated.

Most legislatures are trying to regain control over their wayward progeny. One way is the establishment of select legislative committees to scrutinize all subordinate legislation and report to the legislature, often with the explicit recommendation for annulment. A similar technique is to give the legislature the right to veto executive legislation or to specify that unless the legislature gives its approval within a given period of time, executive orders or presidential decisions will be automatically annulled. Despite these efforts, however, administrative law has gained overwhelming importance and the legislative assemblies have been unable to limit it or effectively supervise it.

Political Functions The political role of representative assemblies lies primarily in the linkages it establishes between the executive and the public. Periodic elections provide for a constant channel of communication between the government and the people. Representatives in most democracies constantly visit their constituencies, interacting with their electors and gauging the mood of the public. Therefore, any government policies that are presented before the legislatures are considered and reconsidered and may be modified according to what the public sentiment is at a given time. The consent of the legislature, even if and when measures are not initiated by any of its members, is required and sought by the government. Even authoritarian regimes seek this type of communication because they can then claim that their policies have been approved by the public at large.

Legitimization is but the corollary of communication. The linkages established between a legislative assembly and the government together with the requirement that the measures of the latter be approved by the representatives of the people enhance the claims of the executive that they are governing on behalf of and with the consent of the community.

Control over the Executive's Term. The executive in all parliamentary democracies can be removed from office if the legislative assemblies vote against it. This may occur in a variety of ways. It may be a vote of censure or a vote of nonconfidence or the rejection of an important bill. Government lost votes of confidence in England in 1979, in the Federal Republic of Germany in 1982, in France in 1962, and frequently in Italy and Portugal. Even in presidential regimes, where this ultimate weapon does not exist, the powers of the legislature over appointments, taxation and spending, treaties and related foreign policy, and military measures provide controls that may force the hand of the executive. Take, for example, an extreme hypothesis: Congress refuses to confirm any of the appointments made by the president! Or take the so-called parliamentary strike used in France in the Third Republic, and which may be used again. The legislature refuses support to *any* prime minister appointed by a given president of the Republic. The position of the president in both cases could become difficult, to say the least!

The Political Function of Debates. Nelson Polsby, in a perceptive essay on legislatures,[6] noted that some legislative assemblies are in fact forums (he calls them *arenas*) where issues are debated, grievances are aired, and policy positions are outlined by the leaders of the major parties. Instead of legislating, these assemblies debate and through a debate they present issues and mobilize the public. They are links rather than decision makers, policy builders rather than lawyers and good accountants. Polsby was drawing our attention to the political role of legislative assemblies, especially in parliamentary regimes with strong parties and strong party leadership, even in cases where legislation and the budget are virtually

6. Nelson W. Polsby, "Legislatures," in *Handbook of Political Science,* Vol. V, pp. 257–310, 1975.

preempted by the executive. The debates offer the government an opportunity to present its overall policies and give the opposition a chance to voice its dissent. The purpose of the debates is to reach a wider public. The legislature thus becomes a forum that mobilizes and organizes opinion. Debate, however, cannot reach the public and mobilize it unless the legislature consists of only a few — ideally two — organized parties or stable coalitions of parties so that the opposing arguments can be presented clearly and cogently. Otherwise the forum may degenerate into utter confusion and end up alienating the public instead of mobilizing it.

Electing the Head of State. Many legislatures participate in the election of the head of state, usually a president of a republic with limited tenure. Such was the case with the French National Assembly and the Senate under the Fourth Republic and it is today the case with the Greek legislature and it is virtually the case in Italy and the Federal Republic of Germany. This is clearly a political function, especially when the head of state is given some independent powers.

Performance. Despite many setbacks, despite the decline of legislative assemblies in the beginning of the twentieth century, and despite the suppression of many legislatures by authoritarian one-party or military regimes or their total subordination to a single party, legislative assemblies have shown remarkable resiliency since World War II. As of 1945, they began to reemerge and they have been restored in the Federal Republic of Germany, Japan, Italy, Greece, Spain, Portugal, France, Austria, and some other countries that had experienced various forms of authoritarianism. They continue to play an important role in England and some of the old Commonwealth countries: Canada, Australia, New Zealand, and India. They are gaining some importance in Argentina, Venezuela, and even Brazil and Turkey. However, they remain brittle in the new political regimes of the Third World where neither time nor the intensity of the existing cleavages have allowed them to gain some degree of acceptance.

Performance should be assessed in terms of the ability of legislatures to handle some specific things effectively, the ability to perform *some* functions well — not necessarily *all* functions. Even more important, performance must be viewed in terms of versatility, whether or not legislative assemblies can shift from one function to another as circumstances and needs change and whether or not they can develop new mechanisms to cope with new situations. If they have the multifunctionality and flexibility to confront new situations, then they gain strength and legitimacy.

Several legislative assemblies have gained a particular degree of recognition for the performance of some functions as opposed to others (see Table 3-1). The British Parliament is known much more as a debating society, airing grievances and discussing issues, than as a legislative assembly or one that makes the budget. It is a true forum, or arena, as Nelson W. Polsby stated. The major political parties confront each other in Parliament with an eye to the public and to mobilizing consent in favor

TABLE 3-1 Some Legislatures in Democracies and Their Functions*

	U.S. CONGRESS	REICHSTAG	FRENCH NATIONAL ASSEMBLY	ITALIAN ASSEMBLY	BRITISH HOUSE OF COMMONS	INDIA
Communication (linkage)	+	+	+	+	+	x
Deliberation and lawmaking	+	+	–	x	+	x
Initiation	+	–	–	x	–	–
Amendment	+	–	–	x	–	–
Enactment	+	–	–	x	+	–
Financial control	+	x	x	x	–	+
Political control over executive's term in office	o	x	x = PM and Cabinet o = President	+	x	+
Investigation	+	+	–	x	x	x
Supervision over subordinate legislation	+	+	–	x	x	x
Participation in electing head of state	o	x	o	+	o	x
Forum	x	x	x	–	+	–

*+ = strong; – = weak; x = partial; o = nil

of certain policies and against others. The American Congress has gained respect for its investigatory powers — the major instrument through which it can check the enormous powers of the American Presidency. The Scandinavians' legislative assemblies have attained a judicious balance between support for the government and for legislative independence. The French National Assembly is only now emerging from a long period of eclipse in which the Gaullist Presidency dominated it by virtue of the Constitution and through a strong and disciplined party. It is only gradually reasserting itself as a debating forum and has been particularly active in the enactment of economic reforms and decentralization. In a number of other European democracies the legislatures have reached a balance between their claim to legislate and their political role in supporting or controlling executive leadership. In the Federal Republic of Germany after almost forty years of democratic government — the longest uninterrupted period in the history of Germany — the legislative assemblies have shown a great ability to protect individual and states' rights. It has also developed a strong and efficient committee system to handle legislation and the budget.

Political Parties in Democratic Regimes

Introduction

The most important and most common vehicle of participation and representation is the political party. It is an association that activates and mobilizes the people, represents interests, provides for compromise among competing points of view, and becomes the proving ground for political leadership.

In this section we are primarily concerned with an analysis of parties and party systems within democratic regimes. The study of individual parties relates (1) to their organization, their history and origins, and their ideologies and (2) to the relationships parties have established among themselves and the functions and specific roles they perform. In the first case we study individual parties; in the second we examine the configuration of parties and their interaction within the democratic regime.[7]

Functions and Characteristics

Functions All democratic parties perform the following functions, although not in the same way and not to the same degree:

1. They represent various societal groups and forces and organize and structure participation and representation.
2. They advocate policies. Policies are embodied in the party program, platform, or manifesto.

7. One of the best analyses is Harry Eckstein, "Party Systems," in *Encyclopedia of Social Sciences*, Vol. XI (New York: Crowell, Collier & Macmillan, 1968), pp. 436–453.

3. Generally speaking, democratic parties have concrete and often limited objectives as opposed to the populist or utopian parties, which advocate a radical transformation of the society. At most, democratic parties aim to reform, not to transform.
4. In their activities, they try to mobilize the citizenry and to aggregate interests and demands.
5. Most democratic parties aim at capturing and controlling the government, but in a number of democratic regimes this is never possible because they can never gain the required majority. It is only by forming coalitions with other parties that they are able to participate in the government or influence it directly.
6. They provide training for future leaders; they recruit men and women who are interested in politics and who can rise to positions of leadership.

Democratic parties are supportive of the democratic regime; they not only draw from the principles of democracy but also legitimize it. By organizing the electorate to participate and to vote, they strengthen supports to the regime and induce loyalties.

Membership Membership in democratic parties has several characteristics: (1) It is open to all and the organization of the party allows free debate to all. (2) In most democratic parties there are recognizable factions that vie for leadership. (3) Decision making within the party (the formulation of the party program) takes place through open debate and voting by party congresses or conventions that meet regularly. (4) Delegates to congresses are elected by the rank and file, and they in turn choose, by majority vote, the various executive organs of the party including the leadership. One thing we hardly ever find in the congresses of democratic parties is a unanimous vote. (5) Members are free to leave the party or join another one.

Membership in democratic parties varies a great deal. In mass parties the membership may reach millions, for example, England's Labour party, which has over 5 million members. In other instances, as with American parties, membership is small. The Social Democrats in Germany have about 750,000 members and the Christian Democrats not more than 600,000. The Conservative party in England has one of the highest memberships among conservative parties in the world, about 2 million. In France the Socialists have about half a million while the Gaullists continue their membership strength with over 700,000. The Italian Communist party, which has a membership of over 2 million, is the largest Communist party in Europe.

Leadership As in all organizations the leadership, the party officials, and the organizers play the most important role. They initiate policy, they structure debate, and they have widespread influence on the decisions made by the members. Although there is leadership control (an oligarchy) in democratic parties, frequent revolts and defections confirm that internal democracy and pluralism also exist. In some instances, the party rebels even managed to unseat the leadership and gain a controlling position in the party, which is what happened with the French Socialist party in the 1970s, the German Social Democrats in the 1980s, and both the Democrats and the Republicans in the United States between 1972 and 1980.

Discipline How disciplined are democratic parties? We ought to answer the question in terms of voter discipline, member discipline, and the discipline of its elected representatives in the legislature. Little need be said about the first since no organizational ties of any kind bind voters to the party. They are free to vote for or against, to change their minds from one election to another. Over time, however, parties become institutionalized, and they develop a hard core of faithful and a periphery of

TABLE 3-2 Voting Strength (In percentages)

		GREAT BRITAIN	
	LABOUR	CONSERVATIVE	LIBERAL
1945	48.0	36.8	2.8
1950	46.1	43.4	9.1
1951	48.8	48.0	2.6
1955	46.4	49.7	2.7
1959	43.8	49.4	5.9
1964	44.1	43.4	11.2
1966*	48.0	41.9	8.5
1970†	43.1	46.4	7.5
1974(Feb)	37.1	37.9	19.3
1974(Oct)	39.2	35.8	18.3
1979	36.9	43.9	13.8
1983	28.0	43.0	25.0 (Alliance)

		GERMAN FEDERAL REPUBLIC	
	SDP SOCIA' DEMOCRATS	CDU/CSU CHRISTIAN DEMOCRATS	FDP LIBERALS
1949	29.2	23.6	11.9
1953	28.8	45.2	9.5
1957	31.8	50.2	7.7
1961	36.2	45.4	12.8
1965	39.3	47.6	9.5
1969*	42.7	46.1	5.8
1972†	45.8	44.9	8.4
1976	42.6	48.6	7.9
1980	42.9	44.5	10.6
1983	38.2	48.8	7.0
			Greens 5.6

*T. T. Mackie and R. Rose, *The International Almanac of Electoral History*, The Free Press, New York, 1974.
†John Sallow and Anna John, *An Electoral Atlas of Europe 1968–1981*, Butterworth Scientific, London, 1982.

sympathizers who vote the straight "party ticket" in every election. Major parties can always count, notwithstanding fluctuations, on a major share of the vote unless and until there are critical elections that cause a realignment of voters. Table 3-2, which gives a rundown of the German and British elections since World War II, indicates a pattern of voting stability until the middle 1970s.

Discipline within the party for party members varies from one party to another. As a rule, left-wing parties, the Socialists (but especially the Communist parties in democratic regimes), are more disciplined than others though some conservative or right-wing parties have at times shown a remarkable discipline. Members are expected to follow the directives of the leadership in the implementation of policy directives or nominations of candidates. The penalty for refusing to do so is often exclusion from the party.

The matter of discipline is particularly important when we come to the elected party members in the legislature, the party representatives. In parliamentary systems, where the political life of the prime minister and the cabinet depends on the support they get from the majority party, discipline has been remarkably tight and defections rare. The members of a party in Parliament vote for their leadership as one, and party splits are seldom seen. The most spectacular one was the recent split of some members of the Labour party in England, which formed its own Social-Democratic party. It is mostly the members of centrist parties, especially in France and Italy, who split and who show the least internal cohesion.

Discipline in overall terms is a matter of centralized control and direction. The control of party funds, the organization of party activities between elections or just before an election, the preparation of documentation and educational services, the ability of the leadership to nominate candidates for various elections and give them support are all important. Most democratic parties have developed such institutionalized instruments of direction and control. Their effectiveness, however, has varied from one country to another, and from one party to another.

The Ideological Spectrum

Ideology is the set of beliefs, ideas, and policies embraced by the party. In democratic regimes the range of ideological variations is virtually unlimited, and many democracies even allow parties that advocate the overthrow of democracy. Freedom of speech and association entitles them to do so as long as they use persuasion and not force in bringing about their goals. In the election of 1973 the leader of a small revolutionary party in France urged the people to vote for him. "If we win," he pointed out, "it will be the last time you will be voting."

In democracies we have regime parties and antiregime parties. In the first case there is wide agreement and approval of the political regime. It is accepted. Common values are shared by all party members and voters, and differences that divide parties relate to concrete policies. Antiregime parties, on the other hand, are characterized by their outright opposition to the regime. It is not accepted. When parties share common propositions about the society and the constitution, we have a consensual democratic regime. When parties divide sharply on fundamental issues, the regime is dissensual.

Antiregime Parties Ever since the emergence of democratic regimes there have been antidemocratic parties and movements organized to destroy the democratic order that we outlined in our second chapter. In the early stages of democracy they came from the aristocracy and the military, which is allied with the aristocracy, and from various religious organizations. The Catholic church rejected the secular and majoritarian assumption of democracy, including popular elections. It was only at the end of the nineteenth century that the Catholic church rallied to democratic governance. In other words, throughout most of the nineteenth century it was the status quo groups that continued to react against both the democratic forces that had assumed political power and the institutions they had shaped (including elections).

There were other antiregime movements, but the major one came from Marxism and the development of the Socialist party and sects. In contrast to conservative forces, they relied on the new socioeconomic forces — the workers. Their purpose was to organize the workers in order to stage a violent revolution and to establish a dictatorship of the proletariat. At first, their strength was small, but by the last two decades of the nineteenth century they grew in numbers and organization. Gradually, however, the socialists reconciled themselves to democracy, as the Catholic church had done, and decided to espouse parliamentary democracy instead of revolution. This was particularly evident in Germany with the development of the Social Democratic party, in France with the organization of a Socialist party and in England with the Labour party. All of them accepted democracy and in a sense became proregime parties.

It was only in the aftermath of World War I, particularly between 1920 and the beginning of the World War II in 1939, that antiregime parties mushroomed in Europe and throughout the world to threaten and seriously subvert the democratic order. These parties consisted of communists who split from the socialists in 1919–1921 and of extremist right-wing organizations: the Fascists in Italy and the Nazis in Germany. Although they had different labels in different countries, they carried the same antidemocratic thrust throughout Europe and even in England and the United States. The communists revived the Marxist appeal for an armed uprising of the workers — for a revolution and for the dictatorship of the proletariat. Right-wing extremists advocated force, the destruction of democratic rights, and the creation of a new authoritarian political order. The democratic regimes, caught between these two powerful antidemocratic movements, virtually collapsed all over Europe. But, after the defeat of Germany and Italy democracy returned, at least in most of

West Europe, and antidemocratic parties declined. Even the West European Communist parties now seem to be following the path the European socialists took at the end of the nineteenth century. They are eschewing revolution, abandoning the notion of class wars, accepting parliamentary democracy including free elections, and recognizing individual and political rights. Eurocommunist parties, as they are called, have accepted democratic institutions; they are willing to operate within the democratic institutions and within the democratic order. This has been the case notably with the most powerful Communist group in Europe — the Italian Communist party — and, with some qualifications, the Spanish and French Communist parties.

THE CATCHALL PARTY[8]

In the 1960s, virtually all the political parties of the Western world and those of the industrially advanced societies began to display a novel characteristic: they began to lose their ideological character. They became brokers of a society that, because of progressive industrialization, had divided into many social, professional, occupational, and interest groups. They became umbrella organizations, encompassing various interests and points of view. They evolved into catchall parties and in the process began to resemble each other in what they offered; they were like two supermarkets that used different labels but in reality were selling the same delicacies to all their customers.

There were many reasons for this development. One was the remarkable post–World War II economic growth that reduced the social and class distinctions. A second was the growing diversity of the working class into many layers and skills for which different incomes and gradually even different lifestyles developed; class was no longer synonymous with party attachments and voting. A third was the remarkable mobility of individuals living in Western societies, which resulted in the weakening of sectionalisms and in the shaping of an undifferentiated body of citizens. They all had pretty much the same concerns, interests, and expectations. The political parties reacted to this change and accommodated it to the point where differences between party platforms were no longer that great. It was the quest of victory at the polls and the gaining of governmental power that became the only issue.

Since the catchall parties appealed to everybody on the

8. The term "catchall" was used by Otto Kirchcheimer, "The Transformation of Western European Party Systems," in Joseph La Palombara and Myron Weiner (eds.), *Political Parties and Political Development* (Princeton, N.J.: Princeton University Press, 1968), pp. 177–200.

same general terms, particular interests and heartfelt ideologies and concerns could no longer use their party as an effective vehicle of expression. The parties became increasingly unable to represent particular points of view and particular interests or even to take sides because they were attempting to represent all and everything. People started to lose interest and to identify less and less with their party — their partisanship weakened. As a result, political action began to manifest itself outside of the political parties — in single-issue organizations, political clubs, direct action and demonstrations, and the emergence of independent candidates running on issues outside the parties. In other words, there was a revival of ideological politics.

Ideologies and Parties Today: Left, Center, and Right

The multiplicity of ideological points of view is greatly simplified thanks to the political parties. It is impossible for every shade of an idea to become a party. If it did, representation would become fragmented, virtually atomized, and the selection of officeholders in the legislature or the executive would become impossible. Ideas, like interests, have to be compromised and accommodated so that comprehensive programmatic formulations can be made. The greater the degree of compromise and accommodation, the less ideological the party becomes. In bringing together many different points of view, the party finds out what is acceptable to as many as possible and offensive to as few as possible.

The configuration of the party system in modern democratic regimes can still be plotted on the ideological map often referred to as left–center–right.[9]

The fundamental criterion for these groups is the socioeconomic positions they take and the policies they advocate, specifically the role of the state in regard to the production and distribution of goods. To the left, Communist and socialist parties advocate, in varying degrees, nationalization of industry and other economic activities, national economic planning, extensive redistribution of the wealth through taxation, subsidies, and welfare spending. Their ultimate goal is to equalize income or at least to reduce inequalities in income as much as possible and to subordinate private incentives and private profit to collective needs. Socialist and Communist parties appeal to those who will benefit from such measures: the workers, the farmers, the underprivileged and the

9. Arendt Lipjhart discusses the ideological spectrum of European parties in terms of socioeconomic, religious, cultural, ethnic, and foreign policy, and also what he calls "postindustrial" criteria. See his "Parties, Ideologies and Programs," in David Butler, Howard Penniman, and Austin Ranney (eds.), *Democracy at the Polls* (Washington, D.C.: American Enterprise Institute, 1981), pp. 26–51.

poor, the unemployed and the aged, and special disadvantaged categories in the population that appear to be in a permanent state of poverty and need. The French Socialist party, the British Labour party, the Social Democrats in the Federal Republic of Germany and in the Scandinavian countries as well as the newly founded Socialist parties in the Mediterranean advocate these policies. In the elections for the European Parliament in June 1984, their combined strength, at least for the 10 members of the European Community (United Kingdom, Ireland, Belgium, Holland, Luxembourg, Federal Republic of Germany, France, Italy, Denmark, and Greece), gave them a total of about 250 out of 511 seats. Portugal and Spain will become members in 1985, and since they have sizable Socialist parties, the socialists in the 12 European countries of the Common Market may have a majority in the European Parliament. Besides the Common Market countries, the Socialist parties are equally strong in Sweden, Norway, Austria, New Zealand, Australia, and Canada. The United States is the exception.

But Socialist parties differ — and sometimes the differences are critically important — both with regard to the urgency with which the reforms they advocate are to be implemented and with regard to the kind of socialism they plan to construct. After a long pause the Labour party in England seems to be reasserting a rapid expansion of the socialist sector in the economy, while the French socialists, after a period of drastic nationalizations and income redistribution undertaken in 1981–1983, have reached a pause and reconsideration while their electoral strength seems to be waning. The German Social Democrats abandoned their commitment to nationalizations and follow an opportunistic path. The Scandinavian Socialist parties emphasize welfare workers' participation in management and ownership, and income redistribution and equalization but not nationalizations. In the Mediterranean, Socialist parties are sometimes extremely radical, as in Greece, and sometimes quite pragmatic and compromising as in Spain and Portugal.

Socialist parties also differ on the kind of socialism they hope to construct. Few remain committed to the notion of state bureaucratic direction of the economy. The socialists in France, in the Federal Republic of Germany, and in the Scandinavian countries have put a growing emphasis on self-determination in the management of the economy. The factories and the farms are run by associations of producers or through complex labor-management negotiations and cooperation. Today, virtually all the democratic Socialist parties seem to have abandoned the Soviet bureaucratic-statist model of national planning and state management. They are all searching for flexible mechanisms to align production to consumer choices and allow for associational and individual incentives. There has been a marked reconsideration by all socialists of some of the market mechanisms that had been rejected in the past.

The same general observations can be made about the parties that fall on the right, mostly the conservative parties in Europe, North America, New Zealand, Canada, Australia and the Republicans (but also many of the Democrats) in the United States. While they have many differences the common trait that characterizes all of them is a marked suspicion of the state and its role in economic and societal affairs. They are against state intervention and heavy taxation, favor free enterprise and the market economy (within limits), extol private incentive and effort, espouse individualism rather than equality (without necessarily endorsing inequalities of income), and generally favor less government spending to deal with social and economic problems such as education, health, unemployment, security, etc. Most contemporary Conservative parties reflect a strong reaction against the welfare state and the government spending that seemed to represent the consensus for almost three decades after the end of World War II, which accounted for the development of the catchall parties. They generally appeal to the well-to-do, the middle classes, the propertied, and financial and industrial interests represented by powerful corporations, but they also receive support from traditional and religious groups, the small bourgeoise, and the farmers. The Conservative party in England, the Republicans (but we repeat many Democrats as well) in the United States, the Gaullists and their allies in France, the Christian Democrats in the Federal Republic of Germany, and in Italy, many of the conservative and religious parties in the Scandinavian countries, Canada, Australia, New Zealand, and the Mediterranean follow the same approach.

The center parties, usually labeled liberals, take an eclectic stance and their programs are often a cross between the positions espoused by Conservative and Socialist parties. They pick and choose different propositions at different times and as a result appear to be the least ideological. The liberals in England (and more recently the Alliance consisting of the old Liberal party and dissenters from the radical program of the Labour party), the Union of French Democracy in France, and the Free Democrats in the Federal Republic of Germany fit this pattern. So do most liberal parties in virtually all contemporary democracies.

In addition to socialists, communists, liberals, and conservatives, new parties continue to appear and disappear. New associations and groups committed to ideological goals attempt to infiltrate existing parties — either at the left or at the right. They include environmentalists who vie for an increment of the vote (3–6 percent); antinuclear proponents and unilateralists who favor unilateral disarmaments, advocates of peace (at any price), antiabortionists, ethnic groups and minorities, as well as the new racist and nationalist groups in France and Italy who seem to favor some of the Nazi and Fascist propositions. There is a constant flux and the ideological profile of both small, diverse groups and the Conservative, Liberal, Socialist, and Communist parties is in constant change. We can only take snapshots of a moving and shifting target. But then this is the very nature of a democratic society and of the democratic process.

Party Systems in Democratic Regimes

As we noted, the term party system covers the general rules and conditions under which interaction among political parties within the regime takes place. However, a number of different and more specific patterns have developed over time.

Two-Party and Multiparty Systems

In a two-party system, two major parties vie for the control of the government in periodic elections. Strictly speaking, however, there is no democratic regime with only two parties. Rather, it is a system where all parties other than the major two have little strength and few members in the representative assembly. In the United States independent candidates who run for the presidency, including third-party candidates (Progressives, Socialists, Dixiecrats), rarely manage to influence the election of the president even if they succeed in getting some of their representatives elected to Congress. The weight of their vote has been negligible. The Liberal party in England, though receiving 5–10 percent of the vote in national elections (until 1970), had a very small representation in the House of Commons and little influence in the formation or the life of the cabinet.* West Germany has been termed a two and a half party system. The two major parties were closely matched and the Free Democrats averaged 7–12 percent of the vote and about 35–55 members in the legislature. One or the other of the two major parties — the Christian Democrats and the Social Democrats — allied with the Free Democrats to form a government. In most other European countries the party system has been multiparty with four or more major parties in close competition with one another but occasionally forming two blocs.

Major, Minor, and Dominant Parties

Major parties are generally assured of a major share of the electoral vote, and occasionally they can assume a dominant position — they become dominant parties. A dominant party is one that manages (over the course of many elections) to gain a large share of the vote, even if it is not a majority. This was the case with the Gaullists in France who between 1962 and 1981 received about 35 percent of the electoral vote, the Congress Party in India between 1947 and 1964 with over 50 percent of the vote, and the Christian Democrats in Italy who have not fallen below 37 percent in a legislative election since 1946. There are also many minor parties with a small membership and a very small share of the vote. They do not expect, as a rule, to see their strength rise, and they have little, if any, influence on the formation of the government. Their political relevance is therefore virtually nil. Unless war or an economic depression cause a drastic change in the political landscape, the following minor parties are destined to

*Except when neither of the two major parties had a clear majority.

remain minor: Environmentalists almost everywhere in Western Europe, the Communist party virtually everywhere except in Italy, and religious or separatist parties.

Competition and Choice

Democratic parties compete for the vote and they compete to gain control of the government. In this sense, they give the voter a genuine opportunity to make a choice and to hold a party leadership or a candidate responsible at election time. There are a number of factors that determine the manner in which political parties compete:

1. The structure of representative government. Is it presidential or parliamentary?
2. The social structure. How strong are the antagonisms between classes and religious or ethnic groups?
3. The electoral system. As we shall see, it can force the hand of the parties and shape their strategy and tactics.
4. Perhaps the most important factor is the degree of agreement or disagreement between political parties on fundamentals, which is a matter of ideology on goals and on the means of bringing them about. The greater the disagreement, the greater the *distance* among political parties. Sharp class cleavages or deep-set ethnic and religious antagonisms account for a great, sometimes unabridgeable, distance. Competition may become confrontation. The stability of the government will be constantly in jeopardy because it will be difficult for competing parties to establish a coalition cabinet, and legitimacy and performance will suffer.

On the other hand, consensual parties are, as noted, those that share common orientations, goals, and tactics, so the distance between them is small. They all appeal across classes and ethnic groups, and become interclass parties. Consensual parties assume a broad national agreement and are most likely to develop in regimes where class, religious, and ethnic differences are not sharp. Sometimes, however, they manage to transcend these differences and amalgamate disparate groups into their organization. In such cases parties manage to create political order and coherence out of disorder and conflict.

Parties of Representation and Parties of Government

Political parties in democratic regimes represent the public and support or criticize the government. The majority party supports the government and the minority party is in opposition. But there are cases where the representative role — that of faithfully representing as many opinions and views as possible — is emphasized more than considerations of governance.

In democratic party systems the most important difference is that between parties of representation and parties of government. Parties of representation usually represent well-defined segments of the electorate in terms of religious, ideological, sectional, ethnic, or class interests. They act and speak on behalf of clear-cut points of view and interests. They may be involved with material issues: the farmers, the shopkeepers, or small businesses. Or they may raise spiritual issues: the church, prayers at school, or subsidies for Catholic schools. They may represent racial or ethnic interests (the Catalans or the Basques in Spain), or class interests, or simply deeply rooted ideological positions on the environment, nuclear proliferation, and war or peace. Parties of representation are not primarily sectarian parties; they do not expect to form a government on the basis of gaining a majority. They represent certain points of view.

In regimes where parties of representation are the rule, it is difficult for a party to win a majority. The government consists of a coalition of the leaders of many parties. In forming a coalition, the emphasis is on the accommodation of conflicting points of view and interests. The formation of a coalition government, usually a cabinet headed by a prime minister, often resembles treaty making: an agreement that defines the common policies but rules out policy making on matters involving disagreements that cannot be resolved. When the parties that make up the coalition are disciplined, the coalition may last a long time: the treaty will be respected. This has happened in the Scandinavian countries and Holland. When the parties are undisciplined, the coalition will not last, which was the case with the French Third and Fourth Republics (1871–1946) and with Italy since World War II.

Parties of representation do not provide the conditions for a clear change of government at an election. In fact alternation from one government backed by a given majority to another backed by a different majority is rare. The same parties represent the same variety of interests and ideologies and every election brings about roughly the same party distribution in the legislature. The strength of the parties shows only incremental fluctuations. This kind of situation was particularly evident in France under the Fourth Republic, in Italy, Israel, Switzerland, and in some Scandinavian countries and Holland.

In contrast to parties of representation, parties of government are primarily concerned with organizing the electorate and appealing to it in order to gain a majority and form a government. Parties of government thus link their representative role to that of governance. As a rule, they are disciplined and coherent; they stand behind their leadership; they become truly national, appealing to all cross sections and classes; and they try to aggregate as many viewpoints and interests as possible. They reconcile interests, avoid internal conflicts, and eschew taking sharp ideological positions. They are pragmatic and they realize that they must reach a comprehensive synthesis of many points of view in order to win a majority. The more they do so, the less the distance between them. They begin to appeal to the same groups and in their quest of a majority they are particularly anxious not to leave out any minorities, since even a small percentage of the vote may make the difference between victory or defeat. Generally speaking, parties of government flourish in two-party systems.

Parties of government, as opposed to parties of representation, are able to form stable governments backed by a stable majority. They give the electorate a clear choice between competing leaders and basic governmental policies. This has generally been the case in Great Britain, Sweden, West Germany, Canada, New Zealand, Australia, and (ever since 1958) in France.

THE CASE OF FRANCE: PARTIES OF GOVERNMENT

France under the Fifth Republic requires special attention. Until 1958 there were only parties of representation, which reflected sectional interests and ideological points of view. After 1962, however, the president was elected directly by the people, and as a result the situation changed. Since the presidential election was limited to the two top candidates selected in a national primary, the political parties were forced to align themselves behind one or the other. They were gradually transformed into parties of government, geared to the choice of the president. Even the Communist party was forced to align itself behind a candidate. Consequently, the party system was transformed. It gradually turned into a two-party, or at least a two-bloc, system: the left and the right, with a dwindling center split between the two. Because the stakes were high — the presidency and the cabinet — the parties became increasingly disciplined and highly distinct: the government party supported the president and the cabinet while the other bloc found itself in opposition. Both parties also took on an increasingly *national* stance. They transcended sectarian and sectional and even ideological points of view and instead tried to bring as many points of view as possible under the same party roof. In 1981 the left-wing bloc ousted the center-right bloc to win the presidency and gain a Socialist majority in the legislature, which supported the president and his prime minister.

THE CASE OF THE UNITED STATES: PARTIES OF REPRESENTATION

In the American presidential system the parties play an important role in the nominations and even in the selection of presidential candidates. But once nominated, the president can appeal directly and personally to the people since he is directly elected by the people. His powers are clearly separated and independent from Congress. He is not beholden to a majority in the legislature and he appoints his own cabinet officers who are responsible only to him. The individual congressmen and senators are therefore confined to the role of representation — so much so that within one and the same party there are ideological and sectional factions that are subdivided into lobbies and groups representing special interests. The primary duty of the representatives is to speak for and advance the interests of their local constituents and the local or special interests. Their reelection or defeat does not affect the position of the presidency, and likewise the president cannot seriously affect their election and reelection. Since representatives draw their funds as well as their inspiration from their local roots, their political life depends very much on winning the approval of their constituency. For all these reasons, the American parties tend to be parties of representation. They are undisciplined and opportunistic coalitions without coherent and binding programs, and they hardly ever use Congress as a forum for national political debates.

Conclusion

Parties of representation or parties of government? Which system is best? Parties of government simplify and streamline the electoral process: the public decides between two competing programs and leaderships. They also clarify the issue of responsibility. Election time becomes a day of reckoning for the government in office and gives the opposition a chance to unseat the existing regime. Parties of government truly nationalize the election by allowing the people at large to consider the issues put forth by the government. Such parties gather interests, combine them into policies, and press them upon the government. The great advantage of parties of government, therefore, is that they provide the means for the selection and the operation of a government, give it majority support, and allow the electorate to hold it responsible at election time.

Parties of representation reflect various opinions and differences and make it possible for these diverse views to be heard and debated in the legislature. Elections are not limited to a choice between two positions or two leadership teams but to the selection of candidates who express a variety of opinions and interests. Instead of allowing legislative proceedings to become a confrontation between the government majority and the opposition that aspires to replace it, parties of representation provide the conditions for a genuine debate on issues, problems, and policies.

It is only by joining the representative function with that of governance that the political parties can play the role they are cast to play: mobilizing interests, providing the necessary supports, and making it possible for the leadership to form a coherent and stable government. It is through this process that the citizenry can be involved in politics and hold the government responsible for its actions. Parties that are exclusively concerned with winning office may lose their representative character and alienate the electorate. Conversely parties exclusively concerned with representation may fail to produce and sustain a government that will be able to make policy and resolve conflicts. It would seem, therefore, that the future of political parties in democratic regimes depends on achieving a mix between representation and governance.

As Harry Eckstein puts it, "The more faithfully divergent opinions are represented the more likely it is that authority will be insufficiently supported." On the other hand, "Maximum support of authority may come from a party [of government] . . . so overarchingly aggregative as to offer no choice at all." The best solution, he concludes, lies in the "search for an optimum between the conflicting values of unity and divergence: the one supports power, the other provides choice."[10] It would be difficult to disagree!

Bibliography

On Participation

Almond, Gabriel, and Sidney Verba (eds.). *The Civic Culture Revisited.* Boston: Little, Brown, 1980.

Barnes, Samuel H., and Max Kaase (eds.). *Political Action: Mass Participation in Five Western Democracies.* Beverly Hills, Calif.: Sage Publications, 1979.

Dahl, Robert. *Polyarchy: Participation and Opposition.* New Haven, Conn.: Yale University Press, 1971.

Key, V. O. *The Responsible Electorate.* Cambridge, Mass.: Harvard University Press, 1966.

Milbrath, Lester W. *Political Participation: How and Why Do People Get Involved in Politics?* Chicago: Rand McNally, 1965.

Nie, Norman H., and Sidney Verba. "Political Participation," in *Handbook of Political Science,* Vol. IV, pp. 1–75, Reading, Mass.: Addison-Wesley, 1975.

Schattschneider, E. E. *The Semi-Sovereign People.* New York: Holt, Rinehart and Winston, 1960.

Verba, Sidney, Norman H. Nie, and Jae-on Kim. *The Modes of Democratic Participation: A Cross-National Comparison.* Beverly Hills, Calif.: Sage Publications, 1971.

Legislatures

Blondel, Jean. *Comparative Legislatures.* Englewood Cliffs, N.J.: Prentice-Hall, 1973.

10. Harry Eckstein, op. cit., pp. 437–438.

Crick, Bernard. *The Reform of Parliament.* 2d ed. London: Weidenfeld & Nicolson, 1968.

Hirsh, Herbert, and M. Donald Hancock. *Comparative Legislative Systems.* New York: The Free Press, 1971.

Jennings, Ivor. *Parliament.* London: Macmillan, 1940.

Kornberg, Alain (ed.). *Legislatures in Comparative Perspective.* New York: David McKay, 1973.

Loewenberg, Gerhard, and Samuel C. Patterson. *Comparing Legislatures.* Boston: Little, Brown, 1979.

Loewenberg, Gerhard (ed.). *Modern Parliaments: Change or Decline?* Chicago: University of Chicago Press, 1971.

Mill, John Stuart. *Considerations on Representative Government.* South Bend, Ind.: Gateway Editions, 1962.

Pitkin, Hannah. *The Concept of Representation.* Berkeley and Los Angeles: University of California Press, 1972.

Wheare, Kenneth. *Legislatures.* Oxford: Oxford University Press, 1963.

On Political Parties

Day, Alan J., and Henry W. Dagenhardt. *Political Parties in the World.* Detroit, Mich.: Gale Research Co., 1980.

Duverger, Maurice. *Political Parties.* New York: John Wiley & Sons, 1962.

Epstein, Leo N. *Political Parties in Western Democracies.* New Brunswick, N.J.: Transaction Press, 1980.

Janda, Kenneth. *A Conceptual Framework for the Comparative Analysis of Political Parties.* Beverly Hills, Calif.: Sage Publications, 1970.

La Palombara, Joseph, and Myron Weiner (eds.). *Political Parties and Political Development.* Princeton, N.J.: Princeton University Press, 1966.

Lawson, Kay. *A Comparative Study of Political Parties.* New York: St. Martin's Press, 1976.

Milner, A. J. *Elections and Political Stability.* Boston: Little, Brown, 1969.

Newmann, Sigmund (ed.). *Political Parties* (especially introductory and concluding chapters). Chicago: University of Chicago Press, 1940.

Ostrogorski, M. *Democracy and the Organization of Political Parties.* 2 vols. New Brunswick, N.J.: Transaction Press, 1982.

Rose, Richard. *Do Parties Make a Difference?* 2d ed., enl. Chatham, N.J.: Chatham House, 1984.

Sartori, Giovanni. *Party and Party Systems.* Cambridge: Cambridge University Press, 1976.

4 Organization of Consent: Elections and Voters

Introduction

In modern democratic regimes elections bring out tens and even hundreds of millions of voters, especially since most democracies have lowered the age of voting to eighteen. Even in the small democracies the number of eligible voters may reach 3 to 5 million. In middle-sized countries — England, France, West Germany, Italy, Spain — it is around 32–38 million. In the United States, it is over 140 million.

The growth of the electorate, however, has not altered the function of an election. It remains the same: to elect our representatives, including those in executive positions, and to hold them responsible for their actions by being able to vote against them and thus put them out of office. The problem of bringing order out of the chaos of millions of individual wills and transforming them into recognizable options is solved by having political parties. The voters emerge as collective entities and are viewed in terms of aggregates: Democrats, Republicans, Conservatives, Labourites, Gaullists, Socialists, Liberals, Agrarians, Greens, and Social Democrats. The voters become organized through a process of reconciliation and adjustment whereby individual interests and choices are boiled down to party formulas, pledges, and candidates. Even parties of representation provide a common denominator for the different points of view. Parties simplify (some say they even determine) choice. But one thing is clear: given the size of the electorate today, there could be no elections and choice without parties.

Criteria of Democratic Elections

An election can be considered democratic if the following conditions are fulfilled:

1. Substantially the entire adult population has the right to vote for candidates in office or running for office.
2. Elections take place regularly within prescribed time limits.
3. No substantial group in the adult population is denied the opportunity of forming a party and putting up candidates.
4. All the seats in the major legislative chamber can be contested and usually are.
5. Campaigns are conducted with reasonable fairness in that neither law nor violence nor intimidation bars the candidates from presenting their views and qualifications or prevents the voters from finding out what they are and discussing them.
6. Votes are cast freely and secretly; they are counted and reported honestly; and the candidates who receive the proportions required by law are duly installed in office until their terms expire and a new election is held.[1]

There are many democratic regimes that have not met these conditions over a sufficient period of time. Spain and Portugal have held free elections only in the last decade. Greece held elections after World War II but it is very doubtful that the conditions of fairness were satisfied until 1974. Turkey's record of elections has been erratic, to say the least. Many Latin American countries have held elections intermittently or under circumstances that only approximate the conditions set forth: Peru, Argentina, Guatemala, Panama, Bolivia, El Salvador, Nicaragua, Mexico, Uruguay, and Brazil are among them. In Africa, as we note elsewhere, there is no regime, even if it is labeled "democratic," that has satisfied most of these conditions for any period of time.

Electoral Systems

An electoral system is the set of rules and regulations that govern the voting process. It determines the election of representatives to the legislature and, in presidential regimes, the election of the president. It has a direct impact on the composition of the legislature, the configuration of the party system, and the formation of a government. The electoral system determines, perhaps more than anything else, the tactics and strategy of political parties and has a direct impact on voters' choices. Since no democratic regime has the same electoral system, however (all of them differ), attempting to make comparative studies of elections and voters' behavior is very difficult.

1. The criteria are set forth in Butler, Penniman, and Ranney (eds.), *Democracy at the Polls* (Washington, D.C.: American Enterprise Institute, 1981), p. 3.

Electing the President

In most democratic regimes with a presidential or a semipresidential system the choice involved — the election of *one* candidate — determines the electoral system. It is necessarily a majority or plurality system. The candidate with the highest number of votes is elected. Primaries are often held by the political parties to select the candidates, but the second round that follows usually pits the two candidates of the two major parties against each other, although third parties or independent candidates are free to run, and they often do. It is not uncommon for a president to be elected by a mere plurality.

In the French electoral system, the final contest is limited to only *two* presidential candidates, and one necessarily wins over the other by a majority. There is a national primary in which any number of candidates can run. If a candidate receives 50 percent plus one of the vote, he is elected. If not, a new election is held two weeks later and pits only the two top candidates. In the election of 1974 the Gaullist-backed candidate won by 50.8 against 49.2 percent. In 1981 the Socialist candidate won by 51.7 against 48.3 percent (see Table 4-1).

The presidential candidate with the greatest number of votes wins. Many have argued that such a system is not fair to the electorate because it leaves a very sizable minority, sometimes half or even more, unrepresented. But since the office of the presidency is in the hands of one person, there is no way, legally or politically, to make his or her election truly representative. Also, once elected, the president is expected to represent the whole nation and act on its behalf. Even those who voted against the president are likely to accept the results of the election since they agreed in advance on the rules under which the choice would be made. It is only in a highly fragmented or divided society, when a majority identified in ethnic or religious terms confronts a large minority also identified in religious or ethnic terms, that the election of the president by direct popular vote and by a plurality, or even a majority, may cause serious conflicts. Yugoslavia avoids this problem by rotating the presidency so that none of the ethnic, religious, and linguistic groups will feel threatened.

Legislative Elections: Majoritarianism and Proportional Representation

In parliamentary systems the authority of the prime minister and the cabinet, as well as their powers, derive directly from their having gained the majority in the legislature. Sometimes this majority backing is achieved through a victory by one party in an election, and sometimes it is achieved through a strong and stable coalition formed by several parties. Thus an election of representatives in the legislature by a simple numerical majority or by a plurality gives one party the edge over another, enabling it to govern. Parties will strive for a majority and may even combine their strength in advance in order to get it.

TABLE 4-1 The French Presidential Election of April–May 1981

FIRST BALLOT (APRIL 26)

Registered voters	36,418,664
Voting	29,529,345
Abstaining	6,889,319 (18.91%)
Valid ballots	29,038,202

	Candidates	Votes	Percentage
Major	Giscard d'Estaing (incumbent; UDF)	8,222,969	28.31%
	Mitterrand (Socialist)	7,505,295	25.84
	Chirac (Gaullist-RPR)	5,225,720	17.99
	Marchais (Communist)	4,456,979	15.34
Minor	Lalonde (Environmentalist)	1,126,282	3.87
	Laguiller (Workers' Struggle — Extreme Left)	668,195	2.30
	Crepeau (MRG–Radical Left Movement)	642,815	2.21
	Debré (Gaullist candidate) (independent)	482,067	1.66
	Garaud (pro-Gaullist Conservative)	386,489	1.33
	Bouchardeau (Socialist Workers' Party–PSU)	321,391	1.10

SECOND BALLOT (MAY 10)

Registered voters	36,392,678
Voting	31,249,753
Abstaining	5,142,925 (14.13%)
Valid ballots	30,362,385

Candidate	Votes	Percentage
Mitterrand	15,714,598	51.76%
Giscard d'Estaing	14,647,787	48.24

(From R. C. Macridis (ed.), *Modern Political Systems: Europe,* 5th ed. Englewood Cliffs, N.J.: Prentice-Hall, 1983)

The opposite of majoritarianism is proportional representation, which makes it possible for many — and preferably all — opinions, interests, ideologies, regionalisms, religious groups, ethnic minorities, etc., to form political parties and to be represented in the legislatures *in proportion to their respective voting strength.* Each vote, no matter where it is cast in the country, counts. Knowing this in advance, voters all over the country can organize themselves into political parties so that they will be able to cast enough ballots to elect even one of their candidates and thus have at least some voice in the legislature. At the risk of drawing what

TABLE 4-2

ELECTORAL DISTRICT: THE WHOLE COUNTRY

	PERFECT MAJORITARIAN SYSTEM (WINNER TAKES ALL)		PERFECT PROPORTIONAL REPRESENTATION SYSTEM (WINNERS TAKE THEIR SHARE)
	A		A1
PERCENTAGE OF POPULAR VOTE	LEGISLATURE: 400 SEATS		LEGISLATURE: 400 SEATS CORRESPONDING TO 50,000 VOTES PER SEAT
Party A 30	Winner: Party A = 400 seats	Party A	120 seats
B 23		B	92 seats
C 18		C	72 seats
D 9		D	36 seats
E 7		E	28 seats
F 5		F	20 seats
G 5		G	20 seats
H 1		H	4 seats
I 1		I	4 seats
J 1		J	4 seats
			400 seats

appears to be a caricature, Table 4-2 shows how a legislative assembly would look under a perfect majoritarian (A) and a perfect proportional representation system (A1).

Note that in A (the perfect majoritarian system) there is only one electoral district: the whole country. Note also that Party A with only 30 percent of the national vote gets *all* the seats in the legislature. This is also called the "winner takes all system," or "first to pass the post," and a plurality of votes is all that is needed. The combined strength of all other political parties and groups represents 70 percent of the votes; they have no representation in the legislature. Note also that under these conditions the prime minister and the cabinet, that is, the leadership of Party A that came in first, will have the absolute support of the legislature but will be just as unrepresentative as the legislature.

In A1 (the perfect proportional representation system) all parties receive a representation proportionate to their voting strength. Party A now receives what it deserves: 30 percent of the 400-member legislature, that is, 120 seats; Party B, 92 seats; Party C, 72 seats; and so forth. The legislature is perfectly representative of the nationwide vote but no government can be formed unless Party A and Party B form a coalition, a very unlikely hypothesis. Perfect representation in this case leads to a very imperfect government, or perhaps to no government at all, just as a perfect government (in the sense of legislative support and stability) leads to a very imperfect representation. In both cases popular support and consent to the government are adversely affected. In the first case because the government is supported by an unrepresentative legislature; in the

TABLE 4-3 Districting: 400 Electoral Districts Electing 400 Representatives

A	A		B			B				C						A			
				D						C	C	C							
														E		E			
							A						G						
							B												
A							C		E								F		
A							D												
				F			E							D					
							F												
B							G					I							
B							H												
H		G					I	H							I				H
H							J												
					J						J						B		
		A															B		
		A															B		
									E										

second because the government without majority backing is unable to govern. Representation or government — this is the question! In our earlier discussion on parties of representation and parties of government, we concluded that there should be a mix that gives a fair degree of representation to the people and enough authority and supports to the government so that it can function effectively. The electoral system must make room for both, and this is precisely what is often attempted.

Majoritarianism: Qualifications There are several ways whereby majoritarianism can be qualified.

Districting. The country is divided into districts, each with about the same number of people and therefore eligible voters. It is the winner in *each* district, by majority or plurality, who is elected. For example, the United Kingdom is divided into 635 constituencies; the United States has 435 districts for election to the House of Representatives; France is divided into 491 districts. Territorial and regional distinctions with their peculiarities and different traditions or economic and occupational characteristics provide for variations from one constituency to another. It is impossible, as shown in Table 4-3, for a party to win in all the districts and capture all the seats in the legislature. Even under this scheme, however, a distortion similar to the one found in Table 4-2(A) is likely to appear. Table 4-4 indicates the so-called "landslide effect" of the British electoral

TABLE 4-4 Majoritarianism vs. Proportionality: A Concrete Illustration

The differences in the electoral outcomes between a majority and a proportional electoral system can be shown with reference to the British election of 1983. The second column indicates the distribution of seats under the present system and the third column indicates what the distribution would have been under proportional representation.

	PERCENT OF POPULAR VOTE	NUMBER OF SEATS	UNDER PROPORTIONAL REPRESENTATION
Conservatives	42.4	397	260
Laborites	27.6	203	180
"Alliance"	25.4	19	165
Other	4.6	16	30
	100	635	635

system favoring the two major parties and discriminating against third parties. It shows how in the election of 1983 the Conservative party, with only 42.4 percent of the national vote, gained an absolute majority in the legislature — 61.1 percent or 397 of the 635 seats — and how the newly formed Alliance party, (Liberals and Social Democrats), with a strong 25.4 percent of the vote, managed only 3.5 percent of the seats for a total of a mere 18 seats! On the other hand, the Labor party that came second, but only with 27.6 percent of the vote, gained 32.2 percent of the seats in the legislature — 200 hundred seats. In the election of 1983 it took fewer than forty thousand votes to elect a Conservative, a little more than forty thousand to elect a Laborite and a whooping 338,000 votes to elect a candidate of the Alliance.

Primaries. Primaries qualify the "first-past-the-post" system. They give many parties a chance to show their strength and to participate in the nomination of individual candidates as well as party leaders. Local and district primaries make it possible for local and regional interests and movements to show their strength within a party and hopefully to elect their candidates and gain representation. Even if new parties and groups fail to nominate their own candidates, they often succeed in gaining a foothold in a major party, broadening the party's program and making it more representative.

Coalitions. To mitigate the rigor of a majoritarian system, parties may form electoral coalitions or agreements or pool their voting strength. In the case of a coalition they appear before the public as one party but their candidates are chosen from among the several (or few) parties that make up the coalition. Thus candidates from different parties are listed under the same party ticket. In this manner smaller parties that had no chance may gain some representation. If no such coalition is formed, parties may run separately but agree in advance to withdraw their candidates from some districts in order to support the candidate of another party, provided the other party does the same. If we go back to Table 4-2(A), parties C, D, E, and F may well agree to do this on the basis of reciprocity, and each one of their candidates in the districts chosen in advance will benefit from the combined vote of all. If small parties manage to make such agreements, they may be able to overcome the obstacles of the system and gain some representation.

French Majoritarianism. The British electoral system (also followed in New Zealand, Australia, India, and Canada), where there are no primaries, has always been cited as a system that represses minority parties. The party candidate that crosses the post first wins; all others disappear. Although the French electoral system that has been used since 1958 penalizes minorities far more drastically, it also promotes the formation of coalitions. This system (shown in Table 4-5) involves two stages. In the first stage, D1, any number of candidates can run in the designated electoral districts. The candidate that wins 50 percent plus one is the winner. Only some 70 to 130 deputies are thus elected on the first ballot, leaving about 365 to 425 seats undecided. Within a week a second ballot is cast in all the undecided districts. Only the candidates that received more than 12.5 percent of the registered voters in the electoral district on the first ballot are allowed by law to run again. This virtually eliminates all small and even middle-sized party candidates, since 12.5 percent of the registered voters amounts to well over 20 percent of the votes cast. Thus only the candidates of three or four of the major parties can run again, but in fact only two run. The major parties and their candidates make reciprocal agreements in advance to pool their votes on the second ballot. As D1 indicates, the Communist will withdraw in favor of the Socialist and the candidate of the Gaullist will withdraw in favor of the candidate of the Union of French Democracy, while the smaller parties that have been eliminated arrange themselves behind the Socialist or the Gaullist. In almost all districts the second ballot becomes what the French call a "duel" between two rival candidates of two rival party blocs. At this stage the French system is practically identical to the British or the American majoritarian system. But, as we noted, there is one difference: there are usually only two candidates, and a majority (not a plurality) decides the election. While the French system penalizes small parties even more harshly than the British and the American systems do, it also allows them to find allies — it promotes coalitions.

In general, majoritarian systems have simplified the party structure and reduced the number of parties. The voter is forced to choose between two party candidates. The parties are forced to form blocs. Thus parties of representation are gradually transformed into parties of government. The coalitions that result give a modicum of representation to smaller parties and a maximum of support and authority to the government.

Proportional Representation: Qualifications Proportional representation is being widely used in most European countries: West Germany

TABLE 4-5 French Electoral System (Legislative Election — An Illustrative Example)

ELECTORAL DISTRICT X REGISTERED VOTES 120,000*

Candidate	D1 PRIMARY (FIRST BALLOT)	D2 RUNOFF (SECOND BALLOT)
1. Communist: Binet	15,000 (withdraws in favor of 2)	
2. Socialist: Trinet	23,000	Trinet 50,700
3. Revolutionary/Trotskyite: Finet	1,200 (withdraws in favor of 2)	
4. Radical: Quinet	13,000 (withdraws in silence)	vs.
5. Union of French Democracy: Traboulet	21,000	Traboulet 53,000 ELECTED
6. Gaullist: Cassoulet	19,000 (withdraws in favor of 5)	Traboulet received his own votes, plus those of the Gaullists, plus the votes of the extreme right, plus at least two-thirds of the radicals and fractions of others.
7. Environmentalist: Le Foret	3,000 (withdraws in favor of 2)	Two thousand voters who abstained on the first ballot voted in the second.
8. Europeanist: Bardoulet	1,500 (withdraws in silence)	
9. Extreme right: Barbaroux	5,000 (withdraws in favor of 5)	
	Total Vote =101,700	Total vote: 103,700 thousand

Candidates 3, 7, 8, and 9 do not receive 12.5 percent of registered voters and do not qualify for the runoff; 1, 2, 4, 5, and 6 do.

*Four hundred and ninety-one electoral districts.

(even in a modified form), Belgium, Luxembourg, Switzerland, Holland, Italy, Austria, Finland, the Scandinavian countries (Denmark, Norway, and Sweden), and the Southern Mediterranean countries (Spain, Portugal, Italy, and Greece). All these countries have been and remain multiparty regimes, and in most of them the government relies on party coalitions for majority support in Parliament.

Districting As we pointed out, Table 4-2(A1) is an extreme case; it applies only to Israel and Holland. In all other countries with proportional representation, however, the districting system is used. Candidates in a district are elected if they win a number of votes that represent the quotient of the electoral district's population divided by the number of seats allotted to it. Thus if the population of a district is 100,000 and the number of seats allotted is three, *any* three candidates of any three parties who received 30,000 and more votes will be elected. Usually a number of electoral districts comprise an electoral region, and there may be five or six electoral districts in each electoral region. All leftover votes, that is, all votes that are in excess of 30,000 for a winning party candidate or below 30,000 for a losing one in any given district, are added up for the whole electoral region and redistributed among party candidates in accordance with their strength. There is usually a third and last distribution where all leftovers in all the electoral regions are added and party candidates are chosen accordingly.[2]

Exclusions In proportional representation every vote counts. Yet there are proportional representation systems that penalize minorities. In West Germany, for instance, unless a party receives 5 percent of the national vote, it is not represented at all — it loses all its votes. This system is calculated to discourage small parties and splinter groups. In other countries, unless a party receives 10, 15, or 17 percent of the national vote, it has no right to the second and third distributions. Thus many of these systems, while stressing representativeness, try to avert a fragmentation so that a party can win an absolute majority of the seats in the legislature.

The disadvantages of proportional representation have already been noted: it perpetuates a multiplicity of parties even when they no longer provide for a genuine vehicle of representation of ideas or interests, and it makes the formation of a coalition government potentially difficult and uncertain. Lack of majority support for a government in the legislature may lead not only to governmental crises but also to crises of legitimacy. The Weimar Republic of Germany has been used as an illustration of these disadvantages. Elections were held between 1928 and 1932 under a proportional representation system but they failed to produce any viable majority support for a government in the legislature until the democratic regime succumbed to the Nazi dictatorship (see Table 4-6).

As we noted, the qualifications of majoritarian or proportional

2. The new electoral law in France, if enacted, provides for proportional representation in each of the 101 French departments.

TABLE 4-6 The German Election of May 1928 . . . under the Present Electoral System

	POPULAR VOTE	SEATS	SEATS UNDER THE PRESENT ELECTORAL SYSTEM
Nationalist party	14.2	73	94
Nazi party	2.6	12	0
German People's party	8.7	35	60
German Country People	1.8	10	0
Peasant party	1.5	8	0
Country Union	0.6	3	0
Economist party	4.5	23	0
German/Hanover party	0.6	3	0
Center party	11.9	62	79
Bavarian People's party	3.9	16	0
German Democratic party	4.9	25	0
Social Democratic party	28.7	153	188
Communist party	10.6	54	75
Others (total)	5.5	4	0
		481	496

Note: The 5 percent exclusion clause that applies today would have eliminated the marginal parties in 1928 and would have made it possible for the Center and the Social Democrats supporting the Weimar Republic to form a coalition with 267 votes. The three democratic parties in 1928 — the Social Democrats, the Center, and the German Democratic party — held between them only 240 votes, not a majority. No stable coalition government was formed and an election followed in 1930 that showed a dramatic increase in Nazi strength.

representation electoral systems try to effect a mix between representativeness and government support. They attempt to reconcile the democratic principles of fair and equal representation of as many points of view as possible with the needs of stable and effective governance. Consent and command have to be linked. It would be foolhardy to say that modern democracies have managed to accomplish this successfully. In England and in the United States minorities remain grossly underrepresented. In France coalitional politics do attenuate, but only to a degree, the inequalities in representation, especially of minorities and ideological groups. In many democracies the few (frequently sizable fractions of the electorate) find themselves without a voice. If they remain outside the appropriate vehicle of expression — the legislature — they will seek to make themselves heard elsewhere. They may move to confrontational politics; they may even resort to violence. On the other hand, a regime that gives a voice to all in proportion to their numerical strength, no matter how small, may deprive a society of the opportunity to attenuate differences and seek compromise. Without such compromise there can be no strong plurality or majority to support a government and its policies. Everyone will hear his or her own voice until no voice can be heard, and there will be no policy and no viable government.

The qualifications we have outlined both to majoritarianism and proportional representation attempt to avoid these extremes and to structure and organize consent and support without stifling dissent or paralyzing governance.

Voter Alignments: Parties and Society

Parties reflect and in turn organize various social forces. They try to be both representative and aggregative. There are several important social and other factors that structure an individual's attachment and vote for a party — his or her partisanship: (1) class, occupation, religion, regionalism, ethnicity, race, language, income, and literacy; (2) tradition and specific historical circumstances; (3) particular and short-term issues, notably the state of the economy or issues of war and peace; (4) considerations involving personality and leadership. and (5) the electoral system in force.

It is virtually impossible to do more than suggest some descriptive generalizations on how people vote in elections and why they vote for one party or another. While the social determinants mentioned above can be clearly spelled out, they have to be qualified in a number of ways because there is no *single* social determinant that accounts for partisanship. There are only *clusters* of determinants that can account for it, and the clustering in one country rarely repeats itself in another. Moreover, there are parties that do not seem to correlate clearly with *any* set of social determinants. As the author Richard Rose wrote, "Because parties may unite support on several grounds [or none] party systems must be perceived in terms of a multidimensional space." It is even possible, he adds, "to have a no-dimension party system, i.e., one in which no party can be placed on a social dimension because all are heterogeneous . . . in terms of major social characteristics."[3] In fact, there is a degree of heterogeneity in all parties. In a democracy it is almost impossible for a party to be exclusively and solely identified with any single social determinant, not even language, ethnicity, or race. Practically all parties are multidimensional.

The most significant dimensions in identifying political parties are (1) socioeconomic, (2) religious, (3) ethnic, and (4) regional. Party programs rationalize the position of the voters in terms of particular groups from whom the party seeks to derive its major support. There have been religious parties; farmers' parties; middle-class parties; working-class

3. Richard Rose (ed.), *Electoral Behavior: A Comparative Study* (New York: The Free Press, 1974), p. 19.

parties; ethnic, linguistic, and racial parties; and parties directly sponsored by business groups. Class has always been considered a key factor but nowhere is there a full identification between a given class and a political party; at best, there is only a rough correlation. In fact, all political parties straddle social classes, particularly in Canada and the United States. In other countries, such as England, France, and Italy, however, the correlation between the working classes and left-wing parties (the Labour Party in England and the Socialists and the Communists in France and Italy) is clearly marked. It is only with ethnic parties, however, especially when ethnicity is associated closely with language, religion, and a regional base that identification is overwhelming: the Flamands and the Walloons in Belgium, the French Quebecois in Canada, and religious groups in Holland. Similarly, in some of the new nations in Asia and Africa there is an overwhelming identification of tribal groups with political parties.

Class

Working-class identification with left-wing parties was a powerful determinant until World War II, but then modernization began to undermine the political coherence of the workers. What was in fact the most homogeneous and self-conscious group in industrial societies in the nineteenth century — the workers — is today fragmented in terms of occupation, income, and lifestyle.

With the waning of the homogeneity of the workers, the correlation between left-wing parties and the workers has declined. Many among the skilled and white-collar workers lose their class identity. They become upwardly mobile, change lifestyles, alter their expectations, and begin to change their political attitudes and attachments. Socialist and Communist parties that used to appeal to an undifferentiated mass of workers now have to straddle classes and appeal to other social and economic groups for votes and support.

As a result, the partisanship (and thus the votes) of the workers goes to different parties. In England it has been estimated that as many as 30 percent of the workers vote conservative; in France even a greater percentage went to DeGaulle when he ran for the presidency. Until 1981, less than half of all French workers voted for the French Socialist and Communist parties. In the United States, during the last thirty years, the workers have generally divided their vote between Republicans and Democrats.

Religion

In countries where religious denominations are many, partisanship based on religion, even if it exists, lacks intensity and continuity. In others, as in France where 90 percent of the population is Catholic, the major distinction is between those who attend church regularly or intermittently and those who are agnostics. It is an important factor, since the believers tend to vote for the conservative parties while the lukewarm Catholics and agnostics vote the center, the Socialists, and the Communists. In the election of 1981, however, the Socialists captured many Catholic votes, but now they seem to be losing them again. In England, the religious factor reinforces class: nonconformist groups that are mostly working class or lower middle class vote Labour, while Anglicans and Episcopalians vote for the Liberal or the Conservative party. In the United States, Catholics voted overwhelmingly for the Democratic party. Recently, however, there has been a marked realignment of the Catholic vote in the direction of the Republican party. Economic and social factors account for it, since many of the second and third generation Catholics from Ireland, Italy, and Eastern Europe improved their living standards. But even among the low income groups ethnic and race considerations accounted for the shift, as blacks identified themselves increasingly with the Democratic party (90 percent voted for the Democratic candidate in the 1984 election). The election of the Mayor of Chicago, a black, showed how race can change partisanship overnight. Most of the Catholic vote shifted to the Republican candidate. Many religious parties that are identified with a religious denomination continue to show strength. In Holland there is the Catholic People's party; in Israel, the National Religious party; in Norway, the Christian Peoples Front; and there are strong Christian Democratic parties in West Germany, Italy, Austria, Switzerland, Belgium, Finland, and Denmark.

Regionalism

Regionalism denotes common political attitudes and orientations that stem from the economic and cultural concerns of a particular region. It may, and it usually is, associated with levels of economic underdevelopment or ethnic and linguistic differences and even an incipient separatist movement.

In general, a number of factors enhance regional partisanships. If a region is predominantly inhabited by people sharing a religious denomination and if historic, ethnic, and national factors have perpetuated a sense of autonomy and independence among them, then it is likely that the great majority of the people will affiliate with a party that espouses autonomy or independence or separation. The cases of the French-speaking Quebecois in Canada and the Flemish and the Walloons in Belgium are good examples. But significantly enough, regionalism in both cases is also enhanced by class, as well as occupational and linguistic factors. It is a combination of many determinants: religion plus class plus regionalism plus language plus given economic conditions. It is a special kind of clustering that accounts for regional voting. One sole determinant does not suffice; we need a number of them that are linked, and we cannot tell which link is the strongest.

Cross-cutting Loyalties

As noted earlier, one of the characteristics of socioeconomic modernization and political development is the weakening of attachments that relate directly to class, region, ethnicity, language, or occupation. Society as a whole has become increasingly homogenized with people sharing common outlooks. One individual may straddle many attachments and loyalties. Consider the following example: an American Catholic worker lives in the South and is married to a non-Catholic high school teacher from Boston, and both are staunch environmentalists. He belongs to the VFW (Veterans of Foreign Wars) and she is active in NOW (the National Organization of Women). No single determinant can structure this couple's politics and partisanships, and it will be hard to find a cluster that does. We can multiply this illustration simply to show that individuals who fit into a number of socio-economic categories, into many determinants that shape their attitudes, may eventually transcend them all. By belonging or being attached to many categories, they may end up belonging to none!

The existence of diverse social forces as well as groups that have multiple, and often contradictory or cross-cutting, loyalties give individuals more freedom to vote their preferences and shape their partisanship. The independent voters, those with no partisanships, vote their choice, regardless of parties and often shift from one party to another. Their decisions and choices are made on the basis of other considerations and factors. What are they?

Judgment, Issues, and Leadership

Besides the theory that social determinants determine partisanship and voting habits, there is also the theory of voluntarism whereby people exercise their own independent judgment. It is a thesis supported by the recent decline in party membership, the weakening of partisan attachments, the growth of independent voters, and the rapid rise and fall of some political parties. Consider, for example, the following developments: the drop of about 15 percent in the votes for the Labour party in the British election of 1983 and the corresponding rise of the Alliance (comprised of Social Democrats and Liberals); the loss of at least 6 percent of votes for the French Communists and the rise of the Socialists by about 11 percent in the French legislative election of June 1981; a corresponding drop in the strength of the German Free Democrats and the emergence of a new party, the Greens, in the election of March 1983; the sweeping victories of the Socialist parties in Spain and Greece in 1981–1982; and the upswing of some right-wing parties in the election of the European Parliament in June 1984. None of these changes can be attributed solely to changes in the social structure and social determinants. The proposition that issues and leaders make an important difference in how people vote and the thesis that they exercise their own judgment should be seriously entertained.

The catchall party, which we discussed earlier, was without any doubt the harbinger of the independent voter. By definition it was a party that was multidimensional: it tried to get the vote by cutting across class, occupation, ethnicity, religion, and regional attachments. In so doing, it gradually moved people from the social moorings (or determinants) they were anchored to. The catchall party, in trying to appeal to so many social groups, did not provide an adequate center of loyalty and partisanship. The voters found themselves increasingly on their own and free to espouse issues and leaders on their own. Choice became more a matter of taste and judgment than organization; particular policy concerns at a given time were more important than long-range policy considerations; and the personality of the candidate grew to new dimensions. Candidates were increasingly viewed in terms of empathy, charisma, leadership qualities, trust and confidence, and honesty.

Leadership traits have played a crucial role in most of the recent elections in Western Europe and in the United States. Party leaders have detached themselves from the party organization and have appealed over the head of their party, and as a result all these elections assumed a plebiscitary character — people began to vote for a leader. Particular issues have also remained prominent. Among them the most important in almost all democratic regimes in the last ten years or so have been the economy and its future; employment; war and peace; nuclear weapons and nuclear energy; law and order; environmental issues, both with regard to the disposal of noxious waste and urban renewal; the legal, educational, political, and economic rights and opportunities for minority groups, including the immigrant workers; women's rights; the degree and extent of welfare spending; attitudes toward the growing confrontation between the Soviet Union and the United States; and abortion and the right to life movements. With issues such as these, the voters selectively exercise their own judgment. Even when deep-felt religious predispositions or economic interests are involved, they are offset by other considerations. Take Catholic workers who have a choice between a candidate who supports the right-to-life movement but is against welfare spending and another who favors abortion but supports welfare measures. What will determine the vote of these people? And how will they form a judgment?

The loss of partisanship and the weakening of the determinants that shape it and structure it are fraught with dangers, however. Without organized attachment and partisan loyalties — without parties — voters relying solely on their own judgments may be swayed by a demogogue. On the other hand, their voting independence may prove to be an antidote to the constraints that the party organization imposes. The parties may be forced to reorient themselves and deal with the issues. They may relax their organizational rigidities so that they can better adapt themselves to the formulation and presentation of solutions to new problems as they arise, before, during, and after an election. They may become more representative.

Parties and Voting Patterns

After an election the votes are added up and the results tabulated. By knowing the number of popular votes that parties receive and by comparing them over a period of time we can establish certain voting patterns. Since World War II we have seen the following patterns: stability with alternation, critical shifts, dominance, and simplification.

Stability with Alternation

Two-party democratic regimes fall in this category. The two political parties are evenly matched and a small shift of votes, a swing, from one party to another of 2 or 3 percent often makes the difference between victory and defeat. This has been the case notably in Great Britain, the United States, Canada, Australia, New Zealand, and to a great extent in West Germany. In these countries the two rival major parties have held the government for about the same length of time ever since World War II. They rotate in and out of office, so to speak. (See Tables 4-7, 4-8, and 4-9.)

TABLE 4-7 Alternation in the United States (1944 to 1986/88)

	PRESIDENCY	SENATE MAJORITY	HOUSE MAJORITY
1944	Roosevelt (D)	Democrats 1944–1945	Democrats 1940–1947
	Truman (D)	Republicans 1945–1947	Republicans 1947–1949
1948	Truman (D)	Democrats 1947–1949	Democrats 1949–1953
1952	Eisenhower (R)	Republicans 1949–1955	Republicans 1953–1955
1956	Eisenhower (R)	Democrats 1955–1979	Democrats 1955–1971
1960	Kennedy (D)	Republicans 1981–1986	Democrats 1971–1986
	Johnson (D)		
1964	Johnson (D)	Total:	Total:
1968	Nixon (R)	Republicans: 12 years	Democrats: 32 years
1972	Nixon (R)	Democrats: 28 years	Republicans: 4 years
	Ford (R)		
1976	Carter (D)		
1980	Reagan (R)		
1984	Reagan (R)		
Total:			
Democrats: 20 years			
Republicans: 24 years			

Table 4-8 Alternation in England (1945–1988)

	Party	Prime Minister
1945	Labour	Attlee
1950	Labour	Attlee
1951	Conservative	Churchill
		Eden
1955	Çonservative	Eden
		Macmillan
1959	Labour	Wilson
1964	Labour	Wilson
1966	Conservative	Heath
1970	Labour	Wilson
		Gallagher
1974	Labour	Gallagher
1979	Conservative	Thatcher
1983–1988 (?)	Conservative	Thatcher
Total	Labour: 22 years	
	Conservative: 21 years	

Table 4-9 Alternation in the Federal Republic of Germany

	Christian Democrats & Free Democrats	1949–1953
	Christian Democrats & Free Democrats	1953–1957
	Christian Democrats & Free Democrats	1957–1961
	Christian Democrats & Free Democrats	1961–1965
	Christian Democrats & Socialists	1965–1969
	Socialists & Free Democrats	1969–1972
	Socialists & Free Democrats	1972–1976
	Socialists & Free Democrats	1976–1980
	Socialists & Free Democrats	1980–1983
	Christian Democrats & Free Democrats	1983–1987 (?)
Totals	Christian Democrats & Free Democrats: 16 years	
	Socialists & Free Democrats: 11 years	
	Christian Democrats & Socialists: 4 years	

Critical Shifts

We see critical shifts when a mass of voters change from one party to another or when new parties develop enough strength to capture sizable blocs of voters. The result is a realignment of groups from one party to another. It is a phenomenon closely associated with periods of national crisis, rapid modernization, the emergence of a strong national leader, or newly gained access by a mass of formerly disfranchised people. The voting patterns in the German Weimar Republic in 1930 indicate a radical shift in favor of the nationalist right: the Nazis; similarly, the Greek electoral picture between 1974 and 1981 is indicative of the same radical change to the left (see Table 4-10). In France in 1962 the shift went to the Gaullists. There was a radical change in the United States in 1932 when the Republicans were replaced by the Democrats — what Walter Dean Burnham called a "critical election," signifying a radical and enduring shift in realignment of voter groups.[4] (See Table 4-10.)

TABLE 4-10 Critical Shifts

GREECE	1974	1977	1981
Center Right:			
Nea Democratia	54.37	41.84	35.81
National Front		6.82	
Center Union	20.42	11.95	3.60
	74.79	60.61	39.41
Left:			
PASOK (Socialists)*	13.58	25.34	48.6
Communists	9.47	13.04	12.3
	23.05	38.38	60.9

WEIMAR REPUBLIC (GERMANY)	1928	1930	1932
Social Democrats	29.8	24.5	21.6
Communists	10.6	13.1	14.6
Center	12.1	11.8	12.5
Bavarian People's Party	3.0	3.0	3.2
Democrats	4.9	3.8	1.2
People's Party	8.7	4.5	
Economists	4.5	3.9	
Nationalists	14.2	7.0	5.9
The Nazi Party*	2.6	18.3	37.4
Other Parties	Approx. 10.0	Approx. 10.0	Approx. 10.0

*The party responsible for the critical shift.

4. Walter Dean Burnham, *Critical Elections and the Mainsprings of American Politics* (New York: W. W. Norton, 1970).

TABLE 4-11 Dominance

THE GAULLIST PARTY: FRANCE	PERCENT OF VOTE
1962	40.5
1967	42.6
1968	48.8
1973	46.3
1978	26.1

THE CHRISTIAN DEMOCRATS: ITALY	PERCENT OF VOTE
1948	48.5
1953	40.0
1958	42.4
1963	38.3
1968	39.1
1972	38.7
1976	38.7
1979	38.3
1982	37.4

THE CONGRESS PARTY: INDIA	PERCENT OF VOTE
1952	45.0
1957	47.8
1962	44.7
1967	40.8
1971	43.6

Dominance

We see dominance when one party receives a large plurality (but not necessarily the majority) of votes in many elections over a period of many years. As a result, it manages to serve as the center of gravity around which other parties revolve and under whose leadership coalitions are formed (see Table 4-11).

Simplification

One observable common trend among some European parties during the last forty years has been the simplification of the multiparty system. First, there is a reduction in numbers, and smaller parties virtually disappear; second, even if small parties do survive, they have little electoral weight and are forced to form electoral agreements and blocs with the major parties in order to support a common slate of candidates. The case of France (Table 4-12) is illustrative.

TABLE 4-12 Simplification of Party Configuration in France from Fourth Republic to Fifth Republic

1956		1978		1981*	
PARTY	SEATS IN NATIONAL ASSEMBLY	PARTY	SEATS IN NATIONAL ASSEMBLY	PARTY	SEATS IN NATIONAL ASSEMBLY
Communist	144	Communist	86 } 199	Communist	44 } 336
Progressist	6	Socialist (and affiliates)	113 } 199	Socialist (and affiliates)	292 } 336
Socialist	100				
Radical	40				
Dissident radicals	20				
Democratic African Rally and Democratic Socialist Union of Resistance	18	Union of French Democracy: Centrist, Independent Republicans, and affiliates	124 } 278	Union of French Democracy: Centrist. Independent Republicans, and affiliates	72 } 155
MRP	74	Gaullist	154 } 278	Gaullist	83 } 155
Independents from overseas	10	Nonregistered	14		
Rally of Republican left	14				
Gaullist	22				
Independents	84				
Peasant	13				
Union of French Fraternity	42				
Other	6				
Totals	593		491		491

*On the second ballot the two major blocs received virtually 98 percent of the vote.

While simplification may be noticeable, there is not enough evidence to allow us to generalize, and the forces moving in the direction of fragmentation should be taken into account. In West Germany a new party, the Greens, has emerged, creating a potential four-party system. In England the party system is in flux with indications that the two-party system may give place to a multiparty system (besides the Conservatives, the Labourites, and the Liberals, the Social Democrats must be added). In the United States independent candidates emerge frequently. In France ever since 1981, there has been a resurgence of new political groups and parties — notably the extreme right-wing National Front that won 11 percent of the vote in the election to the European Parliament in June 1984. Democratic regimes and their party configurations are always in flux, as demands and interests constantly push for realization and in the process the parties are either altered or abandoned altogether. Like all other institutions, large parties that cannot adapt to change become themselves the victims of change.

Financing the Election

The independence of representatives — their ability to fulfill the pledges they made and, more important, whether or not they are obligated to special interests — is of critical importance for the survival of representative government. In advanced liberal democracies the issue of representativeness is directly linked to finances: Who pays the expenses for a party and a candidate? Parties that are financially dependent on certain interests are bound to act on their behalf even if they claim to represent the public at large. Since wealth is unevenly distributed, the rich are fewer in number. But it is the rich who are more likely to control political power: they pay to hire organizers and publicity experts; they control or influence the media; they pay transportation expenses for party officials, candidates, and even voters. Sharp inequalities and sharp differences in wealth, therefore, may account for serious inequalities in representation.

There are at least four sources of funds for a party and its candidates. The first is simply direct contributions by individuals, which may be given directly to the party, to candidates, or to various local committees. The second comes from corporate or group contributions: businessmen, bankers, managerial groups, industrialists, and trade unions. A third source consists of affiliated contributions, dues given by individuals to the groups that are affiliated with or openly support a given party, for example the trade unions that back the Socialist or Communist parties in Europe and the Labour party in England. Fourth, the funds are raised by public contributions, direct or indirect payments and subsidies given by the state to parties and candidates in order to minimize the influence and arbitrariness of the first three sources.

While every effort has been made to disclose all individual, corporate, and affiliated contributions, there are only a few democratic regimes where the candidates or the parties have an obligation to reveal the sources of their financial support. As for direct public subsidies, which are usually prorated on the number of votes a party receives, there a quite a few countries that provide this type of financial support: Austria, Canada, Denmark, Finland, France (for presidential candidates who receive 5 percent of the national vote), West Germany, Italy, Holland, Norway, Sweden, England, and the United States. (Switzerland and Australia are among the few countries that do not provide for direct public subsidies.) In addition, there are a number of services given to parties and individual candidates free of charge, the most common of which are broadcasting and television time, mailing expenses, printing of posters, electoral advertising expenses, voter registration, transportation and use of public halls.

Elections continue to be strongly influenced by the resources that candidates and parties can command. Mass membership and affiliated groups can provide a party and its candidates with a significant amount of funds because they are so large in number. The business, financial, and manufacturing interests that control the major portion of the resources have even more influence. In the United States, where the electoral campaign lasts longer than in any other country, millions of dollars are spent because presidential candidates who can raise funds beyond a certain level in twenty or more states will have (if they also win 10 percent or more of the votes in a number of primaries) their funds matched by public funds. The same applies to congressional campaigns. Hence the importance of raising as much as possible. Political associations and political action committees can organize and collect funds for individual candidates and no matter how strict and elaborate the rules are, many loopholes exist in virtually all democratic regimes. In most countries it is easy for the rich to "stuff the ballot box" and it is precisely to avoid such a situation that public financing of elections, accurate reporting of contributions, and sanctions for violations are crucial to the integrity of elections in all democracies.

Bibliography

Bogdanor, V., and David Butler (eds.). *Democracy and Elections: Electoral Systems and Their Political Consequence.* New York: Cambridge University Press, 1983.

Butler, David, Howard Penniman, and Austin Ranney (eds.). *Democracy at the Polls: A Comparative Study of Competitive National Elections.* Washington, D.C.: American Enterprise Institute, 1981.

Carstairs, Andrew M. *A Short History of Electoral Systems in Western Europe*. London: George Allen & Unwin, 1980.

Dalton, R. J., S. C. Flanagan, and P. A. Beck. *Electoral Change in Advanced Industrial Democracies: Realignment or Dealignment*. Princeton, N.J.: Princeton University Press, 1984.

Penniman, Howard (ed.). "At the Polls." Washington, D.C.: American Enterprise Institute. A series of publications covering the elections held in the last fifteen in many democratic regimes: England, France, Italy, India, Canada, Greece, Australia, Ireland, Israel, New Zealand, and others.

Rae, D. W. *The Political Consequences of Electoral Laws*. New Haven, Conn.: Yale University Press, 1967.

Sallnow, John, and Anna John. *An Electoral Atlas of Europe, 1968–1981*. Stoneham, Mass.: Butterworth's, 1982.

5 The Organization of Interests and Rights

Introduction

It is almost axiomatic that industrialized societies have numerous special interest groups. Interests constantly strive for maximum benefits and hence constantly pressure the government for favors, concessions, help, and even direct or indirect subsidies. It would be impossible to give a detailed account of the variety of interest groups in modern democratic regimes, since the particular issues and concerns they express vary from one country to another. Generally speaking, however, there are three generic types of interest groups: material, spiritual, and promotional.

Material interest organizations are primarily concerned with the preservation and the advancement of material benefits, even if they couch them in idealistic terms. General Motors, trade unions, the American Medical Association, the Trade Union Congress in England, the Jeunes Patrons in France, the Chamber of Commerce, and various other business and professional associations belong to this category. Spiritual interests are primarily religious, philanthropic, and educational. But there are also material considerations linked with these lofty vocations. Would Harvard University stand still if private contributions were not tax-exempt? Would churches consent to a property tax? Promotional interests advocate causes that do not seem to be directly linked with material interests, for example environmentalists, right-to-life advocates, or reform groups (to reform the tax structure or the civil service or local government). Yet if you scratch below the surface of such groups, you will find material interests and concerns underneath. And quite frequently the state itself and its various agencies become pressure groups in order to maintain their autonomy and policies, as for example the military.

Interests and Democratic Regimes: Common Traits

In all democracies, interests share common characteristics and common modes of action that differentiate them from authoritarian or totalitarian regimes.

First and foremost is the fact that there is *freedom* in a democracy. Interests are *allowed* to organize and propagate their claims and points of view. Fraternal associations, veterans of various wars, snake worshippers and sun worshippers, margarine and butter producers, tobacco growers and nonsmokers, homosexuals and polygamists, working mothers and unemployed husbands, private schools and colleges, tax evaders and draft dodgers, businessmen, farmers, manufacturers, spinsters and school teachers, feminists and male chauvinists, divorced women and alimony payers, the young, the aging and the aged — name any occupation, any predicament, any cause, any situation, any loyalty, and you will find an organization, an association, a lobby, a club, or a fraternal association representing it.

Second, the interest configuration in democratic regimes shows a great *diversity*. Interest groups mirror the manifold societal forces, and their very multiplicity attests to the vitality of the societal forces.

Third, interest associations are formed *spontaneously*, and they are constantly mushrooming. They spring from the societal soil. They express common concerns and predicaments, which they hope to promote or alleviate. There is a great degree of creativity in this process, as well as a degree of inventiveness, that provides for change or at least keeps the door open for change.

Fourth, participation in interest organizations is voluntary and interest organizations are *independent* from one another and *autonomous* vis-à-vis the state.

Fifth, interest group activity is a means for the *recruitment* of future leaders and in fact provides a training ground for them. Interest groups also add another dimension to participating in the political process. People who are disenchanted by political parties and government officials find their group to be a center of loyalty and a vehicle of participation that inevitably will bring them to grips with policies and policy makers.

Finally, the configuration of the interest universe is horizontal. *Horizontality* — not a very good term to use — simply means that there is no superior-inferior interest structure in democracies; all interests are heard independently of one another.

Strength and Tactics

Interest groups and associations rely on many sources for their strength: membership, ideology, organization, material resources, and the particular skills of their members.

Membership. In any group, one source of strength lies simply in numbers. How many members does it have? The larger the membership, the greater the potential strength.

Ideology. While the basic beliefs of an association are important, the intensity of these beliefs is even more important. The extent and the degree to which members identify with the overall purposes of the group and how deeply they are involved in it are of critical significance.

Organization. A group with a large and diversified membership may be unable to get its members mobilized and active. Trade unions in many industrialized societies find themselves in this predicament today. On the other hand, a small interest group with a small membership that strongly believes in the same ideology and is well organized can be much more effective.

Material Resources and Skills. Solid financial backing is obviously a major source of strength. And so are the particular professional skills of the members. Small associations whose members have special knowledge and can perform important and sensitive jobs — computer programmers or air traffic controllers, for instance — have greater impact and influence than groups with members who are large in numbers but lacking in skills.

Modes of Action

Interest groups in democracies share common modes of action. They use persuasion and propaganda. Their techniques are usually overt but occasionally they use covert methods as well. The Institute for the Study of Alcoholism in France, for instance, or the Tobacco Institute in the United States are underwritten by alcohol-producing or tobacco-growing and manufacturing interests in an effort to discount many of the evils of alcohol and cigarette smoking. Such covert methods do not remain undetected for long, however, and overt techniques are still the norm. In trying to persuade everybody about the validity of their claims, all interest groups use lobbying tactics, that is, putting direct pressures on legislators and public officials. With dominant interest groups, the tactics may prove successful and, as we saw, efforts are being made to use public funds to underwrite electoral campaign costs in order to safeguard the independence of elected officials.

As to the specific forms of action, they are as follows:

Information and Propaganda. The usual means used to influence public opinion are the press, the radio, and television. Many interest groups have their own newspapers and some control radio and television stations through which they inform the people at large and often help shape public opinion.

Political Organization. These interest groups try to influence elections by actively throwing their support behind certain candidates and against others. They mobilize the electorate and they also provide, within legal limits, direct financial help to candidates. If elected, these candidates can be counted on to defend and promote the interests that helped them get into office. The impact of the Moral Majority or the National Riflemen's Association in the United States in the elections of senators and congressmen in 1978 and 1980 cannot be underestimated; nor can the impact of the nuclear freeze movement or the environmentalists be ignored in most contemporary democracies. As for trade unions and religious associations, their direct weight in elections has been significant almost everywhere.

Threats and Intimidation. Certain letter-writing campaigns for or against policies and officials, as well as street demonstrations and marches, can mobilize fellow members and like-minded people to the point where candidates and policy makers may feel intimidated. Occasionally interest groups go beyond mere demonstrations and resort to direct action: strikes, slowdowns, or even acts of violence. Farmers may throw their fruit on the highways, air-traffic controllers may walk away from their jobs, and wine growers may pour their wine into the town water reservoir! Truckers may block traffic. Powerful financial and banking interests may manipulate the market and artificially influence rates of interest or foreign exchange. The French, for example, referred to the *mûr d'argent,* — the "money wall" — that was aimed at subverting the governmental policies of left-wing governments.

Access

We have already noted that interest groups not only want to shape or influence public opinion, but also they want to get their own candidates elected, or at least avert the election of candidates with opposite points of view. In their attempt to gain access to policy-making, interest groups go after four major targets: the political parties, the legislature, the executive branch (cabinet or presidential), and the bureaucracy.

Interests and Political Parties Three types of relationships between interest groups and political parties can be envisaged: separation, affiliation and collaboration, and fusion.

Separation. Separation characterizes interest groups that claim to be apolitical. They give or withhold their support from a political party depending on where a party stands with regard to their interests and their demands. They may also shift support from one party to another depending on the positions the parties take. They usually reward their friends, whoever they may be, and punish their enemies.

Affiliation and Collaboration. Major interests may align themselves behind one or another political party through collaboration rather than support. This has been typically the case with trade unions and Socialist parties in Western Europe and England. Sometimes collaboration can lead to affiliation: trade union members have automatically become members of the Socialist party, as in the British Labour party. Collaboration with the Democratic party has been a predominant tactic of American trade union leadership since 1932 through the endorsement and direct support of Democratic candidates. French and Italian unions have collaborated with the Socialist and the Communist parties. Similarly, a number of religious and conservative parties in Europe, especially in Holland and Belgium, continue to be supported by and to collaborate with the Catholic church.

Political parties, while welcoming support and collaboration, are generally apprehensive of affiliation, particularly in two-party regimes. The parties want to extend their appeal beyond *any* given interest and avoid an identification that may alienate some voters. They prefer supports and discreet collaboration. In multiparty regimes, however, where no single party is likely to win a majority, a party that identifies with a single interest group may mobilize its members and consolidate its voting strength. This is even more so in regimes that are multiparty and have a proportional representation electoral system. When a party becomes the voice for one powerful interest or a cluster of a few interests, it can count on their votes at election time. In majority and plurality electoral systems, close collaboration and especially affiliation are avoided. Where they do exist, there is constant friction between the political party and the particular interest groups affiliated with it.

Fusion. Fusion between an interest association and a party is rare for the reasons mentioned above. Although religious movements have frequently come close to fusing with a given political party, they have always kept their distance. The Catholic-inspired popular republican party (MRP) that emerged in France after World War II was led and organized by progressive and liberal Catholic Action leaders but it became a lay organization that appealed to Catholics and non-Catholics alike. Indeed some of its younger leaders at the time have now joined the Socialist party. Similarly, the Catholic party of Germany that became the Christian Democratic Union after World War II abandoned many of its ties with the Church. The same may become the case with the Italian Christian Democrats.

Trade unions have had collaborative ties with political parties, notably the Communists and the Socialists, to the point of fusing with them. This was notably the case with the General Confederation of Labor (CGT) in France and the Communist party, as well as the collaboration of the Confederation of Democratic Labor (CGTD) with the Socialist party. The same pattern was followed between the National Confederation of Labor and the Communist party in Italy and between the trade unions and either Communists or Socialists in Spain and Portugal. In all these cases, however, fusion was disclaimed and lip service was paid to the neutral or apolitical stance of the unions.

There is real fusion when an interest group aggressively captures an existing political party or becomes one. Environmentalists, professional groups, and extremist movements from the right or left may achieve real fusion. One of the most spectacular movements of this kind was the formation of the Union of French Fraternity in the mid-1950s, a political movement representing the interests of small manufacturers, artisans, shopkeepers, and small farmers. Similarly, the Greens in West Germany emerged as a party to represent the demands of the environmentalists. We have also seen specialized parties favoring tax cuts, prohibition, tariff reforms, or environmental concerns that have been spawned by interest groups to serve their purposes, but the new parties must develop their own organization and purpose and detach themselves from the interest that gave birth to them in order to survive.

Interests and the Legislature Major decisions about allocation of resources, welfare programs, and taxation are made by the legislature. It is therefore unavoidable (indeed many would argue that it is quite appropriate) for interests to be concerned about the laws enacted and to make themselves heard about impending legislative measures. Frequently there are identifiable groups of lawmakers within a legislature, even cutting across political parties, that are particularly sensitive to well-known interests, often speaking on their behalf, and they can be relied on to advance the aims of these interests. Legislators are approached directly by interest representatives, by lobbyists. Legislative committees are given information by interest spokesmen, who are asked to testify before legislative committees. When legislators are free to initiate legislation, the drafts prepared in advance are made by the representatives of interest organizations.

The impact of interests on legislators, directly or indirectly or in committees, depends to a great degree on the organization of the legislative proceedings. In cases where legislation is initiated by a government that heads a strong and disciplined party, interest representatives must go to the government itself, a difficult procedure. However, in cases where a legislature consists of a number of political parties, interests that gain access to the party leaders in the legislative committees may carry a great deal of weight. Thus the effectiveness of interest groups in the legislature correlates inversely with the coherence of the legislative process.

Interests and the Executive There are very few interests, and only those with a national organization, that can directly reach the executive branch. They can use personal and direct contacts with cabinet members, with the advisors of the various ministers, or with the prime minister or the president. In some cases, such interests may "colonize" a department or a ministry.

The civil service is constantly being exposed to pressure. Since civil servants implement legislation and have considerable discretion in doing so, interest group spokesmen provide information, advice, research papers, studies, and so forth. They establish direct personal contacts with civil servants and develop a consultative relationship pattern. Moreover, interest groups have other means to reinforce their position. They can always provide job opportunities to government officials, military or civilian, at any time these officials resign or retire.

In advanced democracies there is an interchangeability between the skills of civil servants and those of engineers, technical experts, organizers, and administrators in big companies, trade unions, or professional associations. While there are many weapons experts in the military, just as many can be found among the top level executives of private industries. The relationship between the military, the civil service personnel, and engineers and administrators in the private sector is a cooperative one. Similarly, a trade union leader can always feel at home in the Department of Labor. There is so much compatibility between the organization and the operation of big business and big government that cooperation between them in one form or another is necessary and often desirable. The overlap between government and private job skills may, some will argue, be facilitated and even institutionalized if there is mutual access and communication. In fact, cooperation between the state and the bureaucracy with interest groups has already become the rule.

Consultation, Information, and Representation

A number of forces account for the acceptance of interest groups (including trade unions) and the institutionalization of cooperation between them and the agencies of the state: (1) The Catholic church changed its attitude in the latter part of the nineteenth century when it accepted the legitimacy of interest representation, especially workers' interests, in the development of social policies. Without sanctifying interests as such, the Papal Encyclical of 1893 *(Rerum Novarum)* and again in *Quadregissmo Anno* (1933) conceded them a just and representative role. (2) The workers themselves made their voices and claims heard first through their own trade union associations and, second, through a number of political parties, notably the Social Democrats in Germany, the Labour Party in England, the Social Democrats and Socialists in the Scandinavian countries and Austria. (3) The sheer growth in numbers of manual workers accounted for a rapid growth in trade union membership. (4) The militancy of trade unions played an important role: since they could not be licked, they were allowed to participate.

Industrial organization and the outlook of business firms in general also began to change. The family firm gave place to managerial and bureaucratic organizations operating on the basis of well-established and agreed-upon rules. Paternalism yielded to highly organized forms of management. The importance and organization of industry associations increased to the point where they represented large numbers and resources. The many occupational groups that industrialization spawned became more self-conscious and self-confident and began to press their claims. After World War I interest representation in all democracies were in a state of rapid expansion and ferment. It could no longer be ignored or contained.

The first stage in the legitimization of interests begins when state agencies try to secure information from them — through royal commissions, special commissions of inquiry, or investigating committees staffed by civil servants. Facts ferreted out from the professional organizations by such commissions inform policy makers. The second stage comes with the creation of advisory boards consisting of representatives from various interests who participate, even in an advisory capacity, in policy making. The difference between information-gathering groups and advisory boards is that the latter are granted a representative role: they can speak "authoritatively." The very practice of soliciting facts and figures from professional organizations and seeking their advice strengthens them. It elevates them to a position of expertise, and qualifies them as government consultants. Inasmuch as interest organizations develop their own staffs and experts, often recruiting them from universities and top managerial personnel, their claim of expertise injects an element of objectivity and pragmatism in the dialogue between professional organizations and state agencies. The third stage amounts to the granting of deliberative and policy-making functions to representatives of various interests. This is the stage of corporatism, which is prevalent in various degrees in all contemporary democracies. Charles S. Maier defines it as "a partial devolution of public policy-making and enforcement on organized private interests."[1] Most modern democracies have reached this stage today.

Corporatism

Corporatism is the joining of public agencies and private interest groups in the making and implementing of government policy. In its early institutionalization it brings various interests in key economic activities — oil, steel, coal, wheat, corn, banking, etc. — into a "corporation" that includes all those who participate in the same economic activity. The conflicting interests of the participants are reconciled, and, concomitantly, the various corporations are represented in a council or chamber where all economic, industrial, labor, and other interests are discussed and some policies are then made. The rationale behind corporatism is that class conflicts will be muted and through the presence and intervention of the state the collective and public interest will prevail.

1. Suzanne Berger (ed.), *Organizing Interests in Western Europe: Pluralism, Corporatism and the Transformation of Politics* (New York: Cambridge University Press, 1981), p. 49.

Corporatist institutions developed in Italy under the Fascists; in Vichy France — during the short period of that regime's life (1941–1944); in Portugal under the dictatorship of Salazar and his successor Marcello Caetano (1931–1973); and also in Spain, Austria, and elsewhere. As evident from the above-mentioned countries, corporatism was first developed in nondemocratic regimes. The state through a number of agencies — the executive, the legislature, the bureaucracy, or even the military — retained a controlling voice over the corporations, often overriding the interests that were represented. State corporatism was the rule and it put the accent on state controls.

Corporatism practices reemerged after World War II and are very much in evidence in democratic regimes. In democracies that have instituted economic planning, the major guidelines of the economic plan are drafted by assemblies or councils that represent interests; in regimes that have nationalized both industries and other sectors of the economy, the directors are advised by councils elected by the major interest organizations involved; in democracies where there are no nationalizations and economic planning, many decisions affecting the economy are made through direct cooperation between government agencies and the interests involved, often bypassing the parties and even the legislature. Sam Beer has called such practices "collectivist"[2] and they are very much in evidence in England, Italy, Austria, Belgium, France, and to a degree in the United States. In the Scandinavian countries many major social and economic policies are fashioned through negotiations between the representatives of interests and the governmental agencies. We may then speak of the emergence of "democratic" or "societal" corporatism as opposed to "state" or "authoritarian" corporatism.[3]

Societal or Democratic Corporatism Democratic corporatism shares some similarities with democratic pluralism: (1) the development of professional organizations is spontaneous; (2) the dialogue among them and between them and the state is voluntary (they can continue it or break it off); and (3) in their relationship with the public authorities, even when special policy-making functions are given to them, interest associations preserve their autonomy. Societal corporatism has, like pluralism, many voluntaristic traits, but there are significant differences with democratic pluralism. In democratic corporatism interests are organized vertically and include all members of a given economic activity. Professional organizations are monopolistic; that is, common interests shared by individuals in the same profession can be defended or promoted only *within* the organization. As a result, professional organizations are closed —

2. Samuel H. Beer, *British Politics in the Collectivist Age* (New York: Random House, 1965), and *Britain against Itself: The Political Contradictions of Collectivism* (New York: W. W. Norton, 1982).
3. It corresponds to the distinction made by many French authors between *corporatisme d'etat* and *corporatisme d'associations*. See also Philippe C. Schmitter and Gerhard Lehmbruch (eds.), *Trends toward Corporatist Intermediation* (Beverly Hills, Calif.: Sage Publications, 1979).

individuals and organizations cannot leave them without jeopardizing their professional standing and not all interests are free to join. But above all, professional organizations develop institutionalized and legally binding links with the state agencies and consequently they become semipublic agencies, acting on behalf of the state. Their autonomy, even if asserted and reasserted, is always limited by the public role they play. Unlike the democratic or liberal pluralistic universe, the corporatist one imposes structure, hierarchy, and binding ties between the members and their organizations and between the interest organizations and the state.

The cases of democratic corporatism are plentiful and they do not appear only in labor-management relationships. In the United States the National Recovery Act of 1934 provided instances when industrial policies regarding employment and collective bargaining were made by private industry. In Italy, as Schonfield points out, the idea of a "balanced and responsible economic group with quasi-sovereign power administering itself" continues to hold wide currency.[4] Trade unions in Holland show restraint in dealing with the state in order to preserve jobs. In Sweden the interest groups are strongly organized and . . . "their habit of bargaining with the government [is] well established." In fact the process of government in Sweden is "an extended dialogue between experts drawn from a variety" of representative interest associations. The German national business and professional associations have been viewed "as the guardians of the long term interests of the nation's industries." Not so in France, however, where they have been identified by the left and during World War II by the Gaullists as hostile to the national interest and responsible for France's collapse in the 1930s. Yet on a number of occasions business interests have acted together with trade unions in determining wages, employment, and social policies, and they have reached collective agreements that became binding on both business and labor.

CORPORATISM IN ACTION: FRANCE AND AUSTRIA

The French Constitution of 1946 and again the present constitution of the Fifth Republic (1958) established a Social and Economic Council with consultative powers. It consists of 200 permanent members and some sixty specially designated members who represent salaried personnel, civil servant workers, white-collar workers, and the cadres. There are rep-

4. They are discussed in Andrew Schonfield, *Modern Capitalism: The Changing Balance of Public and Private Powers* (New York: Oxford University Press, 1965); see also Berger, op. cit.

resentatives for many interests: industrial, commercial, and artisanal (41); agriculture (40); cultural, scientific, and professorial; (15); social groups (family associations, health, housing, etc. (15); and others. At least two-thirds of the members are elected directly by the professional organizations and the other third are designated by the government.

The Council meets four times a year. It deliberates and gives advice to the government on whatever professional and interest issue it desires. The government in turn may ask for its advice but it also has to ask for its opinion on virtually all economic and social policy issues, except the preparation of the budget. Although the opinions of the Council are not binding they carry considerable weight, and on a number of occasions the government modified its policy either because it anticipated adverse Council reaction or because the Council in effect declared itself against the proposed legislation. At the same time, through a number of Commissions of Study, the Council has managed to initiate economic, social, and professional policies for the consideration of the government. Council members directly advise the government but can also appear before the National Assembly to present their own views. The scope of the Council is very broad indeed, but its powers remain limited. It gives advice, but its main purpose is to improve the collaboration of the different professional categories.

Corporatism in Austria is different from the French version.[5] Corporate practices give a representative role to professional organizations and endow them with a great deal of autonomy vis-à-vis the state. They have the monopoly of representation, tend to be as inclusive as possible, and their representatives are recognized as authoritative spokesmen for the interests involved. They also develop binding and well-structured relations with the public agencies. The state delegates some policy making and enforcement power to these professional organizations. As with the French Social and Economic Council, professional representation and participation in Austria is based on the need for collaboration among professional social groups. The emphasis is on "concerted" action — the French term is *concertation;* the German is *Konzertierte.* The Austrians have given it a better name: "social partnership."

The interest groups are organized into chambers and membership is mandatory. Business, agriculture, and labor, in

5. The Austrian case is discussed by Gerhard Lehmbruch in Schmitter and Lehmbruch, op. cit., pp. 158–160.

effect the Trade Union Confederation, are organized in this manner. Relationships are institutionalized through commissions that include representatives of the chambers, particularly those speaking for labor and business. Through bargaining, these commissions reach agreement and formulate policies on wages and prices. Two members of the government sit in the deliberations of the commission but have no vote. The chambers participate and share decision making on a number of social and economic issues. They are represented in the directorship of the National Bank, which controls monetary policy; they initiate proposals regarding workers' participation in the management of industrial firms; and they administer key social services; insurance, pensions, housing, etc. Although Austria is illustrative of the kind of corporatism we have discussed, Sweden or Norway could have been used as well.

It is evident from our discussion in this section that interests and interest representation, including even corporatist practices, have gained acceptance in democratic regimes. Interests have reached a stage of genuine participation in policy making side by side with the legislature, the public agencies, and the political parties. In the process, interest representation has become institutionalized, something that gives it a greater weight and strength, but at the same time undermines its autonomy and freedoms. We have come close to a pattern of imperative coordination in which the interests and their claims are heard and considered before a policy is formulated but once the policy is made all the interests within a professional organization must comply. Although we are far from the characteristics of imposition and integration associated with authoritarian or state corporatism, we are also moving away from the spontaneity and freedom that characterized interest articulation in pluralistic democracies.

In the last analysis, corporatism in its broadest terms may be due simply to the long overdue realization that interests, like ideas and political parties, constitute an important factor in the organization of consent. They must be accepted and institutionalized, and there is nothing ignoble or necessarily divisive about them. They can speak out through qualified spokesmen and participate in the formulation and implementation of policy. In this sense the question raised by Philippe C. Schmitter about the twentieth century — "Still the Century of Corporatism?" — must be answered in the affirmative.[6]

6. See Philippe Schmitter's essay, "Still the Century of Corporatism?" in Schmitter and Lehmbruch, op. cit., pp. 7–52.

NATIONALIZATIONS: A NOTE

While neocorporatist practices bring together the private and public sectors in deliberations, consultation, and decision making, nationalizations divest private organizations, and the interests associated with them, of their property and freedom of decision. The state assumes the direct ownership and operation of major industries, compensates the owners for their property, and manages them on behalf of the public. The modes of management may vary: it may be statist and bureaucratic whereby it is directed and controlled by state agencies or it may provide the management with autonomy. In some instances, management can make its own decisions on investment, growth, production, employment, and wage policies, and it can set itself up as a profit-making company. In other instances, however, management may have to operate in terms of the public policy considerations set forth by the government.

England and France (and Italy in part) are among the democracies with the most extensive nationalizations. In England the major effort was made in 1945–1951 under the first Labour government. The Bank of England, coal production, air transportation, electricity, gas, land transportation, and iron and steel were nationalized. In 1967 the British Steel Corporation took over all steel-producing firms, which accounted for a total production of about 27 million tons of steel, and nationalizations were extended to the North Sea oil, atomic energy, and the partial nationalization of Rolls Royce and Leyland automobile production.

In France there were two waves of nationalizations. The first occurred right after the liberation of France in the years between 1945 and 1948. It involved partial or comprehensive nationalization of coal, Renault (automobiles), aircraft production and air transportation, railroads, atomic energy, electricity, gas, insurance companies, and of course the Bank of France. The second wave came between 1981 and 1982 under the Socialist government elected in June 1981. Virtually all banks were nationalized and through the nationalization of eleven major industrial conglomerates the state became the biggest producer of aluminum, metals, steel, iron, coal, textiles, chemicals, pharmaceuticals, glass, construction materials, cement, air conditioners, electrical equipment, telecommunications, furniture, kitchen utensils, armaments, and computers. The total assets of the companies nationalized in 1981–1982 amounted to over 650 billion francs, about $130 billion at the rate of exchange that prevailed at that time. Approximately 1,250,000 additional employees were transferred into the nationalized sector. When added to the first nationalized sector, and if we include the post office, which handles mail, telephone, and telegraphs, at least 35 percent of the gainfully employed worked *directly* for state-owned and -operated industrial enterprises, businesses, and services. As for industrial production, the state owns and controls at least 40 percent of the total.

By contrast, in Sweden, except for the telephone and postal services, nationalizations are limited: a good part of civil aviation and the railroads, about half of gas, electricity, coal, and oil, only a small part of banking, and the greater part of steel are directly controlled and operated by public bodies. In the Federal Republic of Germany, Canada, and the United States private ownership and management still remain the dominant form of economic organization.

Organization of Rights

Introduction

Even if individuals are not kingmakers, they are the kingpins of democracy, at least in theory. They all "have a life to live" and they are entitled to live it according to both their whims and their innermost beliefs. According to democratic theory, if not always practice, power, secular or transcendental, stops at the individual's door. His or her conscience cannot be invaded; his or her volition and judgment cannot be forced.

At the very bright dawn of democracy in Athens, around 430 B.C., Pericles proclaimed that the individual has both a public and a private life and that the latter was to be respected and protected.[7] Christianity sharpened this claim — some things belonged to Caesar and others to God. The Reformation opened the gates to religious pluralism, which led to a clear distinction between churches and state. Under the impact of liberalism, especially in the nineteenth century, economic and personal freedoms were added to religious ones.

To the rights against the state and equality of all before the law, new claims were added, which deepened and broadened the substance of individual rights. Since they included material services that were to be provided to all people by the community as well as by the government, the emphasis gradually shifted from equality before the law to equal conditions for all. Individual liberties, defined at first by eliminating some

7. From the Funeral Oration, as rendered by Thucydides in *The Peloponnesian War* ed. by Terry Wick (New York: Modern Library College Series/Random House, 1982). Pericles makes clear the distinction between private and public.

of the state's awesome powers, have been redefined often in terms of what obligations the state owes to its people and what services it must perform for them. In most democracies today, after long and bitter conflicts and sacrifices on the part of so many, the government and its agencies have become the major purveyors of the services without which individual rights cannot exist.

The Legacy of Individual Rights

Assertions of individual freedoms have been made from the very beginning of history. But the institutionalization of such freedoms in the form of procedures and structures that protect and guarantee them and punish violations is a relatively recent phenomenon. "We have also granted to all free men of our kingdom," proclaimed King John of England in 1215 in the Magna Charta, "all liberties written below: No scutage or aid [i.e., taxes] shall be laid in our kingdom except by the common counsel of our Kingdom; no free man shall be taken or imprisoned or . . . outlawed or exiled or in any way destroyed . . . except by the legal judgement of his peers or by the law of the land; . . . to no one we shall deny or postpone right or justice." Almost four centuries later, in 1628, when it was clear that the liberties promised had not been respected, both "lords and commons" petitioned the king to reaffirm them. This was the Petition of Right condemning the king for imprisoning and sentencing individuals without due process of law and the consent of Parliament, for taxing indiscriminately, and for exiling citizens. It petitioned the king "that no man . . . be compelled to make or yield any gift, loan, benevolence, tax . . . without common consent by Act of Parliament." Finally in 1689 the Parliament affirmed in the Bill of Rights

> 1. That the pretended power of Suspending laws, or the execution of laws, by Regal authority, without consent of Parliament, is illegal.
> 2. That the pretended power of Dispensing with laws, or the execution of laws, by Regal authority, as it hath been assumed and exercised of late, is illegal . . .[8]

It was a century later that these affirmations found a mighty echo across the Atlantic with the Declaration of Independence and the Constitution. The American colonies made the same complaints against the king: imposing taxes without the consent of the people through their representatives; depriving persons of trial by jury; abolishing some of "our most valuable laws"; and "suspending our Legislature." The signers stated that all people are endowed with certain inalienable rights — life, liberty, and the pursuit of happiness — and that it is the government's

8. For the major English constitutional documents see R. K. Gooch, *Source Book on the Government of England* (New York: Van Nostrand, 1939).

obligation to ensure that these rights are preserved. The signers also asserted that the powers invested in the government could be given only through the consent of the governed.

The cause for individual rights and freedoms grew all over Europe after the French Revolution (1789). The Declaration of the Rights of Man and the Citizen issued in 1789 proclaimed, like the Declaration of Independence, the inalienable rights of individuals in the most unequivocal and universal terms.

> . . . Men are born and remain free and equal in rights.
> . . . Liberty consists in the freedom to do everything which injures no one else.
> . . . All persons are held innocent until they shall have been declared guilty.
> . . . No one shall be disquieted on account of his opinions, including his religious views, provided their manifestation does not disturb the public order established by law.
> . . . Every citizen may, accordingly, speak, write, and print with freedom, but shall be responsible for such abuses of this freedom as shall be defined by law.

Almost two centuries later during the Nazi occupation of France, the Resistance movement again proclaimed the individual rights that should be guaranteed after the liberation of the country. But the French Charter of the Resistance (March 16, 1944) went for the first time beyond the assertion of individual and civil rights. A set of social and economic rights were enumerated:

> . . . The setting up of a true economic and social democracy . . .
> . . . The rational organization of an economy which will assure the subordination of private interests to the general interests,
> . . . [The] return to the nation of the great monopolies in the means of production, the sources of energy, mineral wealth, insurance companies and the large banks;
> . . . The right to work and leisure . . .
> . . . A complete plan of social security, designed to ensure for all citizens the means of subsistence. . . .

Both the constitutions of the Fourth and the Fifth Republics also endorsed the economic and social rights that were asserted in the Charter of the Resistance.

> Women are guaranteed in all respects equal rights with men.
> The right to work and employment . . .
> . . . Every individual and family must be assured of the necessary conditions for their development. The development of a free of charge lay educational system . . .

> The right of all workers to participate through their trade-union representatives to collectively determine the conditions of their work and the administration of the firms.[9]

Following the liberation of most of Europe from the Nazi occupation, the same reaffirmation of individual freedoms was made throughout the whole of Europe. Spain and Portugal followed in the 1970s, and the Third World democratic constitutions likewise reaffirmed individual freedoms.

The most comprehensive formulation was prepared and proclaimed by the United Nations in the United Nations Declaration of Human Rights (1948):

> . . . All human beings are born free and equal in dignity and rights . . .
> No one shall be subjected to arbitrary arrest, detention or exile.
> Everyone charged with a penal offence has the right to be presumed innocent until proved guilty.
> No one shall be subjected to torture or to cruel, inhuman or degrading treatment or punishment.
> Everyone has the right to leave any country, including his own, and to return to his country.
> No one shall be arbitrarily deprived of his property.
> Everyone has the right to freedom of thought, conscience and religion . . .
> Everyone has the right to freedom of peaceful assembly and association.
> Everyone has the right to take part in the government of his country, directly or through freely chosen representatives.
> Everyone, as a member of society, has the right to social security . . .
> Everyone has the right to work . . .
> Everyone has the right to a standard of living adequate for the health and well-being of himself and of his family . . .
> Motherhood and childhood are entitled to special care and assistance . . .
> Everyone has the right to education . . .[10]

From Individual to Human Rights

The major landmarks in the development of rights are merely the sign-posts of constant political struggle in an ever-widening arena. From the

9. Major French source materials may be found in Maurice Duverger, *Constitutions et Documents Politiques* (Paris: Presses Universitaires de France, 1981).
10. The United Nations Declaration on Human Rights (1948) in B. H. Weston, R. A. Falk, and A. d'Amato, *Basic Documents on International Law and World Order* (St. Paul, Minn.: West Publishing Co., 1980), pp. 161–164.

Petition of Right to the Declaration of Rights of Man and the Citizen to the Universal Declaration of Human Rights, the substance of rights has been deepened and broadened, but only because of political organization, struggle, and often outright violence and confrontation that cost lives.

The right to vote in most democracies has been extended to all who have reached the age of eighteen. Every effort is being made to see to it that the principle "one person one vote" is adhered to; registration for voting has been added to the right to vote with all the attendant protections and safeguards. Similarly, in many democracies individual rights have been strengthened against unwarranted arrests or detention, presumption of innocence until proven guilty, protection against unlawful searches and seizures, and the right of defendants to be assisted by counsel if they cannot afford one. The right of asylum for individuals feeling political persecution is also recognized, which is a sad reminder that many political regimes do not allow for free expression of ideas and do not tolerate dissent. In substance, however, the transition from individual to human rights is due to the incorporation of new economic and social rights into the old individual and civil rights.

The Welfare State

The major instrument for ensuring social and economic rights is the welfare state — the complex of public services and payments that correspond to "entitlements." The very magnitude of entitlements is staggering. In the late 1970s, total government payments to individuals in various forms amounted to from 18.7 percent of the gross national product in the United States to as much as 53.5 percent in France. The corresponding figures were about 20 percent in Austria, 31 percent in Britain, 51 percent in Denmark, 34 percent in Sweden, 31 percent in Norway, and 31 percent in West Germany. In the United States about half of the total for medical expenses came from public funds. In Germany and Holland it was about 70 percent while in Sweden, France, and Britain it amounted to over 90 percent.

To provide for social services and maintain incomes above the poverty level, the state simply extracts, through taxation, a growing percentage of the gross national product (goods and services produced) and redistributes a sizable portion of it in the form of services and cash payments. In most advanced democracies, as much as one-third of the total gross national product is taken from those who produce it and redistribute it to meet group or individual needs.

Major Social Services[11] In all contemporary democracies the growth of social and economic rights calls for a series of choices, and this is what

11. My discussion on social and economic rights and social legislation draws a good deal from Arnold Heidenheimer, Hugh Heclo, and Carolyn Adams, *Comparative Public Policy*, 2d ed. (New York: St. Martin's Press, 1983).

public policy is all about. Which services should be provided for everybody? What groups merit special attention? What are the limits below which poverty exists and should be prevented? The list is long, but by and large most democratic regimes have followed a similar route in establishing similar priority choices. Children and education came first with minimal educational services, but with ever-expanding requirements for schooling, a free college education was added in some countries, the United States being the first to do so.

The aged came next, with emphasis on pensions. In many countries the age limit for retirement is set at sixty for women and sixty-two for men.

The third step came with legislation requiring the state to provide for employment or to cover the unemployed through special benefits (unemployment insurance). It is presently financed through compulsory contributions and public funds, and public subsidies have steadily grown. In Europe after World War II, a comprehensive scheme was developed, which provided for uniform payments and minimum income levels. In the United States, since the Social Security Act of 1935, an ever-expanding number of employees have been included, contributions have been raised steadily, and benefits have increased. In 1983, however, this trend was reversed.

Health care was the fourth step. Originally undertaken by private and religious organizations, it has been increasingly assumed by the state agencies either through insurance programs or through direct payments and services. Germany was the first country to develop a nationwide health program even before the turn of the century. England followed after the turn of the century, and in 1948 it introduced a most comprehensive medical care program: it nationalized all health services and hospitals and incorporated almost all the doctors into the National Health Service. Health care became free, a matter of right. In Sweden a health insurance plan is mandatory and every citizen receives health care free of charge. In France medical expenses are covered through a system that combines insurance paid for by individuals with direct payments by the employer and the state. In the United States it is only after age sixty-five that citizens become directly covered through the medicare and medicaid programs.

Although education, health, retirement, and unemployment coverage do provide some safeguards against unaffordable costs, the so-called safety net is full of holes. Despite this supplementary income, there are millions who find themselves without adequate income — they are the poor.

It is to plug these holes and support the poor that the income maintenance and public assistance programs have been developed. They are aimed at raising minimal income levels to tolerable ones. Minimum wages become a matter of public policy and most democratic regimes have set a minimum floor below which wages cannot fall. But with a family to support, a minimum wage is often inadequate.

Various income maintenance programs are used to raise the family income. Tax exemptions, special benefits in the form of cash payments, rent allowances, food subsidies, special allowances for children, day care centers for working mothers, school luncheons, maternity benefits, and all sorts of other free services are calculated to do so. What the floor income for a family of four is depends on a number of factors and naturally shows a great variation from one country to another.

Public assistance programs and related special treatment and payments are afforded to special categories of the public. Although these programs also vary from one country to another, they are almost always available, at least for a given time. However, their purpose is to provide a family with a minimum income, not to equalize income, even if they lessen the distance between the rich and the poor. The attainment of material equality for all, if ever possible, is full of difficulties and obstacles, and it is not the purpose of the welfare legislation to equalize income. Security and often a small cushion of adequacy are all that can be expected.

Institutions: Similarities and Variations The development of social services, income maintenance policies, and public assistance programs produced one major institutional change in all modern democracies: the rapid growth of the public sector. The number of state employees and civil servants who are responsible for the development of social services and for overseeing their implementation has grown. As a result, there has been a growing need for specialized knowledge and skills to deal with these social services, for instance, health care.

Another result of this growth has been the requirement of administrative discretion, especially with public assistance programs. The civil servants who implement the laws and provide for the stipulated services have a fairly wide latitude in deciding whether or not a particular individual meets the criteria needed. They interpret the law, and in doing so they must exercise prudent judgment. In case of disagreement, special tribunals, administrative ones, review the decision. As a consequence, we have seen the development of a new branch of law designed to deal with litigations concerning the provision of health services, unemployment benefits, public assistance programs, and the like.

Discretion leads to a degree of semiindependence. The civil servants who handle welfare programs acquire a certain degree of autonomy either through the public agency they work for or through legislation. In most cases they are new types of civil servants, adept in handling human services, but also impersonal in the way they administer social services. The large welfare programs have become increasingly bureaucratized, and the beneficiaries have become computerized into unit numbers. Inflexibilities are unavoidable and so are breakdowns in the performance of the services. To the recipients, entitlements seem more like an administrative dispensation rather than the fulfillment of a right. The whole welfare edifice appears huge and impersonal, and the beneficiaries have no say or control over it. The paradox is that the more welfare the state and its agencies provide, the more the intrusion of civil servants is resented!

Welfare Patterns It is difficult to generalize about welfare institutions. There is a *statist* pattern, a *corporatist pattern,* and a *pluralistic* pattern. A fourth may be emerging which, for lack of a better term, we may call a *self-managing* pattern. In no political regime is there one single pattern to the exclusion of all others; there is always a mix.

France, until recently, was the best illustration of a *statist* pattern, where a well-organized bureaucracy and a centralized power gave dominant control to the state in the provision of services. Constant conflicts between government, interest groups, and organizations, including the TUs, were resolved in the form of concessions by the state, which led to reforms. Advisory councils were developed and participation of various groups in policy making was sought, but in the last analysis welfare measures are administered by public agencies, particularly in the areas of income maintenance, unemployment benefits, retraining measures, wage supports, and allowances for families with more than two children. Special councils, set up in various service organizations and in the Social Security Administration, cover both health care and unemployment benefits, but major policies continue to be made by the state agencies.

In contrast, Sweden shows a predominance of *corporatist* patterns: policy is made by well-established representative interests, professional organizations, and the bureaucracy. There are lengthy consultations until a policy is agreed on. The actual administration of the services is often in the hands of the organizations that participate in the making of policy. Similarly, in Germany the health program is jointly managed by doctors, hospitals, and representative organizations that are involved with medical care. Important aspects of wage policies and income maintenance are decided through joint deliberations between trade unions and managerial groups. In other words, in both West Germany and Sweden, there is a considerable degree of participation by interested parties and prospective recipients in the making of policy and its implementation.

Then there is a *pluralistic* pattern where no well-structured consultative processes exist for the elaboration of policies (as in the United States). Instead, there is an interaction of groups, pressures, and counterpressures, within and on the decision-making organs: the legislature, the executive, and more particularly the civil service. In the United States pluralism is compounded because in a federal system there is a constant interplay, as well as friction, between the national, state, and local governments.

Finally, there is a *self-managing* pattern that may be emerging. Decisions about a program and its administration are put in the hands of distinct and autonomous units comprised of those who both administer services and benefit from the services. Funds and services are disbursed to representative associations of the beneficiaries. As with the corporatist pattern, self-management brings the most interested and most directly affected groups into policy making and program administration; it helps counter the remoteness and impersonality of social legislation. The programs set up to provide education, health care, unemployment benefits, maternity benefits, old age pensions, etc., are approved by the recipients, at least in the sense that they have a say in what policies are made and how they are implemented. It is a pattern that is gaining momentum, either through the development of corporatist and consultative practices or through measures of decentralization that give local and functional bodies greater freedom to make decisions, spend money, and organize their services for their own particular needs.

Virtually all democracies show the same trends with regard to interests and human rights. The interest universe, especially economic freedoms and the market economy, have come increasingly, in one form or another, under state control and intervention. Whether through nationalizations or corporatist practices, economic interests have assumed a more public character — the interests speak for the public, but the public asserts its voice, goals, and policies through the state and its agencies. There has been a growing symbiosis between the interest universe and the public sector to the extent that in each and every case private considerations must be rationalized in terms of overriding public themes. Democracies have moved away from the early propositions of liberalism and economic individualism to impose social and public imperatives. Liberal democracies have been transformed almost everywhere into social democracies. The material and economic requirements that now define the notion of individual rights has strengthened this trend everywhere. The welfare state, the supports given to individuals by the state through a number of services (including even direct cash outlays), accentuate the social dimensions of public policy and delineate the new functions and role of the democratic state. To the early battle cry of individual rights against the awesome powers of the state, a new vision, and sometimes a new reality, are emerging that point to the needs of social solidarity and interdependence within the state.

Individual rights — civil, political, and economic — constitute the tripod on which human rights rest. They reinforce one another in providing freedoms and satisfying material wants, giving all of us the means to fulfill ourselves. Democracies and democratic regimes should be measured in terms of the implementation of these rights.

Bibliography

Berger, Suzanne (ed.). *Organizing Interests in Western Europe: Pluralism, Corporatism and the Transformation of Politics.* New York: Cambridge University Press, 1981.

Ehrmann, Henry W. *Interest Groups on the Four Continents.* Pittsburgh, Pa.: Pittsburgh University Press, 1965.

Groth, Alexander, and Wade L. Larry (eds.). *Comparative Resource Allocation: Politics, Performance and Policy Priorities.* Beverly Hills, Calif.: Sage Yearbooks, vol. 13, 1984.

Hayward, E. S., and B. P. Berki (eds.). *Society in Contemporary Europe.* New York: St. Martin's Press, 1979.

Miliband, Ralph. *The State and Capitalist Society: An Analysis of Western Systems and Power.* New York: Basic Books, 1969.

Schmitter, Philippe C., and Gerhard Lehmbruch (eds.). *Trends toward Corporatist Intermediation.* Beverly Hills, Calif.: Sage Publications, 1979.

Schonfield, Andrew. *Modern Capitalism: The Changing Balance of Public and Private Power.* New York: Oxford University Press, 1965.

Wilensky, Harold. *The Welfare State and Equality.* Berkeley and Los Angeles: University of California Press, 1974.

Part Two *Authoritarian and Totalitarian Regimes*

What pleases the Prince has the force of law
ROMAN LEGAL MAXIM First Century A.D.

. . . We control matter because we control the mind. Reality is inside the skull. . . . There is nothing we cannot do . . . about the laws of Nature. We make the laws of Nature. . . .
ORWELL 1984

Introduction Authoritarian and totalitarian governments comprise the majority of the political regimes of our world today (see Appendix A), and while it is relatively easy to distinguish them from democracies it is not always easy to separate them from each other. There are so many similarities between the two that some observers say they represent nothing more than ever-changing variations of the same basic political theme, the same political genus. In both authoritarian and totalitarian regimes, political power is concentrated and the command structure is not subject to the limitations and rules of responsibility that we find in democratic regimes; in both the leadership manipulates and controls consent; in both scant attention and recognition are paid to individual rights — the individual is at the mercy of the wielders of power; both use various methods to subordinate and control interests and interest associations; both utilize the police and other special instrumentalities to ensure the submissiveness of the public; both control the various media of communication; in both, only too frequently, one leader gains ascendancy and is accorded a degree of obedience and adulation reminiscent of the powerful despots of the past.

What is equally striking are the similarities in the internal changes that these regimes undergo. The leadership may shift and change goals: it may be revolutionary and utopian only to change to a defense of the status quo; it may sometimes appeal to the people to mobilize them into political action so that it can gain their support while at other times it may demand only their submissiveness; a frenzy of political activity may alternate with apathy and even indifference. There may also be similar shifts in ideology: sometimes revolutionary and at other times pragmatic, sometimes traditionalist and other times modernizing.

Along with the similarities, however, there are some significant differences that justify a distinction between authoritarian and totalitarian regimes.

Intellectual Origins The models of authoritarian and totalitarian regimes are quite distinct. Those familiar with Hobbes' *Leviathan* and Rousseau's *Social Contract* can trace authoritarianism to the first and totalitarianism to the second. Hobbes argued for the absolute authority of the state over the people in order to guarantee them security in their persons and their property and allow them to pursue their interests in peace. On the other hand, Rousseau argued for direct governance by the people with popular participation and mobilization and proclaimed that the people in their collective capacity were infallible and absolute. The claim for order and security under the state provides the autocratic origins of authoritarianism, while the claim for popular sovereignity and the infallibility of the people provides us with the democratic origins of totalitarianism.

Vocabulary The Rousseauian or democratic origins of totalitarianism and the Hobbesian or autocratic origins of authoritarianism account to a degree for the different vocabulary used. Totalitarianism employs the vocabulary and the terms of democracies: the "sovereignty of the people," the "representation of the people," "individual rights," "representative assemblies," and "responsibility and accountability to the people." It also establishes many of the democratic institutions such as elections, referendums, and parliamentary government, and the political party becomes the vehicle of governance. In form, totalitarian regimes appear democratic. In substance, however, they are at best governance by a well-organized minority — a political party — that knows no limitations of power, bears no accountability, and has no particular regard for democratic forms and individual rights.

Authoritarian regimes, on the other hand, often assert their autocratic traits by dispensing with the democratic vocabulary altogether. The authority of the state and obedience to the state are proclaimed positive values in themselves. In authoritarian regimes there is no political party and if there is one, it is weak and subservient to the state.

Major Differences The major differences between authoritarianism and totalitarianism concern the relationship between the political leadership (the state or the party) and the society with regard to:

1. The extent and degree that the societal forces are penetrated and shaped by the political leadership
2. The degree and extent of mobilization of the people by the political leadership

3. The manner and the degree that the two regimes manage to organize consent
4. The extent and the degree that they manage to institutionalize themselves, to establish stable instrumentalities of governance

Penetration In totalitarian regimes the leadership develops new institutions in order to bring the societal forces under their control. They do so by permeating interests and associations, often destroying some, creating new ones, or reshaping older ones. Among the most important of them are the economy, the family, the churches, the universities and schools, and the various cultural associations. Although authoritarian regimes also impose controls and restrictions, they hardly attempt to reshape and restructure society and the individual actors. Interests and associations often maintain their autonomy and separateness, notably in religion and the economy, even if they remain subordinate. While the aim of totalitarian regimes is the total penetration of society, authoritarian regimes are satisfied with control rather than penetration. As a result, as Juan Linz argues, they allow for "limited pluralism."[1]

The Role of Ideology In totalitarian regimes the penetration of the societal forces is invariably pursued in the name of a new ideology. Totalitarian governments tend to be highly ideological in the goals they posit — the goals are often utopian and transcendental and radically different from the values and goals of the society they seek to control and modify. The official ideology is a highly mobilizing one: it calls for both action and sacrifice, and it is formulated exclusively by the political leadership.

In contrast, authoritarian regimes do not develop the same all-encompassing official ideology. Some of them simply rely on pragmatic considerations: to revive the economy, to do away with foreign competition, to avert civil war, or to maintain law and order. They ask for acquiescence rather than individual devotion and adherence; they do not try to turn the citizen into a believer. Obedience is defined in terms of the absence of any overt resistance to the state. Otherwise citizens can operate within their established associations, groups, or other societal institutions including the churches. They can develop their own loyalties as long as they do not undermine obedience to those who command. But again this may be a matter of degree. Totalitarian regimes may at times find it expedient to give leeway to some societal forces and institutions (the economy, the army, or the church, for instance) or a different ideology (nationalism, for instance) side by side with the official one. The latter was clearly the case with Stalin and the Soviet Union during the "Great Patriotic War" against Germany (1941–1945).

1. In *Handbook of Political Science*, vol. 3., Fred I. Greenstein and Nelson W. Pulsby (eds.), "Totalitarian and Authoritarian Regimes," (Reading, Mass.: Addison-Wesley), pp. 175–411.

Mobilization Mobilization is induced and intensive participation. It brings as many citizens as possible into the regime and creates supports for the leader and others in the command structure. Since it is so extensive it begins with the schools and is continued through a number of associations and organizations set up by the political leaders. The par excellence mobilizing agency is the political party. It consists of the elite, and it is an avant-garde that speaks for the masses. It provides the cues for thought and action and authoritatively interprets the official ideology. It organizes debates, meetings, discussion groups, and even demonstrations. Its members literally branch out and permeate every social activity in an effort to see to it that all act in conformity to the posited goals and policies. No citizen is left out and all are given a chance to speak, but under carefully controlled conditions. In this manner the party appears to be a powerful link between the regime and the people, giving to the latter a sense and sometimes the reality of participation.

In authoritarian regimes, however, we do not find this same emphasis on mobilization. It is not sought by dictators, autocrats, tyrants, military juntas, or bureaucrats. The emphasis is on the authority of the state, which implies and invites obedience, not participation. There was little mobilization under the Franco regime in Spain from 1936–1975, the military-bureaucratic authoritarian regimes in Latin America, or in Portugal from 1931–1968. They did not seek popular involvement; they avoided it. This is equally true with regard to the role of the party. Most authoritarian regimes do not develop a single party in order to indoctrinate and mobilize. Even in many Third World authoritarian regimes where national liberation fronts or parties played an important role in striving for national independence, the importance of the party gradually weakened after independence was attained. It is no longer a mobilizing agency.

Consensus Through the use of ideology and the party a totalitarian regime strives to organize consent and to develop a broad consensus — another characteristic of democracies. It attempts to build supports and establish positive communication networks with the people at large. Every citizen becomes (or it is hoped will become) a "soldier of freedom," a "producer," an "activist," "vigilant" in maintaining legality, "honest and virtuous," sensitive to "treason," which always stalks at night, and so forth. Citizens are made to feel and believe that their regime is the best and that it shelters them against the uncertainties of a threatening world. Totalitarian regimes try to dig deep into the societal soil, to plant roots (supports) that range from acceptance to enthusiasm, and the roots may indeed become solid.

Authoritarian regimes by their very nature do not strive for consensus. They are satisfied with acquiescence, even apathy. They equate stable government with obedience, with the absence of overt opposition. While totalitarian regimes want the individual citizen to internalize the

SCORECARD FOR AUTHORITARIAN/TOTALITARIAN REGIMES

	Authoritarian Weak ← 0	1	2	3	4	5	6	7	8	9	Totalitarian → Strong 10
Penetration of Society											
Mobilization											
Official Ideology											
Single Party											
Consensus Building											
Legitimization											
Institutionalization											

Regimes that score from 0 to 5 tend to be authoritarian, those that score from 5 to 10 tend to be totalitarian.

values they promote, authoritarian regimes simply do not want the citizenry to externalize thoughts that run counter to the political status quo.

Institutionalization Totalitarian regimes not only attempt to legitimize themselves but often succeed. The reason for this is primarily the participatory mechanisms they use and the official ideology they impart and finally manage to inculcate.

While authoritarian regimes also strive to institutionalize the political organizations they develop, the lack of an official ideology and the fact that the political party is either weak or nonexistent make the task far more difficult. Another difficulty is that the particular organizations they rely on — the bureaucracy and the military — are not political organizations properly speaking. They do not link the command structure with the citizenry. Only the charisma of a leader may provide supports for a period of time, but these are likely to wane when the leader disappears.

Differences in institutionalization also relate to levels of modernization. Carl J. Friedrich, for instance, considers modern technology as one of the conditions for the development of a totalitarian regime with a "mass party" and a "totalist ideology." Technology enhances the capabilities of political organizations, especially the party, to communicate with and socialize the citizenry. In a modern industrialized society, for instance, it is easier for the command structure to establish control by penetrating large economic units where decision making is concentrated in a few hands.

In contrast, authoritarian regimes reflect a stage of backwardness in the society and the economy. Since communications, industrial organization, and concentrated decision making lag, the leadership is unable to communicate with and organize the masses. This is the case with many of the Latin American authoritarian regimes and the various military juntas that have plagued Africa, the Middle East, and some other areas of the world including, occasionally, the Mediterranean littoral.

In this second part we will survey the various totalitarian and authoritarian regimes. In Chapter 6 we give an overview of the Communist regime in the Soviet Union, and in Chapter 7 a retrospective account of right wing totalitarianism, Nazism, and Fascism. In Chapter 8 we discuss current trends and manifestations of crisis in some communist regimes in Poland, Yugoslavia, and China and raise some questions about the prospects of a leadership crisis in Cuba. In Chapter 9 we survey major authoritarian regime patterns, including military dictatorships. In Chapter 10 we try to identify the dynamics of change and transformation that authoritarian regimes undergo.

Bibliography

Arendt, Hannah. *The Origins of Totalitarianism.* New York: Harcourt Brace Jovanovich, 1973.

Friedrich, C. J., and Zbigniew Brzezinski. *Totalitarian Dictatorship and Autocracy,* 2d ed. New York: Praeger, 1966.

Friedrich, C. J. (ed.). *Totalitarianism.* Cambridge, Mass.: Harvard University Press, 1964.

Friedrich, C. J., M. Curtis, and Benjamin Barber. *Totalitarianism in Perspective: Three Views.* New York: Praeger, 1969.

Howe, Irving (ed.). *1984 Revisited: Totalitarianism in Our Century.* New York: Harper & Row, 1983.

Linz, Juan. "Totalitarianism and Authoritarianism," in *Handbook of Political Science,* vol. III. Reading, Mass.: Addison-Wesley, 1975.

Neumann, Sigmund. *The Permanent Revolution: The Total State in the World at War.* New York: Harper & Brothers, 1942.

Orwell, George. *1984.* New York: New American Library/Signet, 1961.

Perlmutter, Amos. *Modern Authoritarianism.* New Haven: Yale University Press, 1981.

Popper, Karl. *The Open Society and Its Enemies.* 5th ed. Princeton, N.J.: Princeton University Press, 1966.

Solzhenitsyn, Aleksandr I. *The Gulag Archipelago,* One, Pts. 1 & 2. Trans. by Thomas P. Whitney. New York: Harper & Row, 1974.

Talmon, Jacob L. *The Origins of Totalitarian Democracy.* New York: Praeger, 1966.

Tucker, Robert C. (ed.). *Stalinism: Essays in Interpretation*. New York: W. W. Norton, 1977.
Wolfe, Bertram. *Three Who Made a Revolution: A Biographical History*. Boston: Beacon Press, 1955.

6 Communist Totalitarian Regimes: The Soviet Union

The Communist Ideology: Marxism

The essence of totalitarianism lies in its ideology. It offers a set of overarching propositions about society and human nature in which the existing order of things is to be radically overhauled; it is geared to the refashioning of the economy, the society, family life, education, and culture. Since totalitarian ideologies promise to bring about a transformation of societal relationships, they are future-oriented, and it is for the sake of the future that the present and sometimes the past are manipulated. In the Soviet Union we find this powerful imperative in the Communist ideology of Marxism-Leninism.

A characteristic of all totalitarian regimes is the single-party system. Men and women are tightly organized in the name of the ideology, with the goal of disseminating it and imposing it. What was at first a revolutionary organization aimed against the existing order of things subsequently becomes the official single party: the pillar of the regime. The Communist Party plays this role in the Soviet Union.

Karl Marx introduced the basic ideology that would inevitably supersede capitalism and all the liberal political regimes that had developed in Western Europe. Lenin gave Marxism a particular twist in adapting it to the Russian society, which rebelled against the tsars and staged the Russian Revolution of 1917. Briefly, the tenets of Marxism-Leninism were the following:

1. The capitalist and liberal order was based on the exploitation of the workers, and other average citizens, by the capitalist class of the advanced industrial societies.
2. It was destined to be overcome by the proletariat. A class struggle between workers and capitalists would be inevitable and would ultimately lead to the victory of the proletariat and to socialism. The workers would gain consciousness of their predicament and would realize that the only solution to their problems would be a revolution against the capitalist order and state.
3. A short period of a dictatorship of the proletariat would follow in order to silence all opposition and pave the way for drastic socioeconomic reforms.
4. The economy would come under the control of the collectivity, and the means of production would be socialized.
5. A new society would develop in which the people would control all societal forces, do away with classes, profit, and private property and put production and the economy at the service of all.
6. A proletarian revolution would spread to other countries and create a truly international community.

Lenin's major contribution to this powerful ideological appeal was the organization of an elite party — the Communist party — consisting of dedicated people bound by tight discipline and convinced that their mission took precedence over everything else. The Communist party was to become the true midwife of the Russian Revolution. It would propagate the ideology and nurture the new society.

It is in the name of Marxism that the Communist party of the Soviet Union still operates. Its leadership still views its mission in apocalyptic terms: to liberate the world from capitalism and imperialism; it still considers control of the economy by the state to be necessary in order to fashion the new order of freedom and equality and justice for all; and it continues, as a small elite, to be the custodian of ideological orthodoxy and political power. Marxists view the Soviet Union as the citadel of socialism in a hostile capitalist world, and they believe that its preservation is the single most important condition for the ultimate triumph of socialism.

The political, social, and economic institutions of the Soviet Union have been built and are maintained with these absolute beliefs in mind. Despite many qualifications and "pauses," there is little room for flexibility and compromise in domestic or international politics.

The Constitutional Order

Totalitarian regimes establish the supremacy of the state or the single party. One or the other assumes complete control and power over all societal forces. Lenin's aphorism that "there cannot be two powers in a state" holds true. Political power is centralized and concentrated at the top. Since the powerholders (in the party or the state) do not have to face free and open elections, they are not held responsible or accountable for their actions. The constitution sets a "legal order" that organizes and sustains the rule of a political elite. It establishes the superior purpose of powerholders over individuals and groups and consolidates their position. Separation of powers, checks and balances, and individual rights yield to the concentration of political power.

There have been three constitutions in the Soviet Union since the revolution of 1917: in 1924, 1936, and 1977.[1] Like democratic constitutions, they have embodied the principles of governance, that is, the relationship between governors and the governed. They allocate powers, define procedures, establish limitations, and define individual rights. (Similar documents have been promulgated in other Eastern European countries that have communist regimes.)

The constitutional order of the third constitution — the so-called Brezhnev constitution adopted on October 7, 1977 — does not differ from the basic principles or the organization of political power in the Soviet regime that existed before. It is declared to be a political society where conflicts no longer exist and hence the "dictatorship of the proletariat" is no longer necessary. It is an "advanced socialist system" moving in the direction of communism; the "unity of the Soviet society" has been achieved and as a result, the Soviet state has become "a state of the whole people"; there is a uniform citizenship for all: Soviet citizenship; a "juridical and factual equality" among all citizens has been established; the citizens are required to safeguard the interests of the Soviet state and "enhance its powers and prestige"; the defense of the "socialist motherland is the sacred duty" of all and betrayal of the motherland is the "gravest of crimes against the people"; individual rights, including virtually all the human rights we mentioned in Chapter 5, are granted "in order to strengthen and develop the socialist system" or "in accordance with the aims of building communism."

The present constitution, however, also sets up the machinery of government: elections, representative assemblies, and executive branch, courts, and a federal structure. The basic principle is democratic centralism whereby all state organs are elected and held accountable to the people, but lower bodies must observe the decisions of the higher ones. In this manner the constitution attempts to reconcile central leadership with local initiative, although the central national organs can impose their decisions upon all others. At the same time the constitution establishes the rule of the single party: the Communist party of the Soviet Union (CPSU). It is "the leading and guiding force of Soviet society and the nucleus of its political system, of all state organizations and public organizations." The CPSU, *"armed with Marxism-Leninism,* determines the general perspectives of the development of the society and the course of

1. For the text of the constitutions, see Samuel H. Finer, *Five Constitutions,* op. cit.

domestic and foreign policy of the USSR, directs the great constructive work of the Soviet people, and imparts a planned, systematic and theoretically substantiated character to the struggle for the victory of communism" (Article 6).

Thus the Soviet constitutional order is based on (1) an official ideology, Marxism-Leninism; (2) the single party that is the directing force of the society; and (3) the subordination of all decision-making organs to the Soviet state and in turn its subordination to the CPSU. Everything yields to the superior power of the CPSU.

The Command Structure

What is characteristic of the organization of Soviet governance and what appears to be so baffling to the student is the ingenious mixture of democratic forms and vocabulary with authoritarian structures, which is typical of all totalitarian regimes. After reading the constitution of 1977 one gets the impression that the Soviet Union is a parliamentary regime. The constitution provides freedoms and rights that could be used to criticize the leadership, and even overthrow the members of the top government. Moreover, Article 6, which states that the CPSU is "the leading and guiding force and the nucleus of the political system," does not legally establish a single-party monopoly. The designation of candidates for election to the representative assemblies, both national and local, seems to give a fairly good range of freedom to whatever organizations want to nominate them.

It is the centralized structure of the CPSU, together with its mechanisms for control and decision making, that provides the authoritarian trait. The government appears to derive its powers from below, from the people, but the Communist party as an organization imposes its will and power from the top. The regime thus provides a democratic facade that hides the most advanced instrument of authoritarian political control: the leadership of the Communist party.

The Formal Structure

Technically, the representative assemblies, the Soviets, possess all power. They are found at the rural level, the city level, the various units of the federal structure (the republics, autonomous republics, regions, and provinces) and on up to the Supreme Soviet of the USSR. The Supreme Soviet consists of two chambers: the Council of Union, which is directly elected by the people, and the Soviet of Nationalities, which consists of representatives of each nationality and territorial subdivision of the Union of Soviet Republics (fifteen states) and a number of smaller national groups. All in all about 2 million elected officials represent the people from the lowest to the highest levels of the government. According to the constitution, the Soviets select their own executive organs, from the committees at the local levels to the Council of Ministers at the national level, and hold them accountable for their actions.

Legislation The Supreme Soviet makes the laws, and the constitution is quite explicit:

> The highest body of state authority of the USSR shall be the Supreme Soviet of the USSR . . . and the highest executive and administrative body of the USSR is . . . the Council of Ministers of the USSR. Laws of the USSR shall be enacted by the Supreme Soviet of the USSR . . . The Council of Ministers of the USSR shall be formed by the Supreme Soviet of the USSR [and will be] responsible and accountable to the Supreme Soviet of the USSR. (Articles 108 and 128)

There are, however, some serious qualifications both as to the representative role and to the powers of the Soviets. To begin with, and limiting ourselves only to the Supreme Soviet, it is a legislative body that meets only twice a year for not more than a week each time. It is a body with no genuine legislative functions. If we recall the major functions of legislatures in democratic regimes (p. 60), we will find that the Supreme Soviet scores very low on most of them: low on legitimization and deliberation, and virtually nil on lawmaking, communication, investigation, political control over the executive, airing of grievances, and debate. Laws are in fact made either by a small committee of the Supreme Soviet — the Praesidium, consisting of a chairman (who is the president of the USSR), a first vice-chairman, fifteen vice-chairmen (one from each Union Republic), and twenty-one other members — or by the Council of Ministers. Laws are often submitted to the Supreme Soviet for its endorsement long after they have been in force, and there has never yet been a case where the Supreme Soviet has disapproved legislation by these executive bodies. The various Soviets, especially the Supreme Soviet, and the corresponding executive bodies are controlled by the Communist party. All the members of the Council of Ministers are top members of the CPSU. It is therefore unthinkable that the members of the Supreme Soviet selected by the Communist party will turn against their own leaders in the executive.

What is conclusive, however, with regard both to the representativeness of the Soviets and to their ability to hold the executive bodies accountable, is the manner in which the deputies are elected. Elections are free and the ballot is secret but nominations to run are not! Through a well-orchestrated and carefully controlled process, designation of candidates in each of the electoral districts are made only by the Communist party. Various organizations, including the CPSU, may nominate their respective candidates. However, before the election, all but one have to withdraw, and the one that remains is the candidate approved by the CPSU. At the time of balloting there is only one candidate who, in line with electoral practices in democracies, debates issues, presents the program, answers questions, canvasses his electoral district, and asks for the voters' support. It is always overwhelming. The candidates endorsed by the CPSU (and at least 80 percent are also members of the CPSU) are elected with majorities that amount to more than 95 percent of the eligible voters. There is no opposition, and the election amounts to an enthusiastic endorsement. Its value is symbolic and ritualistic — to show not only the extent of unanimity but also the high rate of participation.

The CPSU makes a great effort to mobilize the voters and get them to the voting booth. Some people vote because they want to show their approval, others because they may be accused of absenteeism, some because they feel intimidated, others because election time is something like a national holiday, still others because there are benefits to be derived from their show of support. The whole process is organized by the CPSU to get the people's support and to consolidate its image and power. There is no competition and no choice, as in democratic elections. It is the CPSU that in fact chooses the representatives, not the electorate. Under these circumstances, the Soviets that are elected and the executive councils they choose are but the creatures of the CPSU. The formal trimmings of election and representativeness hide the hard core of single-party rule.

Federalism The USSR is federal in form. As we noted earlier, however, federalism is designed in many democracies to divide and hence to limit political power, but that only *appears* to be the case with the 1977 Soviet constitution. The Union Republics that comprise a "voluntary" union, the USSR, are sovereign. They have their own Soviets and their own Council of Ministers. They have the right to secede as well as some other powers that do not exist in any other federal or confederal system: the right to enter into relations with other states, conclude treaties with them, exchange diplomatic and consular representatives, and take part in the work of international organizations (Article 80).

Every effort has been made by Soviet writers to show the progressive and advanced form of Russian federalism. It gives self-government to various ethnic, cultural, and linguistic groups in the Soviet Union (there are at least thirty-five major ones). But federalism and self-government also require a clear division of powers between the federal government and the sovereign or autonomous units and the understanding that one power cannot invade the other. It also requires an arbiter, usually the courts, to resolve jurisdictional conflicts. These conditions do not exist in the Soviet Union.

In the Soviet constitution (Article 14) there is an exhaustive listing of the powers of the central government, which includes virtually all aspects of policy making. The powers of the Union Republics are in effect limited to what is not covered by Article 14. Federal organs, like the Supreme Soviet or the Council of Ministers, are given the freedom to interpret the law and the constitution and even to change the territorial boundaries of the various federated units. Further, since the lower organs are subordinate to the higher ones, all Union Republics and all other autonomous republics and provinces are subordinate to the Soviet national government. There can be no recourse to an independent judicial authority to interpret the jurisdictional relations between the national government and the independent but subordinate entities. Also, the majority of the officials, elected or not, are members of the CPSU and act in accord with the directives of the leadership. Finally, whatever the national and cultural aspirations of various nationalities in the Soviet Union, they must be "socialist in content." Soviet federalism, in other words, does not amount to a division of powers or to a genuine pluralism.

In sum, despite the emphasis on the Soviets, it is the executive (The Council of Ministers) that governs. It is a very large body consisting of about 100 ministers in charge of many technical services: health, electric energy, transportation, foreign affairs, housing, education, machine tools, fertilizers, etc. Governance is in the hands of a small committee — its own Praesidium. There is a concentration of decision making comparable only to that of the British Cabinet but without an opposition party and without open and competitive elections. Governmental power is not only centralized but it is unopposed. Yet in the Soviet regime this is not where the real power lies. It is the CPSU that in law and in fact holds unlimited power.

The Real Power: The CPSU

This single party controls all governmental organs and makes decisions about them. It consists of about 17 million members, or about 7 percent of the Soviet populations. It is organized functionally and territorially as a national organization. There are some 450,000 primary organizations, often referred to as "the cells," in neighborhoods, factories, schools, universities, the civil service, or the army. (Each cell averages about forty members, and for each primary organization there is a bureau.) A number of primary organizations form larger units in cities, urban and rural centers, autonomous regions, provinces, and even in the Union Republics. Each one has an executive body, either a committee or a Central Committee. All members of the CPSU elect delegates — about 5,000 in 1981 — to the National Congress, which is convened every five years ostensibly to deliberate party policy and to elect its national leaders. The Congress elects the top executive organ, the Central Committee, consisting in 1981 of 319 full or voting members and 151 candidate or nonvoting members. The Central Committee in turn elects the Political Bureau (Politburo), consisting of twelve to fifteen voting members and varying numbers of candidate members. The Politburo chooses the party Secretariat and the General Secretary, who is the leader of the CPSU. This is the democratic aspect of democratic centralism. It is like a pyramid. (See the chart on p. 139.)

But command, the substance of power, flows from the top down. This is the authoritarian aspect of democratic centralism. There has been

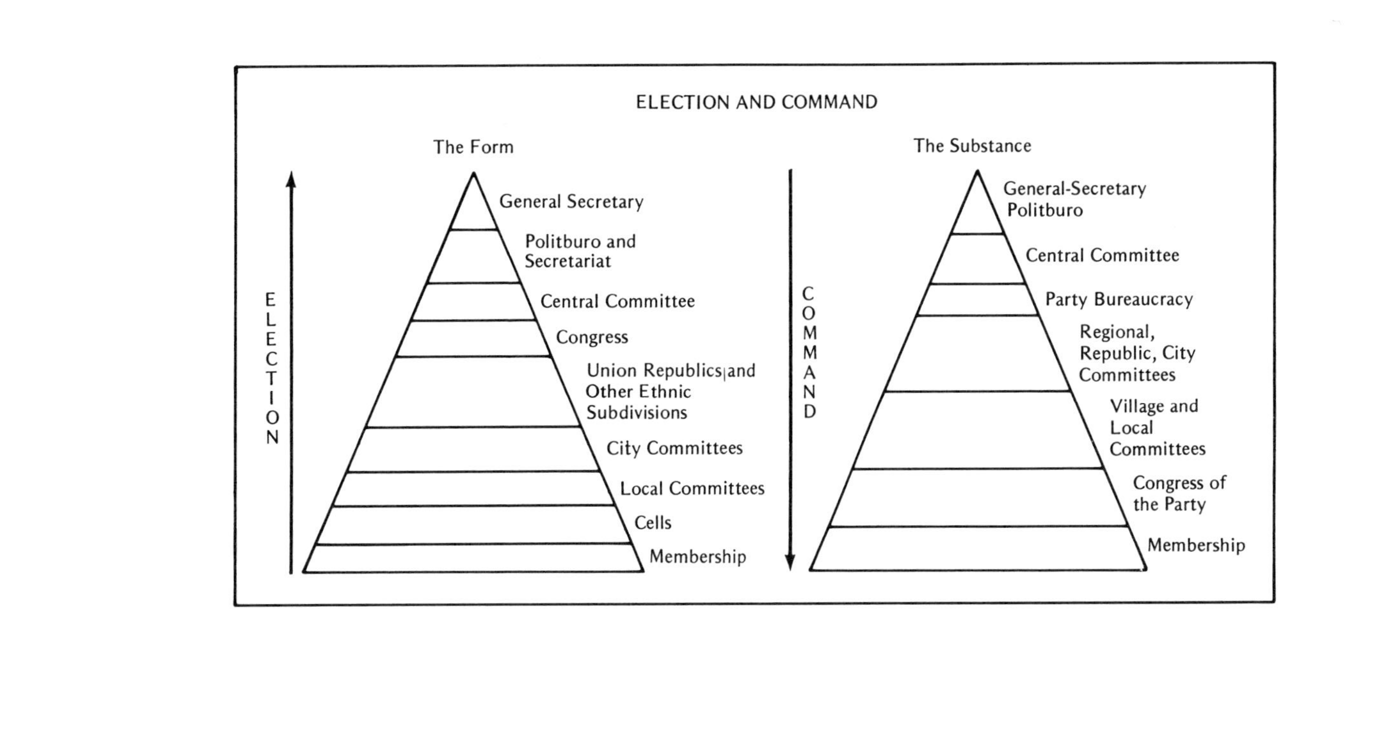
ELECTION AND COMMAND
The Form
ELECTION
General Secretary
Politburo and Secretariat
Central Committee
Congress
Union Republics and Other Ethnic Subdivisions
City Committees
Local Committees
Cells
Membership
The Substance
COMMAND
General-Secretary Politburo
Central Committee
Party Bureaucracy
Regional, Republic, City Committees
Village and Local Committees
Congress of the Party
Membership

no controversy or even debate in the party congresses, and no dissenting vote has been cast in a congress since 1930. Within the CPSU itself decision making and control became increasingly vested in the hands of the top leadership and ultimately the Politburo and the General Secretary. The choice of candidates to be elected to the various posts is made in advance by the top leadership. Party members may be purged and the leadership may order new drives for party members. The official line of the party, its program and goals, are changed at will by the top leadership, always enthusiastically approved by the Congress, and followed by the subordinate units. Thus the subordination of all lower organs to the higher ones — the cardinal principle of democratic centralism — is institutionalized.

But another development in the direction of centralized control has been used, especially from 1927 to 1953: Stalin employed the secret police to intimidate and repress party members, even at the higher echelons. For instance, a majority of the members of the Central Committee were purged, and eventually killed, between 1934 and 1939 during the Great Purge. Stalin had them replaced even though no party Congress was convened between 1939 and 1952. Through the police, Secretary General Josef Stalin managed to secure absolute compliance from all the bodies of the party and to develop absolute personal rule. He was the top of the command structure — indeed the only source of command!

Even though personal rule and the use of the police have been attenuated in favor of a growing emphasis on collective leadership and respect for legal procedures ever since Stalin's death in 1953, the principle of democratic centralism remains very much in evidence. Theoretically, discussions can take place within the party but no factions are allowed to develop. Decisions made by the higher organs bind the lower ones without allowing any room for dissent or criticism. The CPSU continues to control every organ of the government.

Methods of Control: Dual Membership, Overlap, *Nomenklatura*

The CPSU with 17 million members is structured along hierarchical lines. Party committees (for larger units they are called Central Committees) guide the work of the members. More than 4,500 such committees provide the network through which the Central Committee, the Politburo, and the Secretariat, with the General Secretary at the top, organize, structure, and guide the activities of the CPSU. There are about one million members in these committees of whom not more than 200,000 hold important executive party positions. It is they who form the *apparat* and they are known as the *apparatchiks* (party bureaucrats). The rest are in subordinate positions but aspire to future political rewards and promotions to higher positions within the *apparat*. The rank and file, the other 16 million members, work under the instructions of the party bureaucrats, also hoping to receive privileges and rewards in return for their work, loyalty, subservience, and support.

The *apparatchiks* are under the vigilant eye of the top echelons — the members of the Central Committee, the Politburo, and the Secretariat — whose eyes and ears and often brains is the Central Apparat.[2] This group comprises the top central party bureaucracy that looks inward, into the party organization, personnel, and activities, outward to the government officials, and even beyond into every aspect of economic and social life. The Central Apparat is divided into specialized departments: (1) party organization, (2) party personnel, (3) ideology, (4) industry and transport, (5) agriculture, (6) armed forces, (7) Komsomol and Trade Unions, (8) foreign communist parties, and (9) propaganda. Policy questions and options are discussed and formulated in these departments before they are submitted to the Politburo and the Secretariat. Legislation is drafted by experts in the Central Apparat. It reviews or decides directly on all personnel appointments and controls and supervises all decisions about recruitment, transfers, and dismissals in the bureaucracy, the party, and other government organs as well as in the major parapolitical organizations like trade unions. The Central Apparat is in charge of the organization and the personnel of the party, commonly referred to as the *Nomenklatura*. It is the ultimate center of control.

How does the party and its Central Apparat control the government? The diagram below shows that there are three methods used at all levels of the governmental structure. The first is through overlapping (or dual) membership, with higher echelon members of the CPSU occupying important positions in the governmental structure; the second is through the monopolistic choice of all elected or appointed officials; and the third is through the constant surveillance of and control over all government officials by the party cadres.

We have put side by side the hierarchical structure of the CPSU and the government to show the direct overlap between the two. The overlap is not 100 percent because it has varied over time. Stalin was Secretary General, Chairman of the Council of Ministers (for most of his long stay in

OVERLAP BETWEEN THE CPSU AND THE GOVERNMENT AT THE NATIONAL LEVEL

CPSU	Government
General (or First) Secretary	Prime Minister and Council of Ministers
Politburo and Secretariat	The President of the Council of Ministers
Central Committees	Supreme Soviet Presidium
City Committees	Supreme Soviet
	City Executive Committees

There is an almost 100 percent overlap between the Communist party leader and all governmental executive organs. It is only in the Supreme Soviet (the top legislative assembly) that meets only twice a year for not longer than 7 days per session that the overlap is only 80 percent.

2. For an updated discussion of the Central Apparat and *Nomenklatura*, see Vladimir Medish, *The Soviet Union*, 2d ed. (Englewood Cliffs, N.J.: Prentice-Hall, 1983).

office), Chairman of the Praesidium of the Supreme Soviet, and also the Commander-in-Chief of the armed services. Khrushchev's reach was neither so long nor as stable. He became Secretary General and Chairman of the Council of Ministers for a while but never managed to hold all three posts. Brezhnev managed to do so, but only after he had been Secretary General for more than ten years. Chernenko was both Chairman of the Praesidium and Secretary General of the party. Upon Chernenko's death in 1985, Mikhail Gorbachev replaced him as General Secretary but did not assume the chairmanship of the Praesidium for which he nominated the veteran Secretary of Foreign Affairs, Andrei Gromyko.

The overlap of top leaders in the Politburo, the rising stars in the Central Committee, and prominent party leaders with government positions is also overwhelming. The top executive positions — in the Council of Ministers, the Praesidium of the Supreme Soviet, and the Council of Ministers of the Union Republics — are staffed by the top leaders of the CPSU. One may say that the overlap between top party officials and the government's executive bodies ranges from 95 to 100 percent.

The situation is not much different with the Soviets. In the Supreme Soviet almost 80 percent of the deputies are members of the CPSU, many of them in leadership ranks. In the Soviets of the Union Republics, CPSU control is over 60 percent, and as we move down the ladder to reach the local and village Soviets, the overlap decreases, so much so that in the smallest Soviets the CPSU membership represents only a minority. Such a situation, however, is always redressed in favor of the CPSU by the strong presence of Communists in the executive committees and in the bureaus elected by the various Soviets. The CPSU members and leaders control the executive branch at *all* levels of government. They are always in control of the vast command structure — always in command.

The Party as the Government Not only the party officials overlap with the government officials, not only do the government officials owe their election and position to the CPSU, and not only do they operate under its surveillance and are literally at its mercy, but in addition they are frequently superseded by the party officials. The party becomes the government. As we noted, Politburo members and the General Secretary as well as many of the members of the Central Committee wear two hats. They are top party *and* government officials. When decisions are made, laws promulgated, and directives issued, it is very hard to tell which hat the decision makers are wearing, the party one or the governmental one. Sometimes they are not sure themselves. The announcement of the party program by the Secretary General often amounts to policy directives. The Central Apparat, which is divided into functional departments that correspond roughly to ministries, oversee the machinery of the state. They can and do impose themselves. They initiate policies, prepare specific and detailed plans of implementation, and take direct actions to ensure their execution. One would be tempted to say that the party is a state within a state, but this would be inappropriate since the party controls, guides,

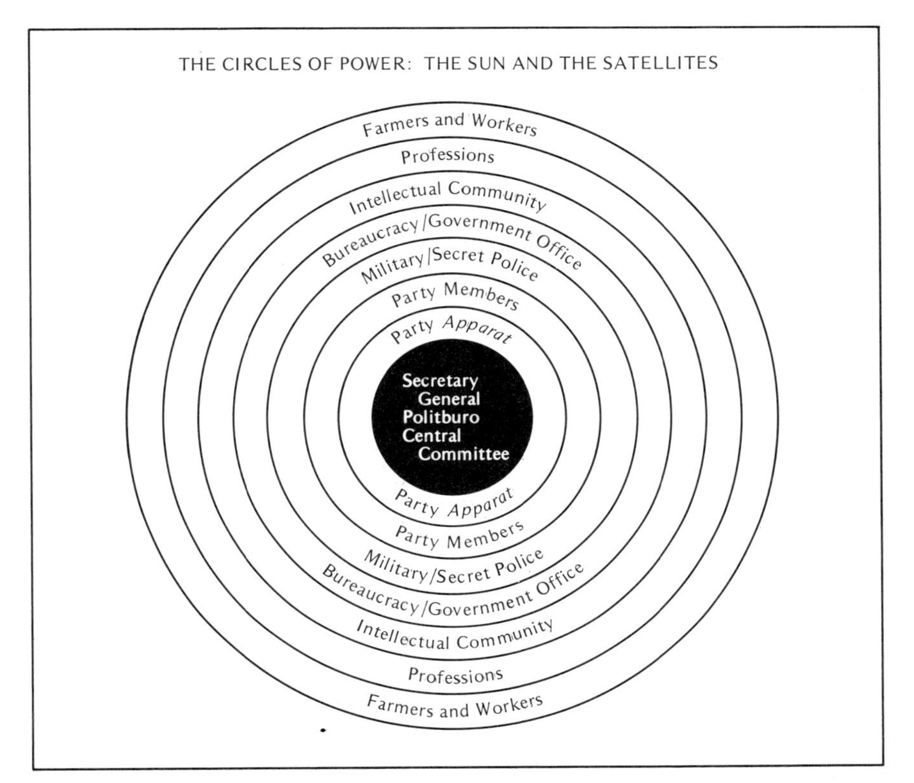

and supervises the state officials and is responsible for their selection. Actually it is the other way around: the state is within the party. It is the party leadership that constitutes the structure of command, which is centralized, monopolistic, and absolute. The state obeys and implements.

The Governing Elite: Characteristics

Let us recall the major traits of the elite configuration in democratic regimes: there are many elite groups; the elite is pluralistic, competitive (within limits), relatively open, heterogeneous, and operates under many limitations. There is also a great deal of interchangeability among political, economic, military, and professional elite positions at the top.

The major characteristic of the elite configuration in a totalitarian regime is that there is *one* governing elite. It is the political elite within the single party. Other elites are like satellites rotating around the party leadership. The party provides the center of gravity; without the Party leadership under which they operate, they would spin off into limbo. Other characteristics include the following: (1) the elite is *monolithic* and it shares a set of values, and official ideology, from which there can be no deviation; (2) it is *exclusive* as one cannot belong to it without the party's approval and consent; (3) it is *integrative* and not competitive. The political

ELITES IN DEMOCRATIC AND TOTALITARIAN REGIMES

Democratic	Totalitarian
Differentiated	Monolithic
Pluralistic	Monopolistic
Multidimensional	One-dimensional (political conformity)
Horizontal	Vertical (dominance of political elite)
Open	Exclusive
Competitive	Integrative

elite shapes the society into its own mold, coopts those who accept it, and seeks members who have particular abilities and skills, especially organizational and administrative skills, and a good grounding in ideology.

Although the party is the ruling elite, there is another elite within the party comprising at least half a million people, and within that second elite there are narrowing concentric circles corresponding to higher leadership echelons. There are several ways of becoming a part of the top elite within the larger elite.[3]

The first is to work for the *Apparat,* the party bureaucracy. There are tens of thousands of positions in the Central Committee, in the various important urban centers, in the Union Republics, and in regional committees. Men and women choose the party bureaucracy as a career and, depending on abilities, loyalty, personal contacts, and sometimes luck, they may succeed. They form a stable and secure group (ever since Stalin died), vigilant of their positions and more vigilant of the regime that gave them these positions. Their major skills and talents are organizational.

A second way is through intellectual accomplishment. These people are the *ideocrats,* the "preachers and teachers." They range from writers, artists, journalists, and media and propaganda experts to the philosophers and the ideologues who have mastered Marxism-Leninism. Many of them are in charge of various Soviet academies or institutes, and they are the interpreters of Marxism. Because of their expertise, they are recognized internationally, and they are the only ones who can give authoritative interpretations of the dogma. They study the course of history in the light of the compass Marxism provides and steer the ship of state accordingly. The early founders of the Soviet regime, the bolshevik revolutionaries, were all (except Stalin) ideologues, but they read the compass differently and turned against one another. After Stalin, the ideologues virtually disappeared and Stalin became the interpretative oracle. More recently ideologues have surfaced again — Suslov died at the age of eighty-two after serving in the Politburo and heading the ideology section of the Central Apparat. Chernenko is believed to have replaced Suslov until he became Secretary General in February of 1984.

3. For a discussion of the major elite roles in the Communist party, see John Rasheter, Jr., *The Soviet Polity* (New York: Dodd & Mead, 1971), pp. 163–170.

A third way of reaching high elite status is to become a *technocrat*. These people have technical skills that they put to use in universities, industries, the sciences, engineering, production, agriculture, medicine, space, and other specialized areas. They can be divided into two categories: one consists of those who while acquiring skills and expertise in their study, research, and work also join the party from their student days or very shortly after their formal academic work is over. Little need be said about them except that many gradually abandon their own academic and scientific pursuits in exchange for organizational and political positions in the party, and quite a few have attained the highest party positions, for example, Kaganovich, Brezhnev, Malenkov, Kosygin, Gorbachev, and Ustinov. They used the party rather than their fields of expertise, and their party loyalty was the primary criterion for their upward mobility.

The second category consists of technocrats who did not join or use the party. They may be considered as a separate quasi-elite stratum or group outside the party. But the CPSU has a number of ways for securing both their submissiveness and their conformity and for utilizing their talents toward its own political goals. Some of them become coopted: the CPSU offers them membership or good positions in the party and in the party-controlled organizations such as a candidacy in the Supreme Soviet, a position in the various scientific or literary academies, a professorship, or a high position in the bureaucracy. In return, these technocrats receive special privileges and stipends, special services and benefits, special consideration for their families, etc. Thus the CPSU can ensure that they become reliable Soviet citizens, even if they are not offered membership in the party.

Should these methods fail, there is intimidation or the threat of force and, not infrequently, outright force itself. They may find themselves expelled from the academy where they teach; their books may disappear from the bookstores and they may discover that no paper is available to print new ones; their circle of friends shrinks, and gradually their aloofness will be interpreted as defiance and a sign of disloyalty. At this point actual force may be used lest the nonconformity of one individual become contagious. The case of the father of the Soviet hydrogen bomb, Sakharov, who has been under house arrest for many years, and has become literally a "nonperson," is the most widely known. Uniformity and submissiveness must be maintained at all costs. Even scientific geniuses cannot retain elite status if they go against the party.

Some of the methods outlined are particularly evident with the military, the police, the bureaucracy, and more generally the intellectual community. The political leadership is sensitive to all four, but especially to the military and the police because they are the only organizations with the physical means to challenge the party. In order to counter any such potential resistance from these groups, the CPSU is constantly taking steps to secure their submissiveness and conformity. The best methods used thus far have been surveillance and cooptation. In army units there is surveillance of the commanders at the top through the appointment of political commissars, trusted Communist party members who report to their superior party officers. There are also primary organizations of the CPSU at the bottom, among enlisted men and junior officers, to carry out political propaganda and instill loyalty and pride in the motherland and, not so incidentally, report on individual failures and deviations. Cooptation, on the other hand, is the process whereby officers are asked and often volunteer to join the party.

In conclusion, as mentioned on p. 143, the major characteristics of the Soviet elite are the following:

It is monolithic. The members of the political elite have to accept and sustain the officially sanctioned values in order to stay in their position. There are two kinds of values: transcendental and instrumental. By transcendental we mean the Marxist ideology that offers a frame of analysis of social events and a set of proposals to transcend these events by building a communist society. This ideology is both a science and a moral and political imperative. The Soviet elite is Marxist in this sense, just as much as the elites in a democracy are or should be democratic. The difference, however, is that while democracy allows for a wide range of disagreement about values, totalitarian regimes demand elite agreement and a uniform acceptance even if they cannot always obtain it.

Transcendental values also lead to a uniform set of instrumental values. These values focus on strengthening and maintaining the regime. CPSU members share by and large the same basic instrumental values: they agree on the rules of democratic centralism, the subordination of the lower organs to the higher ones, unity of action, the subordination of the society to the party, the acceptance of the doctrine and tactics propounded by the leadership, the maintenance of a network of surveillance and control over all citizens, and the role and superiority of the Soviet Union in the world. There may be some disagreements about policies, but we do not know how much because they are not debated in public.

It is exclusive. The political elite is exclusive in the sense that few, if any, attain a position of power and leadership from outside. There is no interchangeability, as in democratic regimes where an army general, a trade union leader, a professor, or an engineer can enter politics at any time, thus moving from one elite position into the political elite. In the Soviet totalitarian regime, political power and leadership can be attained only after a long apprenticeship in the CPSU. It is difficult to imagine a general, a professor, or a scientist outside the party being elected to the Politburo. If it were allowed, it would destroy the image the party has propagated: that of the guiding force and the guardian angel of the society. To allow outsiders to assume responsible positions at the top of the party by virtue of what they did outside the party would be to admit the existence of political wisdom and leadership outside the party. It would destroy the party monopoly.

It is integrative. The elite organization is vertical rather than horizontal. At the top is the political elite and below in hierarchically subordinate layers are the other elites: coopted, rewarded, or intimidated by the CPSU, which integrates them hierarchically in terms of their functions. They may compete within the CPSU for political advancement and power but they can hardly compete with one another about increments of political power. Factional disputes may develop but they are not allowed to become recognizable factions within the party, let alone outside the party or against it.

Recruitment Since the party wants to make sure that the ablest people become members early in their lives, it exerts much effort to recruit them as soon as possible. Early recruitment and socialization are preferable to cooptation, surveillance, intimidation, or force.

Careful recruitment of talented young people is the hallmark of all totalitarian regimes. Plato in his *Republic* begins the search for the Guardians — the top leaders of the state — at the very early age of four or five. After long and careful education and screening, only a few will be chosen by their elders. In the same way, but for different reasons, the CPSU organizes recruitment by providing careful screening and socializing devices to select the future ruling political elite while they are still young. Totalitarian leadership creates and re-creates the political leadership in its own image. In the Soviet Union this accounts, in part, for the relative old age of the top leaders. A system of paternalism whereby the older and wiser members train the young and screen them carefully not only gives legitimacy, prestige, and power to the old but also socializes the young into respect, obedience, and submission.

How does the CPSU recruit its future leaders? First, there are special

ASCENDING TO POWER

Mikhail S. Gorbachev (born in 1931)

Age	Date	Position
21	1952	Entered the party
24	1955	Graduated, Moscow State University
27	1958	Second Secretary, Stavropol Region in the Komsomol
28	1959-1962	First Secretary, Stavropol Region in the Komsomol
31	1962-1963	Party organizer of agricultural administration in Stavropol's Territorial Executive Committee
35	1966-1968	First Secretary, Stavropol' City Committee
37	1968-1970	Second Secretary, Stavropol Regional Committee
39	1970-1978	First Secretary, Stavropol Regional Committee
40	1971	Member, CC CPSU
47	1978	Secretary, CC CPSU
49	1980-	Member, Politburo, CC CPSU
54	1985-	General Secretary, CC CPSU

schools for training in propaganda, agitation, ideology, political organization, and manipulation. These students will become the "political engineers" of the party, destined for important positions in the Central Apparat and higher up. Second, and more important, there is the network of organizations for those between seven and twenty-eight years old. These organizations have a double purpose: (1) to mobilize all the young people around and behind the Soviet regime and the CPSU and (2) to serve as screening devices for choosing the "best."

All totalitarian regimes, communist or not, display the same interest in youngsters and set up organizations to activate and induct them. They spread their tentacles into the schools and even the family. The Soviet youth organizations operate under the CPSU, and those in charge occupy important posts at both the Central Apparat and in the Central Committee. There are three major organizations and each branches out into the family, the schools, and the universities: (1) the Octobrists, young boys and girls between seven and nine; (2) the Pioneers, those between the ages of nine and fourteen; and (3) the Komsomol (The Young Communist League), which is the umbrella youth organization for those between fourteen and twenty-eight. They organize sports, cultural activities, vacations, and classes in Marxism.

The avowed purpose of the Komsomol, with at least 40 million members, is to bring up the new generation "in the spirit of communism"; to inculcate discipline, respect for work, and love for the Soviet motherland. The Komsomol controls radio and television stations, exercises close supervision of school activities and the curriculum, is responsible for the publication of special newspapers addressed to the young of various ages, and also directs the activities of the younger children in the Pioneers and the Octobrists. Belonging to Komsomol can ensure advancement since higher education is almost exclusively reserved to Komsomol members. Young people who have not joined the training grounds of the future political elite are virtually deprived of attaining even subordinate elite positions. They are denied the opportunity of acquiring the special skills and knowledge that higher education provides.

The last and most important test and hurdle is admission to the CPSU. Admission involves careful screening by the elders; applications must be approved by a number of CPSU members; there is usually a probationary period of candidate member status; and a thorough knowledge of Marxism-Leninism is required. Thus for a young boy or girl there is a long period of apprenticeship before the ultimate prize of membership can be granted (no one is accepted before the age of twenty). But once admission is granted, the new member can look upward where most others dare not stare. The late Secretary General of the CPSU, Yuri Andropov, started with the Komsomol and became a Komsomol organizer and one of its first secretaries before he joined the Central Apparat. He was then thirty-eight years old.

The Organization of Consent

Introduction

The differences between totalitarian and democratic regimes are fundamental. As opposed to voluntary participation, totalitarian regimes offer *mobilization* — induced participation; as opposed to representation, totalitarian regimes offer *integration;* while democracies allow for a fairly broad parameter of political competition, totalitarian regimes are more restrictive and the will of the ruling party is often *imposed* on the people; while democracies rely on and value autonomous associational activities, totalitarian regimes try to *penetrate* them, restructure them, and reduce them into subordinate instruments of the CPSU. Mobilization, integration, imposition, and penetration are the hallmarks of all totalitarian regimes, communist or not. The agency through which they are accomplished is the single party; the values and ideas used and the orientation they impart comprise the official ideology.

Soviet communist ideology, despite many twists and turns, continues to pay lip service to the major Marxist propositions. It is being used to mobilize the citizenry, to integrate the society, to impose its will on the people, to legitimize the rule of the CPSU, and to penetrate and restructure all societal forces.

Mobilization

As noted earlier, mobilization is induced participation, which is used to create supports in favor of the ideological goals and policies offered by a political elite. In the Soviet Union the party is the leading mobilizing agency. It sets the tone, provides the cues, and induces participation directly through its organs and members or indirectly through the network of front organizations it controls. At a party Congress, for instance, the general policy guidelines to be introduced are disseminated and discussed in thousands of meetings from the neighborhood level up; special agents of the party known as "agitators" constantly canvass the public about policy issues until an opinion is formed. Similarly, at election time — once every four years — the party candidates stump their districts with answers to the problems facing the country. They too mold public opinion around certain themes, which are orchestrated in advance by the party leadership. Special demonstrations and forums are organized by the party for the same purpose and attendance mandatory. The citizen is not allowed to remain indifferent or apathetic, but the activity of the citizen must be in agreement with the Communist party's ideological and policy propositions.

Mobilization presupposes the control of all media of communication, and the CPSU controls all of them. The daily press, all weekly or monthly publications, and all scientific or literary journals are under party control and direction. The sole private press is clandestine (the *Samizdat*), and it has to circulate from hand to hand. The only other source of information is from foreign radio newscasts, except for American broadcasts, which are jammed. In this sense the monopoly of communication is the same thing as propaganda, and it is a monopoly held by the political elite. Events are portrayed and interpreted in a uniform way; there are no different accounts and no conflicting interpretations or evaluations as in democracies. Both domestic and foreign news events are presented and authoritatively assessed by the party leaders and the ideocrats in the Central Apparat, which is in charge of propaganda. History is constantly being reinterpreted, revised, and rewritten. Powerful personalities become "unpersons" and obscure ones gain prominence. Some events are not reported at all, such as war casualties, airplane accidents, cases of river pollution, or the illness of a political leader. Every effort is made to show that all is well. The people are led to share in the self-righteousness and serenity in which the leadership basks.

The total control of communication is aimed at fashioning a uniform "national mind." People hear and read the same words, look at the same symbols, and listen to the same slogans every day. Even if they could turn off their minds, it would be impossible not to be influenced; it would be impossible to form an independent judgment. Person-to-person contacts with neighbors, friends, classmates, and fellow athletes reinforce the official news, and eventually people submit and join the growing current of uniformity. Such political propaganda has been compared with advertising in the United States, but there is a notable difference. In the Soviet Union, as in other totalitarian regimes, there is only one product!

Two noted authors have argued that instead of mobilizing people propaganda could saturate them so much that they would at first be incredulous and then eventually apathetic and thus the leadership would find itself in a vacuum of indifference and resentment. As a result, it would lose rather than gain mobilization and supports it seeks.[4] In the early years of a totalitarian regime, especially if it faces serious difficulties, this may happen, but the Soviet experience provides no such confirmation. Mobilization and propaganda seem to be succeeding in fashioning a uniform body of citizens who believe that the world as described by the CPSU is what the world is really like.

Integration

In democracies the function of representation is to allow all societal forces to express their viewpoints, articulate their interests, and make their respective weight felt upon the machinery of the government. In totalitarian regimes the political party plays the inverse role. It represents the leadership, not the society, and it coordinates, organizes, and integrates

4. Carl J. Friedrich and Zbigniew Brzezinski. *Totalitarian Dictatorship and Autocracy*, 2d ed. (New York: Praeger, 1966).

all societal activities. In reality representation flows from the top down and not the bottom up. It is the CPSU that provides the values, the cues, the organization, and the policies that guide the society toward communism. It is the link that unites the leadership with the masses just as a staff sergeant links the top brass with the buck privates. The party integrates and molds the societal forces instead of representing them.

The organization of command in the Soviet Union displays marked differences from democratic regimes. Despite the use of democratic vocabulary and democratic forms, governance is highly concentrated and knows no limitations. Although acceptance is sought (no regime could exist without at least some public approval), it is limited to the high echelons of the Communist party. There is deliberation and a search of consensus but only at the top, only in the Politburo and the Central Committee. Under a single-party system, there is no free and open debate within the party let alone beyond it; there are no open elections. There are no formal restraints imposed by a legislature or a judiciary and no political responsibility other than to the top leadership of the party. As noted earlier, mobilization and participation are used to create supports, not to organize dissent and promote different policies. Like all political regimes, the Soviet Union has to meet the ultimate test of performance, but unlike democratic regimes, it does not allow criticism of the performance of its leaders!

Imposition and Penetration

The CPSU either directly or through the governmental organs it controls has penetrated and imposed its will on almost every social organization including the family. The economy is physically in the hands of the state bureaucratic agencies. Banks, domestic trade, imports, exports, insurance, health care and hospitals, and even the corner drugstore and vegetable store are administered by the state. Wages are also controlled by the public agencies and the trade unions are but adjuncts of the CPSU. In short, the state and the party control virtually all economic resources.

Penetration is also the rule with regard to all social activities. Sports, education, the theater, and films operate under public or semipublic auspices and often under the direct administration of the CPSU. This is also the case with universities, cultural programs, cultural exchanges, and literary clubs.

Since the 1977 constitution guarantees religious freedom and the separation between church and state, there is no party penetration into the church, no effort to supplant the clergy and perform the rites! However, operating through a special organization, The Council for the Affairs of Religious Cults, the party does exercise control. All priests have to register; they are not allowed to train new clergy except to replace those who die; special permission is needed to print the Bible or other religious books; many churches have been converted into public buildings; and religion and party membership are incompatible. Yet there is a certain autonomy for religious sects. Despite the overt hostility of the party against religious beliefs, some 50 million people attend religious services, representing about forty religious denominations. Almost seventy years after the revolution, religion has not been extirpated and it continues to be practiced by as many as 15 to 25 percent of the population, virtually all of whom were born *after* the revolution!

Through the youth organizations, not only are children over eight years old being socialized and mobilized by the party, but the family itself is being penetrated. When family relationships and loyalties come in conflict with state and party imperatives, loyalty to the party takes precedence. The Pioneers and the Little Octobrists continue to carry party messages to their homes, influencing and even intimidating the parents. A happy family is a Soviet family first.

A similar mix of penetration and imposition is used with the armed forces, especially the officer corps, which is in charge of the instruments of war and public defense. Military affairs are in the hands of the Politburo and the Central Apparat; the head of the secret police is also a three- or four-star general and only the Secretary General assumes a higher military rank. Communist-trained loyalists act as political commissars who monitor the activities of high-ranking officers. Communist party cells and agitators constantly disseminate propaganda at all levels of the army and are quick to spot incipient dissidence. Also, as we noted, high-ranking officers receive rewards and privileges and many become members of the CPSU.

The net to establish obedient conformity and preempt any potential anti-Sovietism, any possible differences between the army officer corps and the leadership of the CPSU, is as thick as possible, and it is only occasionally that some small fish may slip through. Furthermore, with the coming of second- and third-generation high-ranking officers obedience can be taken for granted. Although cooperation between the party and the military is the preferred relationship, imposition is always present as a matter of last resort. Generals who assume notoriety are quickly removed or shifted to obscure posts. While public pronouncements on military questions come from the political leaders, some public statements by high-ranking military personnel were made during the first year of Andropov's rule (and prolonged illness) both with regard to the installation of missiles in Europe by the United States and on the shooting down of the South Korean plane late in 1983. But the general who made the statements was removed from his position as chief of staff of the Soviet forces, so it is very doubtful that such pronouncements mean that the military has won some autonomy. At best, the army remains a power only within the framework of the all-encompassing monopoly held by the CPSU.[5]

5. Timothy Colton, *Commissars, Commissioners and Civilian Authority* (Cambridge, Mass.: Harvard University Press, 1976).

The Organization of Interests

Introduction

We have discussed the relationship between the CPSU and the various associations — cultural, political, religious, and others. We have also noted some of the patterns of imposition, mobilization, penetration, and control. In this section we will examine how economic associations and interests are organized and structured in the Soviet Union, and we will conclude with a note on the organization and implementation of individual rights: civil, political, and socioeconomic.

A predominant characteristic of democratic regimes is that interests, individual or associational, organize freely to express their interests and articulate their demands. There is a constant dynamic and spontaneity in the democratic interest universe. Interests are always competing in the public forum, and the governmental agencies regulate, distribute, and redistribute goods and services in response to such demands. In totalitarian regimes the situation is very different. The Marxist ideology postulates the total control of the economy in the name of the collectivity, and party control ranges from penetration and imposition to total disinvestiture and direct management. The public interest is determined by the party leadership; interest groups and associations merely implement it.[6]

There are some cardinal rules that apply to all well-established communist totalitarian regimes, not only in the Soviet Union but also in Cuba, Eastern Europe, South Vietnam, and to a degree, China:

1. The state expropriates and manages all productive resources held in private hands. The economy as a whole is nationalized or socialized; it is put under the command of the political elite in the state or the party. This applies to industry, mineral wealth, agriculture, domestic trade, banking, imports and exports, and to all the related economic processes such as price and wage fixing, interest rates, investment policies, allocation of resources between various sectors of the economy. Only minor qualifications to this general rule are permitted, and they relate primarily to artisans and small farmers.
2. The state is the only employer. Nobody is allowed to hire the labor of another person and pay wages. Again, qualifications may be made for household help and individual artisans such as mechanics, plumbers, and the like.
3. All major economic decisions that directly affect every producing unit, every store, and every consumer are made by the central organs of the party and are implemented through a large bureaucratic apparatus. Decision making and often management are centralized, although in

6. Gordon Skilling and Franklyn Griffith (eds.), *Interest Groups in Soviet Politics* (Princeton, N.J.: Princeton University Press, 1971), especially chaps. I and II.

some communist regimes there are varying degrees of decentralization that allow for some managerial freedom in industrial and agriculture production.

4. The right to individual property such as savings, household and personal items, apartments or a house, and the right to pass it on to one's heirs is generally recognized. However, such property rights exist only at the discretion of the decision makers; they can be modified or outlawed.
5. The goal of economic policy is the attainment of equality for all — or, to put it more realistically, to narrow the inequalities. All communist revolutions have been made either *by* or *for* the underprivileged, the workers and peasants, and against the wealthy, the property owners, the business interests, and the landowners.

This overwhelming control of a person's economic life and economic incentives by political agencies may be viewed in two different ways. For some, the virtual elimination of private property and profit in industry, banking, agriculture, and trade liberates the individual from exploitation and intimidation by the property-owning class, the capitalists. State control and direction put an end to class conflicts and exploitation of the many by the few. For others, however, the communist state and the political elite solidify their power by subordinating all economic rights and freedoms and assuming control over them. All individuals become state-employed salaried personnel, free to work for the state agencies but unable to use their incentives outside the economic framework imposed by the state and unable to derive any profit from their activities. Thus the political elite eliminates the last refuge of privacy and individuality. Political power that is totalitarian in scope may become, so the argument goes, just as dehumanizing and exploitative as capitalism is claimed to be in liberal democracies. The socialization of the economy when coupled with the socialization of culture, information, education, and ideological conformity destroys all individual defenses. Some say that economic and political expropriation leads to cultural and political expropriation as well. The society and all persons in it are totally penetrated by the state and totally dependent on it.

Since the bolshevik revolution in the Soviet Union, there have been two phases of policy toward economic interests, both individual and associational: (1) the destruction and restructuring of interest, and (2) the reassertion of interest groups under conditions that still maintain party control.

Destruction and Restructuring

The process of destruction that began after the revolution was followed by a restructuring that emerged after the end of World War II.

It was in 1928–1929, ten years after the Revolution that comprehensive socialism was established. The whole of the economy came directly under the control and ownership of the state. First, all industrial and manufacturing concerns, small or large, were taken over by the state. All the wealthy farmers, those who had been allowed to buy land, to increase their holdings, to hire farmhands, to add some implements to their farms, and to own livestock — the *kulaks,* as they were called — were exterminated by party loyalists and organizers, the police, and special CPSU squads. The trade union leaders who continued to assert their special and separate interests within or outside the party were apprehended and, together with many of the militants and organizers, sent into exile. By 1931 the interests of labor could not be voiced by their independent spokesmen, and trade unions, as autonomous representative associations of labor interests, simply disappeared. Thus in one big sweep, between 1929–1931, the three major and separate interests were destroyed: the independent farmers, the small manufacturers and merchants, and the labor unions.

Restructuring was undertaken in one of two ways: either the interests that had been destroyed were replaced with new organizations or the existing organizations were allowed to go on but under new leadership appointed directly by the party. The whole economy — production, trade, and consumption — was taken over by the state and overall economic decisions were made under the Five-Year Plan. Subsequent versions of the Five-Year-Plan followed and they continue to determine economic policy for the whole of the Soviet Union: the republics, the districts, the localities, and all the firms and all the farms. The policy is implemented by the Council of Ministers, the ministries of the various Union Republics, and smaller territorial subdivisions. Name any important economic activity and you will find a ministry to implement the requirements of the Plan! Through the ministries, directives go down directly or indirectly to the individual units and factories. Each firm is managed by a director appointed by the appropriate state authorities. The planning bureaucracy parallels the party from the top down and administers the economy. It executes the Plan much like a big corporation in the United States. But unlike a U.S. corporation, private initiative and incentive are not allowed. Economic and managerial interests become bureaucratized, and since they operate under the control of the CPSU, they become so politicized that they lose their functional independence.

Agricultural production and food distribution are also planned. Farms have been either collectivized or put directly under state management. In the first case, individual farmers form cooperatives, they lease the land rent-free from the state, and they produce according to the specifications of the Plan. Each collective averages about 600 households. The farmers live in nearby villages and spend a given number of days working in the collective under the direction of the supervising officials who are appointed by the party. They must produce an annual quota determined by the Plan and they are paid wages corresponding to the work they put in plus the price of their product minus taxes. However,

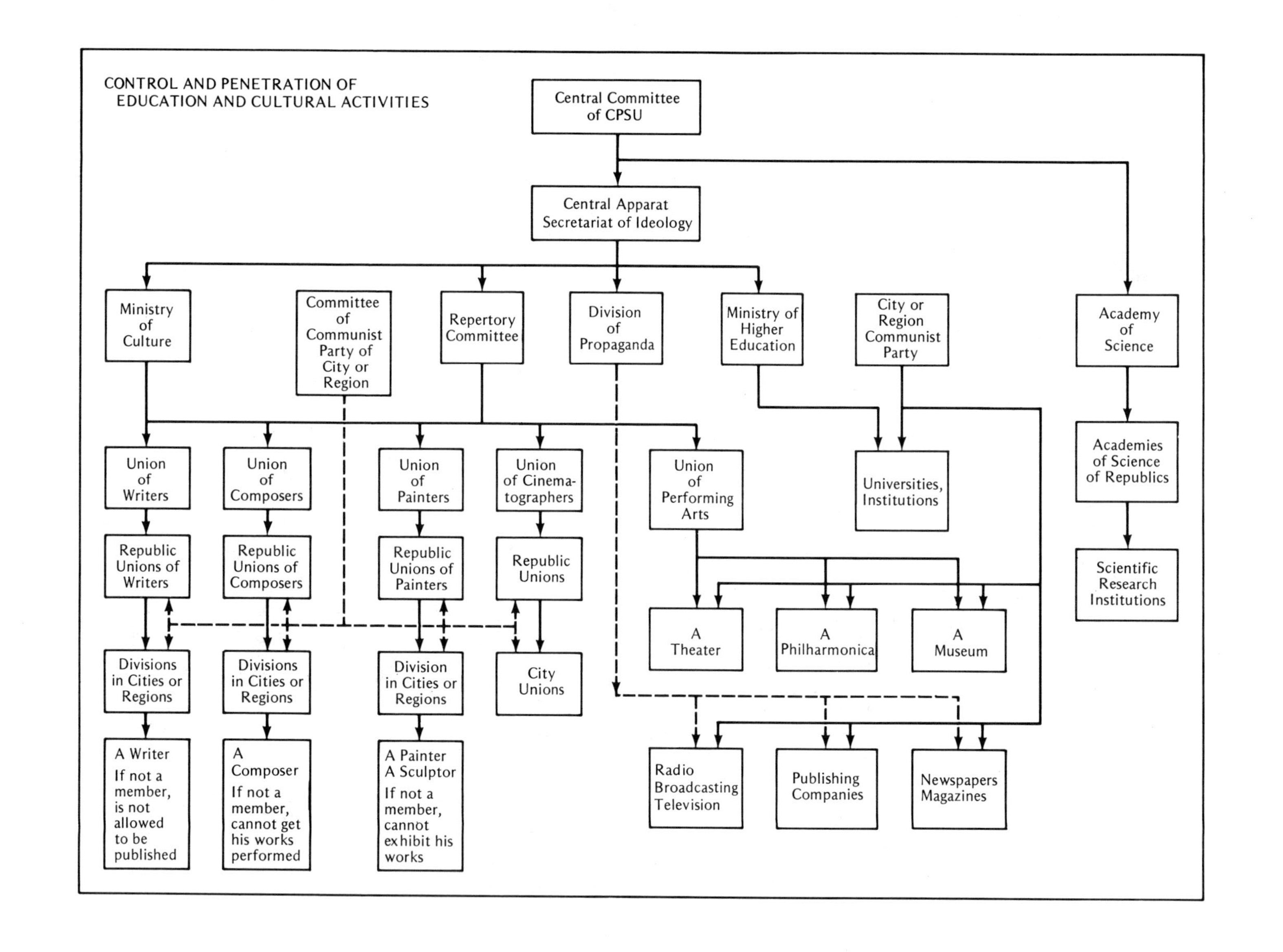
CONTROL AND PENETRATION OF
EDUCATION AND CULTURAL ACTIVITIES
Central Committee of CPSU
Central Apparat Secretariat of Ideology
Ministry of Culture
Committee of Communist Party of City or Region
Repertory Committee
Division of Propaganda
Ministry of Higher Education
City or Region Communist Party
Academy of Science
Union of Writers
Union of Composers
Union of Painters
Union of Cinematographers
Union of Performing Arts
Universities, Institutions
Academies of Science of Republics
Republic Unions of Writers
Republic Unions of Composers
Republic Unions of Painters
Republic Unions
Scientific Research Institutions
A Theater
A Philharmonica
A Museum
Divisions in Cities or Regions
Divisions in Cities or Regions
Division in Cities or Regions
City Unions
A Writer
If not a member, is not allowed to be published
A Composer
If not a member, cannot get his works performed
A Painter
A Sculptor
If not a member, cannot exhibit his works
Radio Broadcasting Television
Publishing Companies
Newspapers Magazines

collective farmers do have what is the last vestige of private property. They "own" a small plot of land (averaging not more than half an acre) and can produce whatever they want and sell it for a market price. It is worth noting that a disproportionately large percentage of the agricultural production (especially in fruits, vegetables, eggs, and poultry) comes from these private plots.

The other unit of agricultural production is the state farm *(sovkoz)* where there are only workers — farmhands. Each state farm employs as many as 600 to 700 workers; each specializes in certain products; and all are mechanized. Called "agricultural factories," they are increasing in number and are considered a more advanced form of production than collectives, because there are no private incentives. They account for at least half of the total agricultural production in the Soviet Union.

Labor interests have had their roles restructured. Trade union leaders are appointed directly by the party; labor representatives in the factory do not participate in any managerial decisions, and the grievances they are allowed to express relate only to day-to-day working conditions. Since the trade union leaders are members of the CPSU, their main job is indoctrination and propaganda: they discuss and support the Plan and extol hard work and productivity. At the national level, trade unions administer vacations, sick leaves, and pensions. They no longer bargain, and they are not allowed to strike.

Briefly, then, the major economic interests are controlled by the state and the CPSU. They make the decisions about what to produce or what not to produce, where to allocate major resources, or where not to, and what values to allocate or withhold.

What is noteworthy is that individual preferences play a very small role and, in times of a limited supply of consumer goods, perhaps no role at all. In other words, the people are deprived of the opportunity to express virtually any choice in the economic realm, as well as in all other aspects of societal life: politics, culture, religion, education, etc. The political regime deprives them of the opportunity to choose their own ideas and values; the economic organization deprives them of the opportunity for choice in the marketplace. Choices are made *for* the citizenry, not *by* the citizenry.

The Reassertion of Interest Groups

It is almost axiomatic that any society that is industrializing fast must undergo some major transformations. There will be a growing social and functional differentiation in employment patterns that are easily identified in terms of new social groupings: skilled and white-collar workers, engineers, scientists, managerial groups, specialized institutions, etc. There will also be a rapid proliferation of groups consisting of people who have specialized jobs to do and who occupy specialized positions. The logic of modernization is the development of many such groups each with similar skills, similar expectations, and similar demands. The most significant demand may prove to be for freedom to participate in political and economic decision making.

Some argue that the modernization and industrialization that have been going on in the Soviet Union have indeed resulted in the formation of new groups with their own know-how, their own loyalty, and their own stakes. It has been said that such groups are not likely to submit to arbitrary governance and are inclined to resist totalitarian controls by the CPSU. They can now participate in decisions and are capable of opposing decisions, at least to a certain extent. Some argue that interest groups have emerged in the Soviet Union and that the process of government is directly affected by their demands and by the interplay of their conflicting claims. Scientists, the legal profession, intellectuals, writers and artists, the intelligence and police community, the industrial managers, the military, and the state and party bureaucrats have become identifiable interest groups, which are directly affecting the political process from their respective positions.[7]

The Role of Interests and Interest Groups

Using interest group analysis to explain the distribution of power and influence and the ultimate allocation of values in the form of decisions has been widely used in the study of policy making in liberal democratic regimes. Interests are defined either in terms of concrete organizations (e.g., the Dairy Lobby or the National Association of Manufacturers) or as activities that unite individuals in pursuit of common values and goals (e.g., the environmentalists). In all cases interest groups try to influence decisions at any level of the political process: electoral, legislative, executive, or administrative. In order to have interest groups, however, and apply interest group analysis to the study of the political process, certain requirements that we found in democratic regimes (Chapter 5) must be met:

1. Interest groups must have an appreciable degree of self-identification. In other words, it is not enough to identify certain groups in objective terms like the industrial managers or farmers or artists. They must have a degree of consciousness of their position; there must be a subjective awareness of what they share in common and what they expect to achieve in common.
2. Subjectivity requires, above all, autonomy — an interaction among the members of identifiable and self-identifying groups or the practitioners of a given profession. Without free and frequent exchanges and interaction, it is difficult to see how commonly shared views can be expressed and formulated.

7. The party *appartchik*, the secret police, the military, the industrial managers, the economists, the writers, and the jurists are discussed in individual essays in Skilling and Griffith, op. cit.

3. To express a point of view a group must have independent resources. There are a number of types of resources to be considered: material resources freely contributed by the like-minded members of a group; organizational resources, the ability of like-minded people to establish an association and recruit members; access to sources of information and the means of disseminating such information; free access of the group to various decision-making units of the government in order to influence decisions; and finally the freedom to influence public opinion, specifically the electorate.

These conditions do not obtain in the Soviet Union or any communist regime. This is not to say that there are no easily identifiable socioeconomic, functional, cultural, or ethnic groups in Russia but simply that they cannot exercise influence from an independent position.[8] Occasionally differences among them are clearly stated and occasionally they can influence policy making (how and in what direction is not at all certain). There are even some powerful groups like the army, the police, the bureaucracy, or the industrial managers who have a certain degree of autonomy within and especially *under* the CPSU, but both their autonomy and control of independent resources are at times only minimal and more often — if we except the police and the army — nil. Since they have to operate within or under the party, their agenda for choice is set by the top party elite. They have no "subsystem autonomy" and not much freedom to reach out laterally to other groups or to bring their case before a wider public.

The Soviet official ideology has created a political and cultural setting in which interests and related interest organizations are viewed as *functions*, cogs in a wheel driven by the guiding force of the Soviet society, the CPSU. As functions, they can be manipulated by the political leadership in order to implement party values. Interests, especially individual spokesmen associated with certain interests, may differ and often do differ about specific policies: how to increase wheat production; how to decentralize, if at all, the economic planning machinery; how to revive socialist art or Soviet literature; or how to deal with political criminals or parasites. However, even differences such as these are controlled and limited: limited as to the number of people that are allowed to express their opinions, limited as to the scope of the debate, and limited as to the time period during which people can articulate their viewpoints. Differences are supposed to deal only with nonantagonistic contradictions, but according to the party propaganda antagonistic contradictions (defined as vital) do not exist! If they do, they will be aired, if at all, at the highest political summit: the Politburo.

8. The conflicts among interest groups and how they are resolved or not resolved are discussed in Skilling and Griffith, op. cit., chap. XI.

Soviet Corporatism?

To the extent that the consultation and the opinions of interests are sought, the Soviet economy has some striking similarities with state corporatism. One of them is the subordination of interests to the party and the state. First, the central planning machinery and the various industrial and economic ministries of the Council of Ministers bring under their respective umbrellas the clusters of particular interests they administer, thus helping to integrate them under their political control and, moreover, under the control of the party leadership. Second, the communications between various interest groups is vertical — it takes place through direct contact between the interest and the ministry. It is not horizontal: the various interests cannot communicate among themselves to reach a common policy unless they do so within the party. Third, the interdependence of the various economic activities in terms of both proximate and ultimate goals is decided, even after consultations with the interests involved, by the highest echelons of the political elite. As we noted, the economic plan is decided by the top party leadership after it has been discussed by the Central Committee. The economy is shaped directly by the political imperatives.

The composition and the role that particular interests play within the party may provide us with a better indication of their activities and their influence. Take, for example, the military. The army officer corps has developed a growing influence, and the top spokesmen of the army establishment are members of the CPSU. The army is one of the organizations that, even if under constant surveillance by the CPSU, possesses a degree of autonomy — it has its own communication network, it trains its recruits, and it has the instruments of coercion. Even if at the service of the CPSU and its leadership, it may exercise a great deal of influence upon it. Consider also the police force. It is likewise a separate organization, an adjunct of the party, but it has access to the media of gathering and disseminating information; it has its own instruments of coercion; and it has a vast intelligence apparatus, with a network of agents placed everywhere — even in the Supreme Court of the Soviet Union!

Since army officers and secret police (KGB) personnel are high-ranking members in the CPSU, they may appear to be acting on behalf of separate interests since they hold enough power to influence major policy decisions. But it is difficult to separate the policemen or the army officers from party loyalists. Do they exercise influence because they are specialists in their own field or because they are loyal and trusted party members? Does loyalty to the party supersede their role as spokesmen for the army and the police? If it does, they are not true representatives of separate interests. They are a part of the political elite. In other words, the political elite within the party maintains its dominance and tightly controls the personnel in all subsystems by penetrating them whether or not they wear uniforms of army officers and policemen.

What has been said about the army and the police applies with far greater force to other interests such as artists, lawyers, doctors, managers, intellectuals, engineers, agriculturalists, bureaucrats, etc. At least the army and the police spokesmen can "speak from where they stand," but other interests cannot: they have no autonomy at all and no access to resources. They "stand" nowhere! As long as the party maintains its tight monopoly over political representation, there can be no representation of interests. It is only if this monopoly is qualified that the minimal preconditions of pluralism may emerge and interest groups may be able to plead their case. In the meantime, interests continue to be defined in terms of their functionality and in terms of the implementation of overarching ideological and policy goals set forth by the party leadership. According to democratic centralism, interest groups, like all inferior organs, remain subordinate to the central authority, and whatever representation there may be is within and under the single party.

The Ideological Imperative and the Economy

Curiously enough, liberal democracies and communist regimes share the same ultimate goals for the economy: to increase productivity through technology and modernization and to increase wealth and spread it around so that all can benefit. However, the basic tenet of communism is that capitalism as an economic system has run its course, that it has entered a permanent state of crisis, and that the only way out is through socialism — the elimination of property and profit and the harnessing of the industrial capabilities by the collective leadership for collective purposes.

The Soviet leadership shares this point of view wholeheartedly. They acknowledge a bad start. Russia, like many other countries where communist regimes gained control, was backward and had considerable catching up to do before it could modernize and provide a higher standard of living. But the leaders never wavered from their credo and their vision: (1) to modernize as fast as possible, (2) to create adequate economic strength to defend their socialist fatherland and socialism everywhere, and (3) to begin ultimately to reap the benefits of modernization in the form of higher and more equitably distributed shares for all.

The early Five-Year Plans that were formulated prior to the 1960s [Russia is going through its Eleventh Five-Year Plan (1981–1986)] put all possible emphasis on capital goods and the building of an industrial infrastructure. The major effort was to develop heavy industries in iron, steel, coal, gas, and electricity; to increase construction; to build up armaments; to erect new factories; and to train workers and the ancillary service personnel that industrialization requires: professionals, technicians, and millions of new blue-collar workers who came from the countryside. New towns had to be built and equipped for the personnel needed, and agricultural production had to be improved to feed them. It was a stupendous task, especially because it was to be accomplished as

TABLE 6-1 Industrial Growth in the Soviet Union

	1928	1940	1950	1960	1970
Electricity (milliard kWh)	5.0	48.3	91.2	292.3	740
Steel (million tons)	4.3	18.3	27.3	65.3	116
Oil (million tons)	11.6	31.1	37.9	147.9	353
Gas (milliard cubic meters)	0.3	3.4	6.2	47.2	200
Coal (million tons)	35.5	166.0	261.1	509.6	624
Cement (million tons)	1.8	5.7	10.2	45.5	95.2
Machine-tools (thousands)	2.0	58.4	70.6	155.9	(240)
Motor vehicles (thousands)	0.8	145.4	362.9	523.6	916
Tractors (thousands)	1.3	31.6	116.7	238.5	459
Mineral fertilizer (million gross tons)	0.1	3.2	5.5	13.9	55.4
All fabrics (milliard meters)	3.0	4.5	4.5	8.2	10.2
Knitwear (million units)	8.3	183	197	584	1134
Leather footwear (million pairs)	58	211	203	419	676
Beet sugar (million tons)	1.3	2.2	2.5	5.3	9.4
Radios and radiograms (thousands)	—	160	1072	4165	7800
Television sets (thousands)	—	0.3	11.9	1726	6700
Domestic refrigerators (thousands)	—	3.5	1.5	529	4100

Source: Alex Nove, "A Note on Growth Rates," in *An Economic History of the USSR,* Penguin Books/Pelican, New York, 1984, p. 398. The list up to 1960 was taken from a 50th anniversary article in *Kommunist* (No. 11, 1967); the figures for 1970 are from *Pravada,* 4 Feb. 1971. Reprinted with permission.

fast as possible. It required sacrifices and hardships, as well as mobilization. Where ideology failed to mobilize, new incentives were introduced, such as differentiated pay scales, special rewards, privileges, and other inducements. And where incentives were not adequate, intimidation and force were openly and blatantly resorted to — more so than the repressive and coercive practices we associate with the early phases of capitalism.

The destruction of Soviet factories, towns, and farms during World War II delayed industrialization until the 1950s, but by 1970 the remarkable growth of production in heavy industry (see Table 6-1) showed that the Soviet Union had indeed joined the ranks of industrialized nations. However, it was precisely at this stage — in the late 1960s — that communist ideology turned out to be an obstacle to modernization and to the achievement of the ultimate goal of communism: a consumer economy of relative abundance and hence economic equality.[9]

Imperative centralized planning was successful in the building of heavy industry because it related to tasks that could be well organized

9. On the Soviet economy, see Alec Nove, *An Economic History of the USSR* (New York: Penguin Books/Pelican, 1984).

through discipline and bureaucratic centralization. Highly regimented organizations deal well with impersonal and environmental forces: how to extract coal or oil, for instance. (Large capitalist corporations dealing with the same economic tasks in the earlier phases of industrialization also built large and centralized industrialization organizations.) But regimented and centralized control is not as appropriate for light industries or the production of household durable consumer goods (radios, refrigerators, electric irons, washers, dryers, etc.). It is even more inadequate for agricultural production and, most of all, for the production and distribution of consumer goods.

It was primarily in the light industries, the heart of modern technology, and in the production of consumer goods, that the Soviet economy began to lag in the 1970s. Tight controls and planning also had an adverse impact on agricultural production. Ideology did not permit a flexible and discriminating policy; it did not allow for market mechanisms, personal inducements, decentralization, and greater incentives among the farmers. It made the dialogue between consumers and producers difficult, and the consumers could not express their preferences without going counter to the ideology. On the one hand, the Soviet Union has surpassed the United States in the production of oil, steel, natural gas, and iron and may continue to draw ahead. Also, it is not only self-sufficient in energy but even exports large amounts. Yet it is a net importer in many agricultural goods, notably wheat and corn. And it remains far behind the Western world in computer technology, in communications, in car production, in household durable goods, and particularly in consumer goods.

The Inertia of Institutions As noted earlier, a key criterion of institutional capabilities is adaptability — whether or not institutions can adjust their organization to new societal or environmental needs or to new demands. The Soviet planning bureaucracy must be judged in these terms. It was originally founded to direct and supervise the early phase of industrialization and the collectivization of agriculture, but today it is confronted with meeting the requirements of the consumers and the consumers' preferences. Many argue, apparently even inside the Soviet Union, that these requirements cannot be met through centralization and authoritative imposition. Yet this is precisely what the rigid and centralized planning machinery continues to do: the millions of bureaucrats have taken over decision-making economic activities that could be better handled by local units and firms. They have expanded the scope of authoritative administrative imposition into areas where personal or group incentives would be more appropriate. They continue to stifle consumer demands even though it is the consumers who can effectively guide supply; they deprive local units of the freedom and the initiative to meet local demands.

Ideological rigidity prevents the Soviet leadership from providing private incentives to firms and managers in the form of monetary rewards (they do not have to be called profits) and some freedom to produce consumer goods that may be in high demand or very scarce. The same is true with agricultural production. Yet the leadership continues to reduce the number of collectives in favor of state farms and thus undermines the incentives that could energize the private farmers into producing more crops on their small plots. Institutional inertia compounds the ideological rigidity. Centralized planning gives little leeway to local and regional needs and precludes lateral agreements among firms and economic regions that could greatly facilitate both the procurement of materials and labor and the distribution of needed materials and consumer goods. Other communist regimes — including Hungary and Yugoslavia, to say nothing of China — have introduced measures for decentralization and private incentives. The Soviet leadership has been unable to do so and the recent efforts made in that direction have been constantly qualified or abandoned altogether.

Conclusion

The rigidity of the official ideology accounts for major institutional flaws. Any institutional changes that decentralize decisions on the economy and give people some freedom and initiative may weaken the power of the political elite, the CPSU, and may strengthen the new managerial groups. Decentralization might also promote centrifugal regional economic interests and claims that may assert themselves in tandem with ethnic ones in the various provinces and republics. Political power is, for all good Marxists, vulnerable to economic power. To allow economic freedoms and autonomy to develop is to open the prospects of challenging the monopoly of political power now in the hands of the CPSU. Any such challenge is a threat to the power of the top political leadership and the total conformity it has imposed thus far.

The Organization of Rights

Introduction

Civil rights, political rights, and economic rights comprise, as we noted in our discussion of democratic regimes in Chapter 5, the expanding range of what is commonly referred to today as human rights. In discussing human rights in totalitarian regimes in general and in the Soviet Union in particular, we will have to be brief. There is an inherent incompatibility between totalitarianism and the individual (and the rights associated with the individual); between the claims of the state and the claims of the individual. In totalitarian regimes all autonomous rights associated with the individual are harnessed to the broad societal goals defined and imposed by the political leadership.

According to a survey, totalitarian regimes score low on civil rights: freedom of expression, religion, the press, the existence of an independent judiciary, etc. The authors who undertook this survey graded political regimes from a perfect score of 1 to the lowest possible score of 7 (where civil liberties do not exist). Totalitarian regimes scored between 5.7 and 7: the Soviet Union, 6.0; Hungary, 5.7; Poland, 5.7; Cuba, 6.6; China, 6.9; East Germany, 6.9; and North Vietnam, 7.0. The score was equally low on political rights: the right to participate in free elections, freedom to form political parties and associations, freedom to be a candidate, and free political competition. The Soviet Union scored 6.6; North Vietnam, 7.0; Rumania, 7.0; East Germany, 7.0; Bulgaria, 7.0; Cuba, 6.9; Poland, 6.0; Hungary, 6.0; Czechoslavakia, 7.0; and China, 6.9.[10]

Civil and Political Rights

The Soviet communist regime is the oldest and most industrialized of all the totalitarian regimes. It is also one where the political practices that have developed over a long period of time have become institutionalized. According to the framers of the constitution of 1977, the Soviet state now represents all the people and not a class. The detailed list of individual rights that are given in that constitution bear a strong resemblance to those enumerated in many democratic regimes.

> Article 39. Citizens of the USSR enjoy in full the social, economic, political and personal rights and freedoms proclaimed and guaranteed by the Constitution of the USSR. . . .
>
> Enjoyment by citizens of their rights and freedoms must not be to the detriment of the interests of society or the state. . . .
>
> . . . Citizens of the USSR are guaranteed freedom of conscience, that is, the right to profess or not to profess any religion, and to conduct religious worship or atheistic propaganda. Incitement of hostility or hatred on religious grounds is prohibited.
>
> In the USSR, the church is separated from the state, and the school from the church.
>
> . . . Citizens of the USSR are guaranteed inviolability of the person. . . .
>
> . . . Citizens of the USSR are guaranteed inviolability of the home. . . .
>
> . . . The privacy of citizens, and of their correspondence, telephone conversations, and telegraphic communications is protected by law.[11]

It is an impressive list and it is generally copied by the constitutions of all other communist regimes.

How genuine is it? Some argue that it is genuine and that even if it is not enforced it constitutes the ultimate goal toward which the regime

10. C. C. Taylor and O. A. Jodich, *World Handbook of Political and Social Indicators* (New Haven, Conn.: Yale University Press, 1983).
11. The Constitution of the USSR, in Finer, op. cit., Articles 28–69.

strives. Others claim that the enumeration of rights is only rhetoric and propaganda calculated to impress outsiders and to gain converts to the ideology of communism and support for the Soviet Union. There are some constitutional provisions, however, that are clearly at odds with the ideology and the practice of democracies. Article 6 considers only one party, the Communist party, as the nucleus of the political regime. It "*determines* the general perspectives of the development of society . . . *directs* the great construction work of the Soviet people. . . ." The fundamental political rights, freedom of speech, association, writing, etc., are subordinate to the determination and direction of the Party. Article 50 guarantees freedom of speech but only when exercised "in accordance with the interests of the people in order to strengthen and develop the socialist system." Similarly, Article 51 grants the right of association if used "in accordance with the aims of building socialism." Article 62 enjoins all citizens to "safeguard the interests of the Soviet state and enhance its power and prestige."

The following provisions of the constitution (Articles 60–63) leave little doubt about the range of conformity and participation mandated upon all citizens:

> Citizens of the USSR are obliged to comply with the standards of socialist conduct, and uphold the honour and dignity of Soviet citizenship.
>
> . . . It is the duty of, and a matter of honour for, every able-bodied citizen of the USSR to work conscientiously in his chosen, socially useful occupation, and strictly to observe labour discipline. Evasion of socially useful work is incompatible with the principles of socialist society.
>
> . . . Citizens of the USSR are obliged to preserve and protect socialist property.
>
> . . . Citizens of the USSR are obliged to safeguard the interests of the Soviet state, and to enhance its power and prestige.
>
> Defence of the Socialist Motherland is the sacred duty of every citizen of the USSR.
>
> Betrayal of the Motherland is the gravest of crimes against the people.[12]

While the state and its agencies, including the judiciary, give individuals protection in their physical persons and their belongings and provide the means for adjudicating differences among them, no similar protection is available to them in their relationships with the state. Despite the rhetoric of the constitution, there is no freedom from arrest and preventive imprisonment. The principle of "no penalty without a law" is not observed, and penal legislation is interpreted loosely: for instance, a person can be arrested, imprisoned, or sent to labor camps for "anti-

12. Ibid.

Soviet" activities. Long detentions, sometimes in labor camps, continue to be administratively imposed, and nobody's house is free from seizures and searches. In spite of restrictions imposed by the Procurator General, the police and the KGB remain free to intimidate or arrest actual and potential dissenters. Freedom to move from one part of the country to another has been restored, but it remains under the surveillance of the police. Freedom to speak and to write remains under party control; so is the publication of books, pamphlets, and newspapers. Without the prior approval of the CPSU, nobody can speak out on any issue, and dissemination of one's opinions through the press is impossible since the party controls all the physical outlets for publication. To violate such controls would mean arrest, loss of one's job, detention, and ultimately a labor camp. Freedoms exist only as long as they are exercised in line with the goals of socialism as defined by the leadership of the CPSU. The criminal code forbids (among other things) the "dissemination of deliberately false fabrications slandering the Soviet State . . ." (Articles 190–191), "organization or active participation in group activities violating public order . . ." (Articles 190–193), and "anti-Soviet propaganda . . ." (Article 70). Such legislation gives wide latitude to the police and enforcement agencies.

The matter of labor camps and political prisoners has been a subject of controversy. In his *Gulag Archipelago* Alexander Solzenitsyn gave us a picture of thousands of labor camps dotting the land in the same way islands dot a sea. That book stunned the world by revealing that millions of people served sentences of five, ten, and fifteen years or more for "anti-Soviet" activities. Among them were political dissenters, conscientious objectors, deserters, former Russian prisoners of war, saboteurs, petty thieves, and even malingerers who refused to go to work or report to work on time. Under the control of the KGB, prisoners did heavy work in mining, forestry, and construction. Although many of the camps appear to have been dismantled since Stalin's death and the scope of arrests has diminished, the picture Solzhenitsyn gives us is still relevant now. The archipelago may have become only a lake but it is a reminder of the intimidation and force that the Soviet regime can use.

Today the number of political prisoners is relatively small (estimated at between 2,000 to 20,000) and political executions have virtually ceased. However, exile to Siberia or elsewhere, forced house arrest, and loss of job and pension continue to be practiced, and a number of minorities, including some two and a half million Jews, find it difficult to enjoy the protections the letter of the constitution provides.

It has been argued that the Russian people have the right to participate in the governing process. They do so, however, under conditions structured and initiated by the party. Neighborhood meetings, larger public meetings, and demonstrations are all organized by the Communist party. While people have the right to criticize, the criticism is orchestrated and also timed by the leadership. There are periods when criticism is allowed and periods when it is banned, and it is the leadership that decides whether it is open season or closed season. These rights of participation have been always touted as an indication of genuine direct democracy as compared to the superficiality of electioneering and national party contests in democracies. Yet, in substance these rights are duties and obligations imposed, sponsored, and organized by party loyalists rather than spontaneous forms of expression. They amount to induced participation, that is, mobilization. The citizenry is given the opportunity to conform, but unless they do conform, there is no opportunity to participate.

Economic Rights

Economic rights — the right to work, paid vacations, education, health care, etc. — again appear to be open to all. When the bolshevik revolution took place, it was claimed that it ushered in "economic democracy" with substantive economic rights and guarantees that were not provided in the political democracies, but the emphasis was on equality and material satisfactions, not political freedoms and opportunities.

The constitution of 1977 provides a comprehensive listing of rights (Article 40):

> Citizens of the USSR have the right to work . . . including the right to choose their trade or profession, type of job and work in accordance with their inclinations, abilities, training and education, with due account of the needs of society.
>
> This right is ensured by the socialist economic system.
>
> Citizens of the USSR have the right to rest and leisure. . . .
>
> . . . Citizens of the USSR have the right to health protection. This right is ensured by free, qualified medical care provided by state health institutions. . . .
>
> . . . Citizens of the USSR have the right to maintenance in old age, in sickness, and in the event of complete or partial disability or loss of the breadwinner. . . .[13]

There is hardly any doubt that economic rights have been expanded to cover more people and to provide a greater number of services. Planned housing construction for the Tenth Five-Year Plan was sufficient to accommodate 60 million people and construction was on target up to 1980. All health care is free and guaranteed by the state. In 1977 there were 120.8 hospital beds per 10,000 people, although there is some regional variation in the availability of health care. Education has been greatly expanded. During 1979–1980 there were 43 million students in grades 1–10. At higher levels students receive stipends tied to academic performance. Retirement benefits, nursing homes, and health care resorts are available and some are administered directly by the trade unions.

13. Ibid.

As we noted, however, democratic regimes have also made great strides in providing for economic and social rights and benefits during the last half century. Moreover, in some democracies (Sweden, Denmark, England, and France) welfare measures and entitlements provide a net of economic safety that is both very comprehensive and substantial. Even liberal democracies like the United States have developed comprehensive welfare, social security, and health programs that were unknown at the time of the bolshevik revolution.

Equality and equal distribution of income were originally stressed in the Soviet Union, but inequalities rapidly developed because of the incentive structure used to promote production during Stalin's industrialization drive in the 1930s, and they have remained a feature of the Soviet economy and society ever since. Special privileges have been granted to some, especially the political and other elite groups, but these special goods, services, and amenities have added to the distance between the few and the many. While economic rights provide a minimum floor for all, as in democracies, there are significant income inequalities, as in democracies. Furthermore, the implementation of economic rights is always at the discretion of the government and party officials. Entitlements are rights for the recipients who display political conformity. Political dissent, even in its mildest form, may deprive individuals of the economic rights they were promised. In summary, the security these rights provide for each and all is dependent upon "good citizenship."

Bibliography

Azrael, Jeremy. *Managerial Power and Soviet Politics*. Cambridge, Mass.: Harvard University Press, 1965.

Berman, Harold. *Justice in the USSR*. New York: Vintage Books, 1963.

Berman, Harold, and James W. Spindle. *Soviet Criminal Law and Procedures: The RSFSR Code*. Cambridge, Mass.: Harvard University Press, 1972.

Bialer, Seweryn. *Stalin's Successors: Leadership, Stability and Change in the Soviet Union*. New York: Cambridge University Press, 1980.

Black, Cyril. *The Transformation of Russian Society: Aspects of Social Change Since 1914*. Cambridge, Mass.: Harvard University Press, 1967.

Brzezinski, Zbigniew. *The Soviet Bloc: Unity and Conflict*. Cambridge, Mass.: Harvard University Press, 1971.

Brzezinski, Zbigniew, and Sam Huntington. *USA/USSR: Similarities and Contrasts: Convergence and Evolution*. New York: Viking, 1964.

Chapman, Brian. *Police State*. London: Pall Mall, 1979.

Cocks, Paul, Robert V. Daniel, and Nancy W. Heer (eds.). *The Dynamics of Soviet Politics*. Cambridge, Mass.: Harvard University Press, 1976.

Colton, Timothy. *Commissars, Commissioners and Civilian Authority*. Cambridge, Mass.: Harvard University Press, 1976.

———, *The Dilemma of Reform in the Soviet Union.* Council of Foreign Relations, 1984.

Conquest, Robert. *The Great Terror: Stalin Purges of the Thirties.* New York: Macmillan, 1968.

Cowden, Nell. *Soviet Agricultural Policy.* Kansas City, Mo.: Northwest Missouri State University, 1980.

Davies, Robert William. *The Industrialization of Soviet Russia.* Cambridge, Mass.: Harvard University Press, 1980.

Fainsod, Merle. *How Russia Is Ruled.* Cambridge, Mass.: Harvard University Press, 1958.

Feofanov, I. V. *Soviet Citizens and the Law.* Moscow: Navosti Press, 1976.

Gregory, Paul R. *Soviet Economic Performance & Structure.* New York: Harper & Row, 1981.

Hutchings, Raymond. *Soviet Economic Development.* Oxford, England: Basil Blackwell, 1982.

———, *The Soviet Budget.* Albany, N.Y.: State University of New York Press, 1983.

Kassof, Allen. *The Soviet Youth Program.* Cambridge, Mass.: Harvard University Press, 1966.

Kolkowicz, R. *The Soviet Military and the Communist Party.* Princeton, N.J.: Princeton University Press, 1967.

Lenin, V. I. *What Is to Be Done: Burning Questions of Our Movement.* New York: International Publishers, 1943. (First published in 1903.)

Medish, Vladimir. *The Soviet Union.* 2d ed. Englewood Cliffs, N.J.: Prentice-Hall, 1983.

Meyer, Alfred G. *The Soviet Political System: An Interpretation.* New York: Random House, 1965.

Nove, Alec. *An Economic History of the USSR.* New York: Penguin Books, 1984.

Reshetar, John S. Jr. *The Soviet Policy: Government & Politics in the USSR.* New York: Dodd, & Mead, 1971.

Scott, H. F. *The Armed Forces of the USSR.* 2d ed. Boulder, Colo.: Westview Press, 1981

Shapiro, Leonard B. *The Communist Party of the Soviet Union.* New York: Random House, 1960.

Simons, William B. (ed.). *The Soviet Codes of Law.* Rockville, Md.: Sijthoff & Noordhoff, 1980.

Skilling, H. Gordon, and F. Griffith (eds.). *Interest Groups in Soviet Politics.* Princeton, N.J.: Princeton University Press, 1971.

Solomon, Susan G. *Pluralism in the Soviet Union.* New York: St. Martin's Press, 1983.

Tucker, Robert (ed.) *Stalinism: Essays in Historical Interpretation.* New York: W. W. Norton, 1977.

Veselow, Nikolaie A. *The Communist Party and Mass Organizations in the USSR.* Moscow: Navosti Press, 1973.

7 Totalitarianism without Communism: Nazism and Fascism

Introduction

In briefly discussing fascism in Italy (1922–1944) and nazism in Germany (1933–1945), we are dealing with two noncommunist totalitarian movements that emerged and conquered political power in the interwar years, lasted for a relatively short time, and disappeared in military defeat. Nazism and fascism are often referred to as totalitarian regimes of the right, because they assumed power on behalf of many vested economic interests and against the left-wing parties and trade unions. Yet in many of their ideological and political manifestations, especially with regard to the role of the single-party, ideology, and mobilization, they bear a marked resemblance to communist totalitarian regimes. They are also similar in that the basic structural changes they made were in the direction of centralization and concentration of political power.

Centralization and Concentration

Decision making in Italy was centralized in the hands of the top governmental organs. In Germany the governments of the individual states were taken over by the central government. Thus federalism — one of the ways to divide power in democratic regimes — was set aside. Local governmental units were dismantled and taken over by the central government. In Italy the Minister of the Interior dismissed everybody in the provincial administration (the provincial assemblies) and appointed new administrators and local councils — all members of the Fascist party. In Germany the administration of the states and local units was put in the hands of an appointed official: the *Reichsstatthalter*.

There was no separation of powers, a hallmark of democracies, and command flowed from the top. Either through enabling acts or the direct assumption of powers, the government legislated by decree, and the legislative assemblies simply disappeared. Both the Reichstag in Germany and the Parliament in Italy lost (while they lasted) any role other than to unanimously endorse decisions already made by the governmental leaders who were also the party leaders. The Italian Parliament is the only one in history to have unanimously voted for its own abolition!

In both regimes executive and legislative functions were concentrated in the hands of the party leader, the Fuehrer or the Duce. In both regimes elections were controlled by the party leadership; all candidates were nominated by the party; and the voters could vote for only one candidate, who (understandably) received over 99 percent of the votes cast. The process was the same for referenda held on a number of issues in Germany and some in Italy, and all were approved overwhelmingly.

Both governments proceeded to destroy all existing or potential centers of opposition. All parties other than the Fascist or Nazi parties were outlawed. The Fascist laws passed between 1926–1928 withdrew permits from the publishers of all anti-Fascist newspapers, banned all organizations that might take a hostile position toward the regime, and inflicted penalties and imprisonment on all those who committed or "*who manifest the intention*" to commit acts that "*may* cause the subversion of the social, economic and national order." In Germany the Reconstruction Act of 1934 authorized the government to create a new constitutional law that gradually evolved to include the following: the suppression of all freedoms; censorship and the elimination of newspapers inimical to the regime; the establishment of people's courts to try political offenders; the subjugation of the judiciary; punishment of all forms of dissent; abolition of trade unions; the formation of new police organizations; and the establishment of racial laws that deprived Jews of their rights and ultimately ordained their destruction. In both regimes it was not only existing opposition and dissent that were suppressed, it was also the *potential* political dissent, which was to be nipped in the bud.

The Single Party

In both regimes the single party — the Fascist party in Italy and the Nazi party in Germany (the NASDP) — set up a highly centralized leadership and organized consent through intensive mobilization. Everything was organized along hierarchical lines with local, provincial, departmental, or state sections operating under a top executive committee headed by the Duce or the Fuehrer. Annual party congresses were convened only for the purpose of hearing and applauding the leader and confirming his policy guidelines.

The Fascist and Nazi parties had several things in common with the CPSU in the Soviet Union:

1. They monitored and controlled the government at all levels.
2. There were interlocking arrangements between party officials and governmental ones.
3. There was a wholesale infiltration of the government by party officials.
4. There was a subordination of all inferior organs, party and government, to the superior authorities and ultimately to the leader who acted both in the name of the government and the name of the party.
5. There was a careful network of front organizations through which the party recruited new members and leaders.
6. There was an increasing use of intimidation and force to ensure the compliance of both party members and government personnel.

In both regimes, despite the apparent duality between the government and the party, there was only one power: the power of the party leadership, sometimes exercised independently of the government and sometimes through governmental offices.

The structure of command was therefore very similar, although not identical, to the Soviet pattern. In Nazi Germany the party gained ascendancy over the state. The state was considered to be only part of the party; it was created by and acted for the party in the role of a subordinate organization. The party was the elite group that spoke on behalf of the people and for the people. In Italy the state appeared to be above the party: "Everything in the State; everything for the State; nothing outside the State" was the celebrated dictum of Mussolini. Yet the Fascist party infiltrated the state and all its organs through massive appointments of Fascists until it became only a shell that the party used to legitimize itself and to infuse with Fascist purpose and substance.

The Leader — Absolutism

The force that amalgamated the people, the party, and the state into one entity was the leader. Leadership was defined in terms of the personal characteristics of the leader — his charisma. He possessed the ability to both command and represent; to elicit both full support and total obedience; to infuse the people, the party, and the state with will and give guidance to all. The leader is not a "sovereign" that imposes itself upon others: "Leader is the Party; the Party is the Leader"; "Leader is the opposite of Sovereign" — these are not phrases taken from George Orwell's *1984*. They were the actual slogans used in Nazi Germany by Hitler and other leaders for the party. The Fuehrer was portrayed not as an arbitrary and supreme commander, but rather as he who *follows* the goals set by the people, even if the people do not know what the goals are. The "Leader . . . *knows* the goals and the direction." This is what became known in Germany as the *Fuehrerstaat*, the leader-state. It revealed the starkest form of absolutism cast in mystical terms.

The Duce in Italy claimed the same qualities. He represented both the state and the party and embodied the interests, goals, and ambitions of the nation and the people. He "never sleeps"; "with closed eyes he reads our innermost thoughts"; "he knows everything"; "he is the pride and honor of the nation."

The absolutism of the leader was the substance of the new constitutional order in the Nazi and the Fascist totalitarian regimes. Actually it was no order at all. It prescribed no procedures and no goals other than those emanating from one person, and we should note the differences vis-à-vis Soviet totalitarianism. For example, even though Stalin as Secretary General established his personal rule with the aid of the police, it was never rationalized as a new legal order and did not become part of the Soviet legal order. In fact, after Stalin's death personal leadership and personal government were sharply criticized as a deviation from the rules guiding the CPSU and as contrary to Marxist doctrine. For nazism and fascism, however, personal leadership was the very essence of the legal order.

The Governing Elite

Both Nazis and Fascists attempted, like the Communists, to fashion a new political elite that absorbed or subordinated others. But they were not as successful, and for a number of reasons. In both Germany and Italy the Nazis and the Fascists did not "make" a revolution, as the Communists had in Russia, even though they appeared to be revolutionary and anti-regime parties. They were helped into power by older, more traditional elites: the President of the Republic in Germany or the King in Italy, the army, the business community, the conservative political leaders and parties, and even the churches and the Parliament. Their revolution was "legal." They took over the state. They did not promise, as Lenin did, to "smash it to pieces." They accepted many of the formal instruments of governance and used them. Hence both the Fascists and the Nazis accommodated many segments of the existing elites, at least at first. In Italy, for instance, the monarchy, though reduced to a symbol, continued nonetheless to be feared by the Duce and the Fascists because it was widely supported by the army and the aristocracy; the army itself was not tampered with and many of the old generals continued in their posts throughout World War II. The organization of the economy, even if calculated to impose the will of the state, allowed the industrialists and businessmen wide autonomy. Also, despite their efforts, the Fascists never managed to undermine the autonomy of the Catholic church and its organizations, even among the young.

In Germany, the older, more traditional groups also found a niche in the party while others gave it their support. The Catholic church, while neutralized, retained its autonomy and so did the army until the beginning of World War II. As for the industrial and business community, in spite of state intervention and war time controls imposed by the Nazis, it too enjoyed a great deal of independence, especially when we compare its position to its counterparts in the Soviet Union after 1917. Neither the Fascists nor the Nazis attempted to eliminate the ownership of property and to socialize the means of production as the CPSU had done. In short, the Nazi and Fascist parties represented a cross section of the society. They were not the avant-garde of a new class.

Recruitment

A common characteristic of fascism and nazism is that they both appealed overwhelmingly to the youth. Every effort was made to "form" the young people as early as possible and train them into the new order of the two respective regimes. Both countries established an elaborate network of youth organizations for children ranging in age from under ten up to eighteen. It was only at eighteen that membership in the party and a career of political leadership became open and at this stage special schools were set up to train youngsters.

The members of the Nazi party were selected on the basis of their courage, their unswerving loyalty to the leader, obedience to the higher authorities in the party, anti-semitism, and racial purity (an "impurity" that dated back to 1800 made a person ineligible). The following skill categories (job description, we would say) were sought:

1. The *coercers*, or experts in the use of force. They were recruited primarily for the SS in Germany and the militia in Italy, which numbered about 700,000. In both countries, the military had their own source of recruitment, the young army draftees, but in Germany "the best" among the young were increasingly attracted to the elite paramilitary formations (the SS), which grew rapidly in strength.
2. The *administrators*. These people worked within the central organization of the party (the counterpart of the Central Apparat of the CPSU). They gradually occupied the various local, provincial, regional, and national bureaucratic and governmental positions that replaced the old governmental elites.
3. The *ideologues*. They were the propagators of the ideology, the interpreters of the will of the leader, and the experts in propaganda. This group included prospective philosophers like Carl Schmitt or Alfred Rosenberg in Germany as well as journalists and manipulators of the mass media. It also included some intellectuals, even teachers, who both in Germany and in Italy had made a personal commitment to propagate the new doctrine and adhere to it without mental reservations.

Nazism and Fascism

Ideology

Both nazism and fascism projected ideologies as total as communism; they both organized disciplined political parties and relied on the single party to monopolize their control, mobilize the people, penetrate the society, and impose their vision; and they both tried to integrate all the societal forces into a uniform mass. This ultimate goal was to get everybody to march to one and the same tune played by the party leadership. This was the meaning of the term *Gleichschaltung* ("marching in step").

Unlike the communists, neither the Nazis nor the Fascists, however, had a formalized body of doctrine to fall back on. Their ideology was a hodgepodge put together from many sources: antiliberalism, anticommunism, racism, communitarianism, socialism, antiparliamentarism, all wrapped together in one package labeled "nationalism." What characterized both was a profound irrationalism — a rejection of the values of the scientific age and a direct appeal to will, vision, and instinct. The Fascists went back to Roman authoritarianism and the Nazis reverted to early tribalism looking for unifying symbolisms and traditions. National unity and the subordination of the individual to the state were the two major ideological propositions in both regimes.

For the Fascists the legacy of the Roman Empire evoked conquests in the Mediterranean and North Africa; for the Nazis nationalism meant the domination and perhaps the extinction of inferior races and supremacy in Europe and ultimately in the world. Nationalism became an ideology, transformed into a powerful political movement, that promised conquest and subordination and proclaimed it "natural" for a superior race to dominate inferior ones (which was in essence the character of German nationalism under the Nazis). As a result, it lacked the universalistic appeal of communism. Today, only fragments of the Nazi or Fascist ideology remain and surface here and there: racism, nationalism, communitarianism, antiparliamentarism, or authoritarian leadership. Efforts to bring them together again into one unifying and mobilizing ideology under a single leader or party have failed thus far.

Nazism: Mobilization and Organization of Consent

Upon Hitler's assumption of power in January 1933 the mobilization of the German society began in earnest. First there was the elimination of all actual and potential centers of opposition. Then there was the establishment of a network of new associations, to replace or take over the existing ones: cultural associations, athletic organizations, philanthropic associations, literary clubs, guilds, and professional and educational associations. In 1935, only two years later, Nazi organizations had mushroomed in every sector of the society: the Nationalist Socialist Automobile Corps, the Hitler Youth, the National Socialist Women's Association, the National Socialist Students Association. the National Socialist University Teachers Association, the Association of German Jurists, the National Socialist German Medical Association, the National Socialist Association of German Engineers, the National Socialist Organization of German Veterans, the German Labor Front, and the Strength Through Joy organizations (to structure the leisure time of the people).[1]

All independent sources of information and opinions were destroyed. The party simply took them over or established new ones. Daily and weekly newspapers, radio stations, scientific and literary journals — every word addressed to or written for the public was generated by party officials or persons operating closely under their control. There were only two exceptions: mouth-to-mouth communication, preferably in a whisper, and the pastoral letters occasionally issued by the higher clergy for their flock.

With all communications securely in the hands of the party, mobilization intensified. The party membership rose rapidly; the youth and popular organizations, including the Hitler Youth and the Labor Front, quickly gained new converts; the nation as a whole endorsed policy measures submitted to it in referendums; annual party congresses assumed the character of national holidays; new symbolisms and salutes were introduced to give tangible evidence of acceptance; and acts of violence against opponents or Jews provided solid proof of the determination of the Nazi leadership and the loyalty of the rank and file.

Penetration and Imposition

The full impact of mobilization can never be felt unless it is accompanied by imposition and penetration. No totalitarian political party can grow, any more than an army can "march," if it leaves behind powerful centers of resistance. The Nazis successfully penetrated the trade unions and restructured their organizations; they totally penetrated the educational system; they destroyed the free press and restructured it; through their youth organizations they penetrated the family and shifted the loyalties of the children to the party, the Fuehrer, and the state; they also penetrated the home by organizing leisure time activities; they gained control of all agencies of the state through direct assumption of official duties or through a careful system of offices "interlocking" the Party and the State. When such interlocking did not work, the party imposed its will through direct orders. The rationale was that the party had the right to give orders to the new state since it was the party that created the state in the first place.

For a while, the army seemed to be beyond the control of the party. It had formed a solid and autonomous organization with its own symbols and loyalties and a history that often had put it above the state itself. By 1934, however, officers were required to take an oath of loyalty directly to the Fuehrer. Although the top generals and the reconstituted General Staff maintained their aloofness, it was not to last long. By 1938 many of the top generals were discredited and new ones were promoted by the

1. In Fritz Morstein Marx, *The Government of the Third Reich*, 2d ed. (New York: McGraw-Hill, 1937), p. 69.

Nazis. By 1941 the army came directly under the domination of the party leaders. The regular army was gradually subordinated to the elite SS formations. Hitler himself assumed full command of the armed forces on the Russian Front, and a combination of personal loyalty to him plus intimidation from the SS and the Gestapo subdued the army into silence and obedience. It lost its autonomy and for all practical purposes became absorbed into the party.

The churches, both Protestant and Catholic, maintained a certain autonomy all along, but their field of action was limited. At the beginning there was full acquiescence of the Nazi takeover of power — for the Catholic church it meant anticommunism and for the Protestants, stability and the reassertion of national identity. Early antireligious demonstrations and even acts of violence by Nazis tapered off and in return the churches maintained their silent neutrality (even complicity) with the new state. There were few overt condemnations of the initial racial laws and the anti-Semitic acts of vandalism or, for that matter, of the concentration camps and the exterminations that took place. The churches withdrew from all lay and temporal activities, allowing the party and the state the monopoly of education, mobilization, and socialization. Many religious leaders found themselves unable to resist the spiritual and ideological claims of the Nazi state, although resistance did crop up whenever the Nazis tried to directly control their organizations or set up rival Nazi-inspired church organizations. World War II, particularly the phase against the Soviet Union, put heavy constraints on the clergy because any criticism of the state would be considered unpatriotic and treasonous. Criticisms that did surface were muted by intimidation and occasionally force. At best the churches maintained a very narrow autonomy.

Intimidation and Force

The political party was the major vehicle for mobilization, constantly organizing demonstrations and overseeing activities in every locality, every governmental office, every school, and even the family. But besides mobilization there was intimidation by the police force, which became virtually a state within the party, operating under Hitler's deputy, Heinrich Himmler, who controlled both the SS units and the Gestapo.

By 1938 the police had assumed a predominant position. A number of commentators refer to the rise of the "SS state"; others speak of the "bureaucratization of terror" — the development of an intricate bureaucratic machinery to intimidate potential opponents and to sanction nonconformist behavior. Prevention of dissent through massive arrests, direct acts of violence, and summary executions became commonplace. The SS and the Gestapo administered justice swiftly and directly. The Office of the Security Police became something like a parallel government with various departments and a vast bureaucracy operating under it. Specialized bureaus dealt with communism, churches, religious sects, homosexuals, "Austrian affairs," and the concentration camps, as well as with economic, agrarian, and sociopolitical problems. They also supervised broadcasting, the press, and general intelligence gathering.

The scope of police action was comprehensive and it spread throughout the whole of Europe in the wake of the German armies. Special SS units were entrusted with the job of cleaning up the conquered territories, transporting prisoners and civilians into labor camps, and collecting Jews and shipping them off to the death camps, which were also operated by the SS. At home, activities such as "seditious behavior," "defamation of the swastika," "insulting leaders," or "being asocial" were dealt with swiftly. Looting, tortures, indiscriminate killings, and deaths by starvation were all justified in the name of protecting the state. As early as 1935 some fifteen concentration camps had been set up in Germany, and the number multiplied when the German armies moved into Eastern Europe. The reality of the German state was beginning to lie with the police. Its omnipresence, together with the "Gulag Archipelago" it built even within Germany at first and in the great part of Europe between 1941–1944, was the best instrument of intimidation and the most irrefutable evidence of its power. Side by side with the leader-state there grew the police-state. "The establishment of concentration camps as instruments of both reeducation and terror," writes Karl Bracher in the most authoritative study of the German dictatorship, "and their development into pillars of mass arrests and mass extermination were simply consequences of [this] totalitarian authority. It went considerably beyond that of the Stalinist system of the 1930s."[2]

Can a system that relies on arbitrary and discretionary will, force, and terror ever become institutionalized? Only if the ideology and the leader allow it, some will answer. But if the very source of the ideology lies in the arbitrary and capricious will of the leader, can stable political structures ever develop? In the last analysis, one of the major differences between nazism and Stalinism may well be that the first was not amenable to any kind of institutionalization — nazism was inherently hostile to routinization and the establishment of norms regulating behavior. Stalinism, on the other hand, might be viewed as a violation of the framework of rules inherent in Marxism. Nazism was bound to remain an explosive ideology and force until it had reached a point of self-destruction by virtue of the very forces it had set in motion. Soviet communism, on the other hand, despite Stalin, carried the seeds of an institutionalized and structured political behavior even if totalitarian. Nazism was unrestrained and unrestrainable; Soviet communism recognizes institutional restraints even when it breaks them!

2. Karl Bracher, *The German Dictatorship* (London: Weidenfeld & Nicholson, 1970), p. 233.

Fascism: Mobilization and Organization of Consent

The Italian fascists mobilized, penetrated, and imposed their will on all the societal forces as much as nazism did. The steps taken in the two regimes were parallel: destruction of old political parties and trade unions; total control of the press and all media of communication; and the penetration of all associations: economic, philanthropic, athletic, professional, youth, and educational. Every effort was made to infiltrate and regiment people both at work and in their leisure time. The *Dopolavoro*, a Fascist-controlled national organization with the same overall purpose as the Strength Through Joy Nazi movement, organized the leisure time of the Italians by providing entertainment. It had almost 5 million members. The Ministry of Popular Culture controlled all media and attempted to promote a Fascist culture. In the universities professors were required to take an oath of loyalty to the Fascist party. At least 75,000 university students belonged to the Fascist University Organization, preparing for positions in the party and watching carefully over the performance of professors and non-Fascist students.

By the mid-thirties more than half of all Italians between the ages of ten and sixty were involved in activities and organizations controlled by the Fascist party. Fascism was a far greater mobilizing force than any other movement in the history of Italy, including the movement for national unification throughout the latter part of the nineteenth century.

Nazism and Fascism: Organization of Interests

While all communist regimes that came to power had a blueprint of the economy and a plan for the relationship between the state and economic interests, nazism and fascism did not. "To endorse an economic program," Hitler stated in 1928, "would be the most foolish thing I could do."[3] The Nazis resorted instead to broad slogans such as the "supremacy of politics over economics," "the subordination of materialistic incentives to communitarian values, and "the harnessing of the economy to national goals." Both the Nazis and the Fascists borrowed from the antiliberal and anticapitalist doctrine and often from the communist vocabulary.

When they came to power the Nazis and Fascists tried to impose their ideology on the economic elites. They used some of the techniques of destruction and restructuring, as well as penetration and imposition, that we discussed with regard to the Communist party in the Soviet Union. But they never went as far in the takeover of economic power. While some economic interests were subordinated to the state and the

3. Marx, op. cit., p. 150.

party, others lived side by side with the party, and few were destroyed. The heart of the economic system continued to be private property and private incentives (and profits) and neither big capital, the bourgeoisie, or the farmers were singled out for expropriation or destruction. Labor was the only sector that came under the direct control of the party and the state.

The relationship between the Fascist and the Nazi regimes and the economy show some of the limits of Nazi and Fascist totalitarianism. They did not destroy the centers of economic power. Instead, they established close relationships, (even if they claimed supremacy) with the industrial and entrepreneurial forces and guaranteed their property rights and profits. Since the capitalist order of the economy was maintained, business and industrial interests could coexist with the state and the single party. In fact, powerful economic interests managed to attract the Nazi and Fascist political elite into a symbiotic relationship that was profitable to both. Yet this cooperation between economic elites and the political leadership imposed restraints and limitations on the latter, and also injected potential conflicts within the political elite about the division of rewards and spoils. Under such circumstances, totalitarian control encountered far greater obstacles. The centers of economic power were not swept away, as in the Soviet Union and other communist regimes.

NAZISM, FASCISM, AND COMMUNISM: A COMPARISON

The forms of totalitarianism that we have discussed — the communist regime now well entrenched in the Soviet Union (with many offshoots elsewhere) and the Nazi and Fascist regimes, long defunct — show remarkable similarities. Their official ideology projects a new order of things; a strong and well-disciplined party implements the ideology; a governing elite speaks for the masses; the official ideology and the political party reach out to encompass and subdue the societal forces and create conformity; and intensive participation and mobilization are very much in evidence.

Yet the differences are profound and fundamental. We have already hinted at some:

The Nazi and Fascist regimes were leader-regimes. They were based on the leadership of one person and the organization of supports and government were built around the leader. As a result, they lacked institutionalization. They were likely to disappear when the leader did, although fascism and nazism collapsed in military defeat.

The social classes that supported the Nazis and Fascists were radically different from those that backed communism.

The Nazis and Fascists were supported by the middle- and lower-middle-class strata and received generous support from elite groups: the military, the landowners, the bankers, and the industrialists. In contrast, all communist movements turned to the workers, the underprivileged, and the peasantry for support.

The type and nature of support had a direct bearing on the organization of political power under nazism, fascism, and communism. In the case of nazism and fascism political power stemmed from an alliance between many of the elite groups and the middle and lower classes, but, as we noted, alliances create reciprocal restraints. The Nazis and the Fascists were never able to overcome them; they remained bound to the forces that supported them. They did not destroy the centers of economic power; they maintained the capitalist structure and defended the property-owning classes. In contrast, the Communist party, by appealing to the workers and the poor, were able to mobilize them into politics for the first time. From the very beginning, there were limits on the totalist reach of the Nazis — their totalitarian regime had to face powerful enclaves that at times were more difficult to penetrate and occupy than it was to occupy the neighboring countries. On the other hand, the communists had only enemies, and it was easier to deal with them!

Nazism and fascism in Germany and Italy were primarily political revolutions, while the communist revolutions have been both political *and* economic. They called for a total restructuring not only of political loyalties but also of economic relationships.

However, the most basic difference lies in the ideologies they projected. Communism is an egalitarian and universalistic ideology, based on rational propositions. It is addressed to the resolution of social and economic problems in order to satisfy human imperatives, such as freedom, individual dignity, equality, and economic well-being. Communism appeals to everybody everywhere — it is universalistic. Conversely, Nazism and Fascism were addressed to the specific circumstances and the grievances of their respective societies. In Germany the ideology also promised the domination of one nation, defined in biological terms, over all others. Since nazism and fascism set forth the permanent dictatorship of the few over the many, it lacked the universalistic appeal that communism generated. Moreover, the intensity of Nazi nationalism was neutralized by the intensity of the hostility it provoked among other nations and peoples.

Yet, another significant difference can be found in the

respective institutions they built. Communist regimes, even when the personality of the leader is of critical importance, as was the case with Stalin in the Soviet Union, Mao in China, and Castro in Cuba, establish mechanisms for collective deliberation and decision making among the top leaders. Collective leadership provides for succession and a degree of internal restraint that is inherent in the whole process of collective deliberation — even if only at the very top. The General Secretary in the Soviet Union speaks for the leadership — not for himself. In contrast, the government structures built by the Fascists and Nazis relied on the personality and the leadership of one man. The leadership of Hitler and Mussolini knew no bounds and was not subject to any procedural or substantive restraints. They represented the people because of their foresight and their superior, even if intuitive, understanding of history. It is difficult to see how such intensely personal regimes can establish stable institutions over a period of time.

Communist totalitarianism may have greater capabilities of survival and institutionalization. It is based on a broad, coherent, and universalistic ideology; it undertakes a drastic overhaul of all societal forces; it organizes a carefully selected new elite and gives it the mechanisms of participation and consultation; it sets forth rational and objective standards of success in the society and the economy that serve to measure achievement or failure, no matter how much manipulation of the ideology may slant objective reality. Not so with nazism and fascism, which were intensely emotional and nationalist movements. They represented a reaction against the value of rational discourse, equality, and universality among all people and nations. They embodied a frenzied reaction against liberal values, and the passion that they generated — especially in Germany — accounted both for their early successes and their ultimate destruction.

Bibliography

Allen, William Sheridan. *The Nazi Seizure of Power: The Experience of a Single German Town, 1930–1935.* New York: Quadrangle, 1965.

Aron, Robert. *The Vichy Regime.* New York: Putnam, 1958.

Bracher, Karl D. *The German Dictatorship: The Origin, Structure and Effects of National Socialism.* London: Weidenfeld & Nicholson, 1970.

Bullock, Allan. *Hitler: A Study in Tyranny.* New York: Harper & Row, 1971.

Delzel, Charles F. (ed.). *Mediterranean Fascism, 1919–1945.* New York: Walker, 1971.

Gregor, A. James. *Interpretation of Fascism.* Berkeley, Calif.: University of California Press, 1974.

Hohne, Heinz. *The Order of Death's Head: The Story of the SS.* London: Sacks Warberg, 1969.

Kedward, H. R. *Fascism in Western Europe, 1900–1945.* Glasgow, Scotland: Blaki, 1969.

Krausnic, Helmut, Hans Buchheim, and Martin Broszat. *Anatomy of the SS State.* New York: Walker, 1968.

Laqueur, Walter (ed.). *Fascism: A Reader's Guide.* Berkeley, Calif.: University of California Press, 1976.

Lyttleton, Adrian. *Italian Fascism: From Pareto to Gentile.* New York: Harper Torchbooks, 1973.

McKale, Donald. *The Nazi Party Courts.* Lawrence, Kan.: Kansas University Press of Kansas, 1974.

Newmann, Franz. *Behemoth: The Structure and Practice of National Socialism, 1933–1944.* New York: Octagon, 1963.

Nolte, Ernest. *Three Faces of Fascism: Action Francaise, Italian Fascism and National Socialism.* New York: NAL, 1969.

Overy, R. J. *The Nazi Economic Recovery.* London: Macmillan, 1982.

Paxton, Robert O. *Vichy: The Old Guard and the New Order.* New York: Columbia University Press, 1982.

Payne, Stanley G. *Fascism: Comparison and Definition.* Madison: University of Wisconsin Press, 1980.

Speier, Hans. *Inside the Third Reich.* New York: Macmillan, 1970.

Stephenson, Jill. *The Nazi Organization of Women.* New York: Barnes & Noble, 1981.

Tannenbaum, Edward R. *The Fascist Experience: Italian Society and Culture, 1922–1945.* New York: Basic Books, 1972.

Vajada, Michaly. *Fascism as a Mass Movement.* London: Allison & Busby, 1976.

8 Communist Regimes: Variations and Crises

Introduction

Most communist regimes have been founded on the basis of the Soviet model. During 1944–1945 all Eastern European countries and the Balkans, with the exception of Greece, established communist regimes. In 1949 the Chinese communists took over the government, and in 1961 Castro proclaimed Cuba to be a Marxist state. Since then Vietnam, Mongolia, Ethiopia, Angola, and Mozambique have joined the ranks. In Central America, communist-led guerrilla movements in Nicaragua and El Salvador are either in complete control of the state, as many claim to be the case in Nicaragua, or may gain control, as some claim to be the case in El Salvador. North Korea is also communist, but the rule of Kim Il-Sung is closer to a personal dictatorship. All in all there are seventeen established communist regimes today (see Appendix A).

Although inspired by the same ideology, there are many variations among communist regimes, and even if they profess to follow the Soviet model there are many differences between them and the Soviet prototype. But above all, virtually all the communist regimes that were established after World War II have faced and continue to face serious crises, primarily those of legitimacy and institutionalization. As a result, they have been unable to establish their control over the society, gain public acceptance, and develop solid institutional mechanisms of governance.

We have portrayed totalitarian regimes in terms of their ultimate goals and aspirations. In their drive for power they invade all the old institutions and ideas in order to totally revamp them. Sometimes, however, they march too fast, leaving behind them large pockets of potential resistance, and they may find it difficult or impossible to neutralize them. This is one source of crisis they may face.

Another source of crisis relates to serious conflicts within the political elite itself, conflicts about developmental strategy, about the new institutions being set up, and about the tempo of economic modernization. Since most communist-led revolutions have succeeded in relatively underdeveloped societies, the particular strategy for modernization becomes of critical importance. The governing elites even within the party may split; it happened in the Soviet Union in the 1920s and it seems to have been the major source of crisis in China after Mao came into power. In Russia the CPSU managed to control the factional disputes that developed and Stalin implemented his modernization scheme through drastic socialization of the economy, central planning, and collectivization of agriculture, but the Chinese Communist party has not been able to do the same. Divisive strategies about economic modernization are constantly being reflected in the organization and structure of the institutions — they become crises of institutionalization.

A third source of crisis is the need to consolidate not only the power of the new elite but also that of the society that went through a revolution. The major problem is the disparity between the utopian ideology and goals that led a movement to success and the fulfillment of the social and economic everyday needs. People must be fed and clothed, transportation must be adequate, health care and education must be provided, there should be work for all, and the goods the people need should be available. The revolutionary elite may be hard pressed to adjust to these new and pragmatic requirements. In 1921 when Lenin discovered that the Soviet economy was in a state of collapse he introduced market incentives and freedoms in commerce, agriculture, and manufacturing in order to revive it, but many party members were deeply disillusioned by this move. Some even committed suicide. The dichotomy between revolutionary and utopian goals versus utilitarian and pragmatic (often economic) considerations constitutes an endemic source of crisis, especially in the years immediately following the takeover of political power.

There is also a fourth source of crisis that is typical not only of totalitarian regimes but other political systems as well: personal conflicts among the top leaders. To the degree to which the institutions put in place by a revolutionary regime have not crystallized into accepted rules for the resolution of conflict, (i.e., to the degree to which they have not gained legitimacy), personal conflicts are difficult to contain or resolve. This type of crisis played an important role in the CPSU between the death of Lenin and the ascendancy of Stalin (1924–1927), but it seems to have been circumscribed since Stalin's death. It has been equally important in China even when Mao, the "Great Helmsman," controlled the ship of state.

Inability of a revolutionary party to do away with pockets of resistance and to integrate the society, severe conflicts about modernization strategy, the built-in contradiction between the revolutionary forces and those favoring consolidation and governmental authority, and personal antagonisms — these are the major sources of crisis in a totalitarian regime. They invariably account for a crisis of legitimacy, which in turn leads to withdrawal of supports that may range from simple indifference to overt opposition. It is manifested in a loss of confidence in the leadership and in the institutions of governance. In this chapter we will survey the crises in Poland, China, and Yugoslavia, all communist and totalitarian regimes, and we will conclude with a discussion of Castroism in Cuba.

The Crisis in Poland

The crisis in Poland and what appears to have been a breakdown of a communist totalitarian regime is due to three separate but mutually reinforcing reasons:

1. A strong feeling of nationalism held by the Poles against Soviet presence and control, even if indirect. Since the Polish Communist party increasingly became the spokesman for the Soviet Union, it also became the target of Polish nationalism.
2. The presence of a powerful and separate organization within the regime. With its autonomous powers and the material means of organizing and gaining supports, the Catholic church has identified itself with Polish independence and Polish nationalism.
3. The economic crisis that developed in the mid-seventies that transformed the disillusionment of the workers into overt opposition against the regime.

Gradually the Communist party lost its ability to mobilize and regiment the workers who, under the direction of Lech Walesa, formed their own union — Solidarity — and began to make demands upon the state. First there were economic demands concerning wages, prices, hours of work, and conditions of work, and then there were political demands concerning freedoms and political representation through agencies other than the Communist party. As a result, a parallel and independent political organization began to develop within the regime. It challenged the monopoly of the Communist party and soon translated its demands into militant action. There were local, regional, and nationwide strikes that threatened the stability of the government. The members of the Communist party, all Polish nationalists at heart, wavered. It was the first crack in Poland's totalitarian shield.

The workers' protests and organizations, however, could not have manifested themselves without the existence of the Catholic church and its special position in the regime. It had maintained its autonomy and had kept its distance from the Communist party. It had a large following, and it increasingly became the symbol of Polish nationalism. Because of this factor, the workers' movement could operate in a friendly environment. The Communist party gradually lost control, first over the citizenry and then over its own members and cadres. As a result, the regime appealed directly to the military, to establish internal order and avert outright intervention by the Soviet army. A military dictatorship and martial law were instituted in December 1981 and formally speaking it lasted until the spring of 1984. In reality, however, it continues to exist today.

The crucial factor that accounts for the crisis and the breakdown of the communist regime in Poland is the position that the Catholic church has enjoyed as a separate and autonomous force. The communist regime has been unable to bring the church under control. As long as it is allowed to compete for the loyalties of the citizens and to mobilize them, the conflict will continue and so will the crisis of the regime.

Yugoslavia: Crisis or Breakdown?

The blueprint of the Yugoslav communist regime that emerged after the liberation of the country and the elimination of all opposition (1944–1946) was but a photocopy of the Soviet model. Both with regard to the organization of the state and the organization of the Communist party, it was a totalitarian regime. The position of the six federated republics — Serbia, Croatia, Slovenia, Bosnia, Macedonia, and Montenegro — and the two provinces — Vojvodina and Kosovo (in Serbia) — was similar to that of the republics in the Soviet Union, except that they were not formally granted the "right to secede." The Communist party, which later became the League of Communists of Yugoslavia (LCY), adopted democratic centralism, assumed the role of the avant-garde of the proletariat, became guardian of the new communist society, and, as in the period of Stalinism, remained under the personal control and rule of its leader, Marshal Tito. Its ideological inspiration was to refashion the society and to follow the path of the older (it turned out the bigger) brother in building socialism and in confronting the "forces of imperialism."

Domestic factors and the dispute with the Soviet leadership accounted for the gradual loosening of totalitarianism. The dispute with the Soviet Union (1948–1949) called for new ideological and modernization formulas to oppose Stalinism, and it was accomplished by decentralizing the economy, the bureaucracy, and the state apparatus. The domestic factors involved the particular nationalisms of the various units of the federation and their insistence on greater autonomy from the central organs of the government, including the LCY.

Space does not permit a detailed account of the development of Yugoslavia's economic, state-administrative, and party institutions ever since the Soviet-Yugoslav split of 1949. However, three major trends should be emphasized: (1) The growth of regional nationalisms, (2) economic decentralization in the name of self-management, and (3) the weakening of the cohesiveness of the party and its gradual loss of control over decision making. Each one of these developments began to be reflected increasingly in the pluralization or the fragmentation of the societal and the political forces.

Regional Nationalisms

As we have seen, a federal system can provide the central government with much power as long as that power derives from the people and as long as decisions (even within a limited area) can be made by simple majority in the federal representative assemblies. In the United States, Australia, Canada, West Germany, Switzerland, and other federal regimes, including India and Nigeria (when it was a democracy), this has been the case. In the Soviet Union, on the other hand, federalism is vitiated by the dominance of the central government, the overlap between federal and state ministries giving primacy to the former, the ubiquitous control of a highly centralized party that claims to speak for the Soviet people, and the interpretation of democratic centralism according to which lower organs (the federated units) obey the higher ones — the Soviet government.

In Yugoslavia the six republics and the two provinces began to press for more powers, requesting that all problems that affected them should be discussed with them until an agreement was reached. Since 1966, representation of these regions has evolved in the direction of equal representation in the Federal Executive Council (which corresponds by and large to the Soviet Council of Ministers), and in the office of the president, which has become a collegial body of regional representatives in the federal bureaucracy. Gradually the six republics and the two provinces "colonized" the legislature and the executive. The preparation of legislation now requires prolonged consultations between the representatives of the regions until an agreement is reached. Many decisions are made through a unanimous vote. Although there are also provisions for a two-thirds vote, the practice is not to act until there is unanimity. Thus each republic and province has veto power over all federal decision making, which means that the central authority does not have the power to act for the whole country.

While the nationalities have been pressing their claims for representation, they have been equally insistent on diluting the powers of the central authority. The presidency consists of nine members and the presidents are "rotated" — that is, each nationality takes turns in having one of its own members in office. The major function of the presidency is to promote consultation among representatives of the nationalities. Since the federal government — the Federal Executive Council — must provide equal representation to all national units, its formation is a laborious process with an eye to a balancing act rather than political coherence and competence. The allocation of funds for public works, investment, and other purposes pits representatives of the various republics against each other. They act as ambassadors of the particular interests of their respective republics. Special social councils and other bodies that parallel the legislature are entrusted with the task of harmonizing the various positions of the republics before decisions are made. It is a lengthy process and often a futile effort. In brief, decision making on most issues has shifted to the individual republics and their governments, while national legislation and executive decisions are increasingly taking the form of treaties made by autonomous bodies. Since interregional bargaining puts heavy emphasis on the particular interests of each republic, the end result is often a stalemate. To avoid this situation, special interrepublic committees have been set up, and prior consultations are required before a law is passed or an executive decision made.

The inability of the central federal authorities to reach out directly to the people for support on policies that apply to all contrasts sharply with the coherence and the strength of the Soviet executive. In Russia the command structure remains unified and dominant. In Yugoslavia it has become increasingly pluralized and impotent. Totalitarianism is a hallmark of the first; the dismantling of totalitarianism results from the second. Particular nationalisms in Croatia, Serbia, Kosovo, and other republics have occasionally asserted themselves against the federation — and the Federal Executive Council. They embody mini-nationalisms that not only block the operation of the federal agencies but also affect the unity of the LCY.[1]

Self-Management

After the split with the Soviet Union, Yugoslavia's communist leadership launched a new socioeconomic program of modernization different from the Soviet model based on central planning and bureaucratization. It attempted to combine central planning with the market economy. The system that developed is referred to as Workers' Self-Management, or the Pluralism of Self-Managing Interests. Workers and citizens practice self-management in all enterprises: in public services such as health, education, culture, etc.; in regional, local, and municipal units; and in organizations like trade unions and youth organizations.

Self-management is therefore an all-encompassing formula, which affects various social and economic activities, not just industrial and economic enterprises, but the principle for all of them is the same. Decisions within the units are made by those that participate: workers, managers, doctors, nurses, patients, farmers, tradesmen, artisans, managers, technical and white-collar personnel, public officials, recipients of public services, consumers, etc. Although the size of the unit may vary,

1. Steven L. Burg, *Conflict and Cohesion in Socialist Yugoslavia: Political Decision-Making Since 1960* (Princeton, N.J.: Princeton University Press, 1983).

the principle remains the same: autonomy. In industry it allows the workers to participate in the formulation of all decisions, from checking the budget and the accounts of the firm to having a say on investment and production policies. They also share in the benefits and profits, and selling for profit (within limits) determines the efficiency of the firm.

Self-management has strengthened the growing autonomy of the republics. Economic, social, educational, and self-managerial units operate on behalf of the local interests and local predispositions. Investment policies, public works, tax policies, and distributive and redistributive measures to be undertaken by the central government are assessed in terms of the needs and interests of an individual republic. There are of course interests and policies that transcend a single republic. In such cases, the conflicting interests reach a compromise out of which one may weave the fabric of a general or national interest. To attain it some republics may suffer and others benefit in terms of goods and services; some may experience short-term deprivations for the sake of long-run gains. But it is almost inevitable that without a common arbiter and a common perception of the national interest, and without spokesmen for the national interest, self-management units will use various forms of internal consultation and decision making to advance the interests of their own republic at the expense of the others. Self-management, aside from its economic and strictly operational traits (which we do not discuss here) organizes the social forces into a great number of autonomous and even competing ethnic and regional units. In other words, while democracy within each unit is attainable, it comes at the price of national unity. However, Yugoslavia does have a powerful force that should speak for the whole nation and impose its will upon the whole nation: the LCY. How unified is it and is it coherent?

The Erosion of the Party

The internal developments in the LCY parallel, indeed they seem to reflect, the pluralization and regionalization of political and economic power and decision making. During the last decade, and even more so since the death of Marshal Tito in 1981, the central direction and organization of the party reflect the nationalist forces at work. The following trends are noticeable.[2]

1. The leadership of the party, the Praesidium, has been weakened. Its members cannot be nominated (and elected by the Central Committee) unless they hold prior consultations with the republican communist leaderships.
2. Rotation of about one-third of the members of the LCY Praesidium (consisting of twenty-five members) occurs every year, thus reducing the coherence and stability of the supreme body in the LCY.

3. The members of the Secretariat of the Praesidium serve only one term and are not eligible for reappointment. In contrast to the top executive organs of all the other communist regimes, the Secretariat in Yugoslavia is subordinate to the Praesidium. The tenure of its members is short and they have only a limited staff.
4. The principle of democratic centralism has been seriously qualified: "The obligation of members whose opinions and proposals remain in the minority in an organization or organ of the League of Communists to accept and carry out the decisions adopted by the majority" is maintained but *"with freedom to retain [their] own opinion."*[3]
5. In general, representation in the central party organs follows the principles of equal representation of the republics. In fact, assignments to high party positions must be made in accordance with the instructions and decisions of the Communist party organs of the republics. Communist leadership, even if collective, is viewed as representing the interests and positions of the party organization in the constituent republics.

In theory, the LCY is considered the avant-garde. It is supposed to develop the broad outlines of the general interest, to educate the masses in socialism, and to preserve national unity. It transcends particularisms and local nationalisms and acts as an antidote to the pluralistic trends in the system. It is supposed to represent unity while tolerating and at times even encouraging diversity and particularism. But the reality is different. The party is increasingly succumbing to ethnic and regional particularisms. For instance, it is now the function of the national congress of the LCY to "synthesize" the resolutions of the regional party congresses of the republics. The party is becoming increasingly fragmented and its top spokesmen are viewed as ambassadors acting in the interests of *their* republics. Moreover, the League of Communists in each republic virtually has the right to recall them.

The erosion of the cohesiveness of the party leadership and its federalization may well prove to be the best indication of the inability of the command structure to impose its will. It is indicative not only of the decay of totalitarianism in Yugoslavia but also of the gradual dismantling of the national government. If the communists can no longer speak for the whole country (there are about 1,100,000 members in the LCY), if they begin to identify and speak for *their* particular nationalities first and for communism and Yugoslavia second, then there will be no force to counteract the centrifugal force in the republics and the self-managing organizations in the economy and society. Unless it is the army!

The Yugoslav Army

The Yugoslav army — the Yugoslav People's Army (YAP) — has remained a strong force since the period of the Resistance (1941–1945). It

3. Ibid., p. 63. (Emphasis added.)

took a defiant posture in 1949 during the Yugoslav-Soviet split and it again showed its apparent readiness in 1968 when the Warsaw Pact countries, under the control of the Soviet Union, invaded Czechoslovakia and threatened others. It has a quarter of a million officers and enlisted personnel and half a million reservists, and there is a territorial defense force consisting of about one million. It has been totally under party control since 1945. Only once, when the Croatian nationalist movement appeared particularly active, was its use considered. Tito himself, in a speech on December 21, 1971, referred to it as the "last savior" of the country and of the communist system.

> There is no question of the Army's role in preserving the achievements of our revolution. Although the primary task is to defend our country against foreign enemies, our army is also called upon to defend the achievements of our revolution within the country, should it become necessary.[4]

Although the army operates under the federal government, the basic Law of Defense stipulates (Article 14) that "each constituent Republic and the two autonomous provinces [will] have *[their]* Defense Ministry that will *cooperate* with the central defense agencies in Belgrade in organizing the defense of each republic and province."[5] The Council of National Defense consists of eleven persons who represent the republics and the autonomous provinces. Furthermore, the whole territorial defense force — one million strong — even though it is directly under the federal presidency and the Council of National Defense, is responsible to the organizations that established them: the republics and the provinces.

About 100,000 army personnel are also members of the LCY, many of them officers. There are about twenty-five officers in the LCY Central Committee, and here again representation by nationality (as equal as possible) is emphasized: eight are Serbs, five Croats, two Slovenes, two Montenegrins, two Macedonians, one Albanian, one Moslem and two "Yugoslavs." In the officer corps also, despite a disproportionate number of Serbs, every effort has been made to have equal ethnic representation, as in the LCY.

While there are many indications that the army remains a centralized force under national direction, the weakening of the central institutions of governance also undermines central direction and control. As the central control of the state and the party weakens, so will the central control of the army.

Particular centrifugal forces seem to have penetrated the central command structure of the state, as well as the LCY and the Army. The spread of particularisms of one kind or another is not harnessed by a coherent, unifying vision of the society and the state, even though the

4. Quoted in Slobodan Stankovic, *The End of the Tito Era: Yugoslavia's Dilemma* (Stanford, Calif.: Hoover Institution Press, 1981), p. 35.
5. Ibid., p. 44.

Communist party continues to claim to have one. Totalitarian controls and ideology have splintered into many special, local, particular, national, and interest claims, so much so that the crisis of the totalitarian regime now imperils the integrity of the multinational state itself. Some argue that the party was destined to encounter resistance from various ethnic groups and that its effort was doomed from the start. Others see in the present crisis some of the general characteristics of a crisis of legitimacy that can affect totalitarian regimes and even bring them down.[6]

Some Concluding Observations

Both Yugoslavia and Poland illustrate some of the pervasive reasons for a crisis that may affect some totalitarian regimes:

1. After coming to power, the regime is unable to counter other centers of loyalty and to mobilize the society enough to gain its support.
2. The regime is stymied by strong ethnic minorities and regions that insist on a great degree of internal autonomy, strong representation in the institutions of the central government, and the power to veto decisions made by the central government. However, a pluralized political regime with semi-independent constituent parts is incompatible with totalitarianism. Developments in all totalitarian regimes must be carefully followed with this in mind.
3. The ultimate guardian of a totalitarian regime and its ideology is the single party. It makes policy for all and is the custodian of the unity of the regime. However, if ethnic and regional party units demand equal representation and participation in the party central organs, then the party itself becomes pluralized. Do the subordinate party organs obey the higher central organs or their ethnic and regional constituencies? The moment this question is raised, there is a crisis in totalitarianism.
4. Likewise, decentralization can induce the development of regional and local loyalties, which will impede the overall control and effectiveness of the single party.
5. Demands for local and functional autonomy by different associations invariably allow for greater initiative and freedoms for a number of societal forces, such as workers, managers, educational institutions, and elite groups. These freedoms invariably create a situation where genuinely representative institutions may develop, even under communism. They are incompatible with totalitarianism and their presence indicates a breakdown in the totalitarian model of governance.
6. An economic crisis, if it lasts long, erodes many of the supports a totalitarian regime requires. The process of erosion may be slow. An established totalitarian regime (like an established democracy) can survive it for a long time. But sooner or later it will have to face the test of reconciling conflicts and providing for services.

6. On the processes of legitimization, see Bogdan Denitch (ed.), *The Legitimization of Regimes: International Framework of Analysis* (Beverly Hills, Calif.: Sage Studies, 1979).

These are some of the flash points of crisis. They constitute a syndrome: many of them must appear at the same time in order to have a crisis, and it is their combined weight that may topple a totalitarian regime.

China: In Search of Institutions

Introduction

It is way beyond my purpose (and competence) to give an account of the institutions, ideology, and modernization strategies in China. As with Yugoslavia we are concerned only with the phenomenon of crisis. In China there has been an embedded crisis of a regime that came to power with aspirations for totalitarian control and that at first copied the Soviet institutional mechanisms in order to integrate and modernize the society. The crisis has been due to different strategies of modernization that still remain unresolved and to the Maoist ideology that undermined (and may continue to undermine) institutional consolidation. Also, China's problems cannot be fully understood unless they are discussed against the background of Chinese history and society, something that space does not allow here.[7]

The communist regime — the People's Republic of China — was formally established on October 1, 1949. More than thirty-five years later the leadership is still trying to consolidate the regime: to establish the political institutions through which policy priorities are deliberated, agreed upon, and implemented. As we noted earlier, institutionalization provides for the development of stable, widely accepted, and legitimized political organizations that can make authoritative decisions. That goal has not yet been realized in China.

The contrast with the Soviet Union is striking. After the first decade or so of internal conflicts at the higher levels of the Communist party and Stalin's rise to power, the consolidation of Soviet institutions had been achieved. The state bureaucracy expanded its role, the army became a powerful ancillary force to the Communist party, and within the party a small elite tightened its hold over the rank and file and over the population as a whole. Gradually all centers of loyalty or power were subordinated to the party and the Soviet state. Both in agriculture and industry centralized planning and centralized controls were adopted. There was little conflict about the institutions, and their particular functions and roles became progressively consolidated. In China, however, there is no comparable evidence of consolidation and institutionalization. Even for the three major institutions of governance — the army, the central government and the bureaucracy, and the Communist party — no stable division of roles and functions has been reached.

7. For an excellent overview see James R. Townsend, *Politics in China,* 2d ed. (Boston: Little, Brown, 1982).

The Party

In theory, the party continues to be supreme, making overall policy while the role of the central government and the bureaucracy is merely to implement it.

The party (today there are about 40 million members) has been the vanguard of the people and the major instrument of mobilization and indoctrination. On paper its organization resembles that of the Soviet Union: the party congress elects the Central Committee (its membership has varied significantly over time), the real depository of power between party congresses; it in turn elects the Politburo, consisting of some twenty-five members; and there is a General Secretariat, primarily in charge of organizational and membership matters, that determines the composition and roles of the party officers. The Politburo is the policy-making organ, but it is too large, so a standing committee of five members headed by the party chairman acts on its behalf. Although it is the real center of power it has to report regularly to the Politburo.

The major principle that guides the party's work is democratic centralism, which we have already discussed with regard to the Soviet Union: the higher organs are elected by the lower ones and by the members of the party; lower organs obey the higher ones; and a majority decision is binding on the minority. However, a second principle — which seems to be diametrically opposed to democratic centralism — is "from the masses to the masses." According to this principle, the party cadres take their cues from the masses with whom they are in constant touch, refine and clarify various positions and demands, package them into programmatic statements through the party and its major organizations, and take them back to the masses. The cadres are thus brokers between the masses and the leadership. They may thus be caught between democratic centralism, which is authoritarian, and mass democracy, which is participatory and populist. The cadres may be caught between conflicting loyalties and roles and may split for or against certain policies.

The Government

The national government — consisting of a National People's Congress (the legislature), the State Council (the executive), and a vast array of departments, technical ministries, and subordinate regional and local units — execute policies. The Chinese officialdom has always claimed technical competence, integrity, and administrative skills. In the course of China's turbulent history it was often the only existing apparatus that could legitimately act for the state.

With the victory of the communists in 1949 there was a period of effacement for the central government and its bureaucracy. It was followed, however, by a rapid growth of the bureaucracy both in numbers and in effective and competent administration.

> The government had to strengthen its administrative and technical capabilities . . . and the Party [between 1952 and 1958] made [the] most impressive achievements in bringing effective centralized government to China. The bureaucracy that emerged under Communist control was the most efficient institution in Chinese history. . . . The government reached down further into society than any previous administration, penetrating into villages and urban neighborhoods where officials in the past had tolerated a great deal of autonomy.[8]

However, constant frictions developed between the bureaucracy, the party, and the army. Furthermore, beginning in 1958, policies initiated by the party undermined the bureaucracy, and many competent administrators were removed.

The Army

The People's Liberation Army, the third pillar of governance, had played the key role in the victory over the nationalist forces. Many of its officers joined the cadres of the Communist party, and in fact there has never been an army so thoroughly politicized as the Chinese army. The doctrine of guerrilla warfare, developed by Mao, emphasized the value of political weapons in combat. The war waged against the nationalist forces was a war of attrition in which political organization and propaganda were even more important than military competence. As a result, the military became great communist loyalists and inseparable from the Communist party. But for a long time it was also an administrative organization. It administered territories and provinces long after the defeat of the nationalist forces and the establishment of the People's Republic, and it became one of the best recruitment sources both for bureaucrats and the party cadres.

Traditions die hard, and the relations between the three major organs of government were fraught with frictions. Governmental units managed to insulate themselves from the party; many high-ranking party leaders led a number of factions that undermined central party control; and others developed their political bastions, their fiefs one might say, in a city, county, or province or within the bureaucracy. An intricate network of power centers, crisscrossing and overlapping each other, developed within the Communist party and the state officialdom.

The same situation existed in the relationship between the central organs of the party or the central government and the subordinate territorial units (provinces, regions, communes, or villages). In a manner reminiscent of the war lords, when individual political leaders and generals assumed virtually autonomous powers in the provinces, party or governmental officials under the communist regime resisted or deflected orders from the center. Although there was almost never an open de-

8. Lucien Pye, *China: An Introduction*, 3rd ed. (Boston: Little, Brown, 1983), p. 174.

fiance, the result was to weaken central authority, including even that of the party.

Army officers, even if communist, also showed some of the old tendencies of the war lords. They tried to gain autonomy and develop their own territorial fiefs against the central government and even against the party. Lin Biao, Commander of the Fourth Army, became virtually the head of the central and southeast areas and attained a national reputation before he attempted to seize power from Mao. Peng Dehua, another general who administered the Northwest as head of the First Army, openly objected to Mao's policies and was purged.[9]

Thus the regime seems to have been unable to clearly define the position of the army and assign its duties accordingly. Together with the cadres, the army maintains order and discipline and protects the interests of the revolution; together with the bureaucracy, it has administered and governed for a long time. Even though it has progressively withdrawn from administrative work it still remains an essential organ of integration and indoctrination, and it is the pillar of the central government and administration. At the highest echelons of the party hierarchy, its spokesmen deliberate and participate in policy making. The army is often the only organization that can settle major disputes, the only organ capable of maintaining national unity. During the last decade, however, the professionalization of the army has necessitated a reconsideration of tactics and strategy and a separation between political and defense matters. A professional army subordinate to the party and the state organizations may yet emerge.

Shifts and Changes

Since 1949 at least three major occurrences illustrate the flux in institutions and policies. The first, The Great Leap Forward, from 1958 to 1961, was initiated in order to fully socialize agriculture, do away with small agricultural units and cooperatives, and industrialize the countryside. Large communes were established under the control of the state and the party, and thousands of collectives were incorporated into these communes. They became the major units of agricultural production and, in exchange for their work, the farmers were given wages and provided with food, shelter, clothing, schools, health care, etc. But the farmers balked because the services the commune provided were inadequate, and because of their attachment to their family plots and their smaller cooperatives. As a result, agricultural production fell rapidly, the size of the communes had to be reduced, the farmers returned to their plots and cooperatives, and individual incentives had to be reintroduced Similarly, an effort to industrialize the countryside by promoting local initiatives and decentralizing manufacturing also failed. The Great Leap produced famine and industrial dislocation.

9. Ibid., p. 177.

Another major change, the Great Proletarian Cultural Revolution, began in 1965 under the direction of Mao himself. It was a movement against the communist institutions and organizations, both political and economic. It was addressed against the party, the bureaucracy, and even the army, although to a much lesser degree. New political forces were mobilized, such as the high school and university students who became known as the Red Guards. They attacked all symbols of authority as well as the state and party officials themselves. Revolutionary committees mushroomed to supervise all the officials; the officials and cadres in turn fought against each other and against the revolutionary committees. Tens of thousands of party officials, from the Central Committee down, were unseated or disappeared. The result was total institutional dislocation, and China did not fully recover from it until after Mao's death in 1975.

It was in 1977–1979, and only after a number of succession crises had been resolved, that the new leadership undertook a yet new wave of reforms, most of them aimed at the economy and modernization. The emphasis on central planning and the socialization of industrial production (except for the major industrial sectors) and especially agriculture was abandoned. The new leadership began to introduce market mechanisms for pricing and for meeting consumer demands. This policy was clearly confirmed in the plenum of the Central Committee of the Communist party on October 20, 1984.[10] First with regard to agriculture, family households again became the major farming units, although cooperatives continue to be encouraged. Farmers can produce and sell directly in the marketplace. In industry, the managers can make their own decisions. Prices are to be determined by the market; subsidies for consumers are to be gradually reduced; and central planning is to be seriously qualified. If these reforms last, they will mean the definitive abandonment of the Soviet blueprint of central direction and bureaucratic control — indeed the abandonment even of socialism. Competition and consumer choice will become the major forces for increased productivity and economic growth. In the words of the Central Committee,

> On the basis of public ownership and subject to the control of state planning and laws, and for the purpose of serving socialist modernization, our enterprises are put to the test of direct judgement by consumers in the marketplace so that only the best survive. . . . There is an urgent need . . . to unclog the channels of circulation . . . for the increasing amount of agricultural products and satisfy the rising needs of the peasantry for manufactured goods, science and technology as well as culture and education.[11]

10. *The New York Times,* October 21, 1984.
11. Ibid.

During the 1980s the Chinese leadership has progressively expanded not only economic but also cultural contacts with many capitalist countries, notably the United States. Western industrial firms have been allowed to operate in China; foreign investments have been encouraged; foreign banks have been able to establish themselves; and Western technology, much in demand, is being imported. There has been a remarkable increase in the number of Chinese students studying in Western European and American universities, and exchanges among European, Japanese, and American academies as well as business and professional organizations have also increased significantly.

In spite of the many changes during the past thirty years, however, there is no assurance that the new economic policy with its liberal tendencies will continue. Powerful forces within the Communist party are opposed to the recent reforms and to the opening of China to the Western economy. Also, there are pro-Soviet groups who favor economic and trade relations with the Soviet Union and a renewed commitment to socialism and centralized planning. There may yet be many twists and turns in economic policy that will reflect political conflicts between the top leadership and the party, and the different factions may try to mobilize the masses behind their own particular view of how the economy should be run.

The Constant Flux[12]

The Great Leap Forward (1958–1961) and the Great Proletarian Cultural Revolution (1965–1969) were dramatic and extreme upheavals. However, China has gone through numerous shifts and changes of lesser severity. There have been constant factional disputes about every policy aspect including modernization and economic growth: how to plan, if at all, or how not to plan; whether to develop centralized controls or to decentralize; how much to collectivize; what should be the size of the collective; how much personal and material incentives to allow; and what concessions, if any, to make to the market. The Chinese leadership moved at times from complete communalization of the land under state ownership and central direction to cooperatives and small collectives and family farms, from state-controlled distribution to a modified market system. Similarly, in the organization of the state institutions various forms of centralization and decentralization were attempted with the role of the provinces and regions constantly changing and with constant modification of the size of the various territorial units.

There were also shifts and changes in the relationship between the party and the masses. Characteristically enough, China is perhaps the only communist regime that has on occasion espoused and practiced

12. For the flux in Chinese political institutions, see Townsend, op cit.

open and spontaneous debate and criticism. The first occasion was in 1956 when Mao launched the Hundred Flowers campaign, which allowed for the free expression of viewpoints, but it led to criticism of many aspects of the regime and was quickly ended! Another opportunity was provided by the constitution of 1982, which specifically gave people the freedom to express their views on large posters on walls. It was widely practiced and became known as the Democracy Wall, but it had to be abolished within a year. The message *from* the masses was often the opposite of the message given by the party cadres *to* the masses!

For a regime that is considered to be totalitarian, the lack of coordinated institutions to impose total control is striking. The army, the party, and the state officials have vied with one another openly. But the curious thing about China is that none of these three organs has attained control. Shifting alliances keep breaking down. What is also unique in a totalitarian regime is the tendency of the leaders to appeal directly to the masses. In the Soviet regime, disagreements among the leaders were never (except on the eve of the Russian Revolution) brought before the public. In China virtually the opposite is true. The masses have therefore become a genuine and indispensable element in the struggle for leadership. They are brought directly into politics because the leaders have to build constituencies in order to gain support or maintain it.

There is another distinguishing characteristic about China. When conflicts have surfaced in other totalitarian regimes, whether about leadership or about policies, they have been invariably resolved by giving the victor all the spoils. The losers were shifted to insignificant posts in a remote area, or expelled from the party, or subjected to banishment, imprisonment, or execution. Not so in China. Many losers reappear because the victors are not strong enough to fully impose their will and their power. There is a precarious balance arising from these constant confrontations.

Whether induced or spontaneous, there is a great deal of direct action and mass participation in Chinese politics. When this type of action and participation is used by a united leadership to mobilize the masses, such a mobilization has, as we noted, all the earmarks of totalitarianism. But in China, where it has been used by different leadership groups in conflict to gain support, it injects a populist and a participatory dimension that cannot be found in other totalitarian regimes. If the vigilance of the citizen organized in various groups is constantly solicited, such vigilance becomes legitimized and may exert its weight and become a strong restraint on the leadership.

In conclusion, let us return to our original question: Since there are no strong institutions — because the party, the army, and the state are in constant flux and none of the three has enough strength to assume top position in the command structure — can we say that China is a totalitarian regime? The answer has to be: not quite!

THE LEADER AND COMMUNISM: THE CASE OF CUBA

Introduction Cuba is a communist totalitarian regime in which communism as an ideology and as a pattern of political organization is pronounced and where mass mobilization, penetration, and integration under the leader and the party are total. It is the only communist regime that came to power through a noncommunist movement and under a noncommunist leader. The followers of Fidel Castro, drawn mostly from among the leaders of the revolutionary guerrillas, were able to use and ultimately absorb the Cuban Communist party — the People's Socialist party (PSP) — and create a new Communist party. The new party was formed in 1965 and since then many of its former leaders have been purged. Only those who cooperated with Castro's movement and accepted his leadership have been allowed to continue to play an important role. The new Communist party that rules Cuba is more *fidelista* than communist — or at least it has to be *fidelista* in order to be Communist!

The aim of Castro and his original guerrilla companions became clear, even before he discovered and accepted Marxism-Leninism. His short but intensive guerrilla war against the Batista dictatorship caused the regime to collapse shortly before the end of 1958. Batista, who had seized power for the second time in 1954, was forced to leave the country. All of Castro's democratic pledges were then quickly shelved and he and his followers imposed their control. The manner in which they did it revealed their ultimate goal: to establish total control over all facets of political, social, and economic life. It is admirably outlined by Professor Edward Gonzalez.

> . . . The old anti-Batista political parties were ignored. . . . The judiciary was attacked . . . the opposition press had been curtailed or closed down, [and] other forms of mass communication virtually nationalized . . . the labor unions and student-movements were purged of dissident elements, in the end becoming docile instruments of the regime during 1960. In still other areas, the regime moved in totalitarian fashion to extend its control over formerly independent or private spheres of activity after late 1959, dissolving as it were the boundaries between state and individual. Much of the non-agrarian sector of the economy was . . . nationalized. . . . The educational system was also nationalized . . . and the Catholic Church . . . was brought to heel . . . the interest group associations of

the prerevolutionary period [were] either dissolved or incorporated under state control.[13]

The transformation that Castro wanted to accomplish required radical measures. In effect, it required setting up *another* dictatorship. All the old political leaders, even the liberals, were ousted, and all the existing societal, economic, and cultural centers of power were dismantled. Castro's revolution can be readily distinguished from other authoritarian movements and dictatorships in Latin America in that its objective was to wipe out the existing social order and replace it with a new one. It was both a political and a socioeconomic revolution, and a strong ideological fervor was injected into it for a number of reasons, some of which were particularly germane to the Cuban situation:

1. It was intensely nationalistic. It was directed not only against Batista but also the United States and its instruments of economic and military power.
2. It was a youth movement. There was clearly a generation gap between the young guerrillas that followed Castro, his two brothers, and Che Guevara and the old political leaders and forces. The revolutionaries completely discarded the past and looked far ahead toward a different (and brighter) future.
3. It was a particularly adventurous revolution, if boldness can be equated with adventure. It pitted the will of a few leaders and their handful of followers against the establishment despite overwhelming odds. This boldness stemmed mainly from the guerrilla experience where acts of daring against a mass of dispirited soldiers often win the battle, and the revolutionaries began implementing their goals in the same manner. They launched what some have called "guerrilla economics" or "guerrilla social engineering" to industrialize the society and the economy. They wanted to build communism fast, even if it meant telescoping the stages of economic development that some of the leaders of the pre-Castro Communist party in Cuba considered necessary. The guerrilla mentality also prevailed in international politics where Castro took many chances and made many bold moves, most of the time with success.
4. It was a profoundly ideological movement, designed to change the individual, to inject voluntary participation and work in a common endeavor, and to build a new moral order. Communism in the mind and utterances of Castro was to do away with selfishness, individual gain, material

13. Edward Gonzales, *Cuba Under Castro: The Limits of Charisma* (Boston: Houghton Mifflin, 1974).

wealth, and consumerism. They would be replaced by collective efforts, egalitarian considerations, individual sacrifice, and, above all, dedication to collective virtues. The Cuban men and women would thus undergo a profound transformation whereby a new social being would emerge. The ideology was all-encompassing and all-demanding and, as we noted, the kind of ideology that generates totalitarian regimes.

Institutionalization Institutionalization has taken a number of forms. First, the revolutionary transformation that began in 1959–1960 has continued and in 1961 Castro officially accepted Marxism-Leninism. All centers of economic power that continued to provide some autonomy to individuals or associations were eliminated; every company, every economic activity, domestic or foreign, was nationalized; every form of trade, down to individual vendors, was taken over by the state and run by state agencies; and under the auspices of the National Institute of Agrarian Reform (INRA) all private landholdings and farms were transformed into cooperatives and state farms with the state providing technical information, seeds, fertilizers, etc. Not even small plots of land — the "kitchen yards" that the Soviet farmers can own to produce what they want and sell in the market place — have been allowed to the Cuban farmers. All economic activities and all resources are owned, managed, and distributed by the state. No communist regime has gone so far in reducing the individual to such complete economic dependency upon the state.

Second, all media of communication were taken over and managed by the public agencies. The newspapers were seized by the new government and the communist newspaper was merged with *fidelista* newspapers. Intellectuals and artists were given freedom to write and express themselves but only "within the Revolution." The Catholic church, never a powerful force, was gradually undermined as an institution and the educational and cultural services it performed were secularized. All social and cultural associations were dissolved, and every trace of individual expression separate from the official one was done away with.

Third, the restructuring of political controls went through a number of stages. First, all political parties except the Communist party were abolished. Some liberal leaders who had cooperated with Castro withdrew or were forced to withdraw when he failed to live up to his pledge to hold an election. The *fidelistas* and the communists remained the only two political forces. Castro proceeded, however, to bring together his followers and the communists into one single formation — the Integrated Revolutionary Organization — in which the communists occupied leading positions for a while. But in 1965 the new Communist party of Cuba (CPC) was formed and here the *fidelistas* took over the most important positions. Henceforth the CPC under the leadership of Castro became the only recognized party. It held its first congress ten years later in 1975.

Between 1965 and 1975 governance was in the hands of Castro and the party leaders and was exercised directly by the party through its national, regional, and local branches. But even more important, the party began its penetration and mobilization of the society and the implementation of all policies, including major economic ones. Thus it not only consolidated its position but also expanded its power over the population and developed supports for the leadership. Consolidation and mobilization in Cuba took the usual forms employed in all totalitarian regimes. Some were direct, such as the party reaching out to all segments of the population and providing the linkages to the leader. With a membership of about 75,000–100,000 (not more than 3 percent of the population) it was an elite force that made and executed policy. It was also the *only* political organization designated to guide the whole society and to disseminate and enforce the ideology. As with the Soviet Union, the party became, and still is, the supreme guiding force, the vanguard of the society.

Side by side with the party (but naturally always under the party) a number of ancillary organizations have been formed. Foremost among them is the Revolutionary Armed Forces (FAR), which numbers about 200,000 on active duty and another 100,000 reservists — the largest military force in the American hemisphere except for the United States.* In addition to their defensive role, they carry the legacy of the guerrillas. They are ready to be sent into combat in faraway places for the sake of revolutionary internationalism and against American "imperialist" designs. They are the "Jesuits of the Revolution," and they are preaching their gospel in some of the most unlikely spots of the world: Ethiopia, Afghanistan, Mozambique, Angola, and the Middle East, in addition to the Caribbean and Central America. But they also play a no less exalted role at home. They are present in demonstrations and parades, they help organize volunteers for the realization of crash programs in road construction and transportation, and they form the backbone of the squads that help with the harvest. Every Cuban must serve in the armed forces for three

*The corresponding figures given in *The New York Times* (June 23, 1985) are 160,000 active, and 130,000 reservists. Others, however, give much higher estimates.

THE STRUCTURE OF GOVERNANCE: CUBA

Communist Party of Cuba (CPC)	The Government
Secretariat	The President
Politburo	The Executive Committee of the Council of Ministers
Central Committee	
Congress of the Party	The Council of Ministers
Members	The Council of State
Society	The National Assembly
Electorate	Local and Regional Assemblies and Officials

years, and it is a period of intensive political indoctrination as well as military training.

Side by side with the FAR, but closely allied with the party, there are the Committees for the Defense of the Revolution (CDRs), about 3 million strong. Their function, in one word, is regimentation. They induce conformity and participation within their own ranks as well as the rest of the society; they generate mass supports; they provide the local or regional leadership with information about their own members and also those outside their organization; they preach the ethic of voluntary work; and they organize mass demonstrations and marches in honor of Castro. Some of them belong to special paramilitary formations, the Militia, that are particularly active in the countryside where they enforce the ideology, execute the policies, and oversee the performance of common tasks.

The massive regimentation of the population is enhanced by numerous front organizations, all of them controlled by the CPC, such as the Communist Youth League with over a million and a half members and the Federation of Cuban Women with over a million members. And of course there is the Confederation of Cuban Workers (CTC) with over 1.5 million members. Their role now, however, is only supportive: to implement economic policies as effectively as possible and to meet the quotas of production set by the leadership.

Since practically all adults belong to one organization or another and since many Cubans belong to more than one,

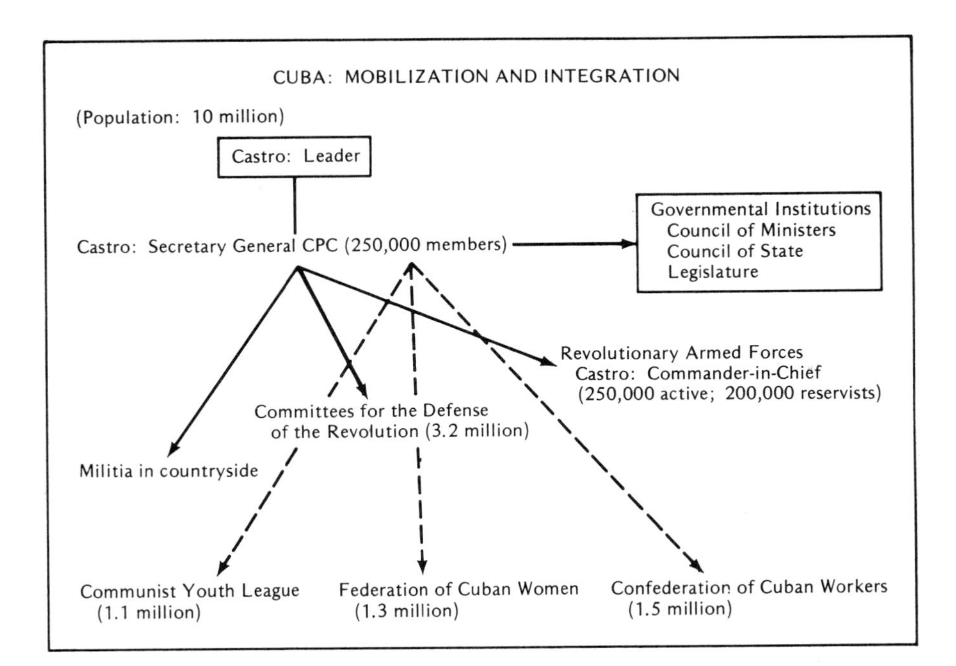

there is an overlap, which reinforces mobilization. In Cuba virtually no individual is left out. No room is left for spontaneous activities or nonregulated forms of expression. Wherever they are found, they are branded as antisocial.

The Structure of Governance Since Castro and the CPC made and implemented the policies, provided for massive mobilization, and ensured the regimentation of the people, there was never a clear distinction (even if formal) between the party and the government, such as exists in the Soviet Union. The leader and the party institutions were the governmental institutions as well. But in 1975 separate governmental institutions were established and an effort was made to distinguish the party from the government. This was done in a new constitution that was adopted in a referendum in 1975 and came into force in 1976.[14] It established a framework of governance, a set of institutions entrusted with policy making and policy implementation. The party, however, as with the Soviet constitution of 1977, remains the animating and guiding force to which all governmental agencies must yield.

Outside of some minor exceptions, the Cuban constitution copies the Soviet constitution. Elections are held to select local assemblies which in turn elect regional ones which in turn elect the members of the legislature. In contrast to the Soviet

14. On the Cuban constitution, see Judy M. del Aguila, *Cuba: Dilemmas of a Revolution* (Boulder, Colo.: Westview Press, 1984), pp. 141–152.

elections, the Cuban elections are indirect. Technically, the legislature is the supreme body (note that it is a unicameral legislature as opposed to the bicameral one in the Soviet Union), but like the Supreme Soviet, it meets only twice a year in two sessions that do not exceed two or three days each. Thus, technically speaking, the legislature makes the laws, but in reality it simply confirms the legislation proposed or already enacted by the higher organs of government.

In Cuba the top level of government consists of the Council of Ministers, headed by the President and elected by and responsible to the legislature. Technically speaking, this system, as with the Soviet Union, is parliamentary. Within the Council of Ministers there is a small executive committee consisting of the president, the first vice-president, and the four other vice-presidents (it is in fact analogous to the Soviet Praesidium of the Council of Ministers). This executive committee can at any time act on behalf of the Council of Ministers and overrule its decisions as well as those made by or the legislature. Democratic centralism determines the relationship of the various governmental organs: the superior organs control the lower ones; the lower ones yield to the higher ones. Elections are from the bottom up but command is handed down from the top: the president, the executive committee of the Council of Ministers, the Council of Ministers, and down to the national legislature and the regional and local bodies.

What is the functional division of labor between the CPC and the governmental structure? Technically, the party provides the ideology, mobilization, and overall guidance, and the government implements the policy. In practice, however, the separation between government and party is, as in the Soviet Union, far from clear. There is the same overlap and dual membership between party posts and government positions. The top governmental organs, including 90 percent of the members of the legislature, are staffed by high-ranking members of the CPC. The members of the Council of Ministers are high-ranking members of the CPC in the Politburo, the Secretariat, or the Central Committee. Fidel Castro is First Secretary of the party, Commander-in-Chief of the Revolutionary Armed Forces, and President of the Council of Ministers. His two brothers occupy the corresponding highest positions in the army, the party, and the government. Members of the Secretariat and the Politburo generally occupy the top positions in the executive committee of the Council of Ministers and in the Council of Ministers.

The party officials permeate the governmental structures. The latter provide only a beginning of institutionalization. Formally, the government officials make decisions, implement policies, provide a channel of representation through elections, and handle criticisms. The existence of a separate, if not autonomous, governmental structure enables the party to stay aloof from matters that might affect its credibility and supports and to devote its energies to national or critical areas, such as defense, foreign relations, the building of socialism, and the strengthening of the ideology at home and its dissemination abroad.

Although the revolution in Cuba started without reference to Marx or Lenin and without Soviet support, its leaders have gradually erected an apparatus of total and centralized control that is virtually indistinguishable from that of the Soviet Union. But there is an important difference: Fidel Castro. Whatever institutionalization has taken place in the CPC and the governmental structure, it has in no way diminished the intensely personal element of leadership that Castro provides. He remains the ideologue, the guerrilla leader, the founder, the heroic figure who defied not only foes (Batista and the United States) but also friends (the Soviet Union). He has the loyalty and affection of his immediate associates, and he is the inspirational source of political mobilization and support. Marxism-Leninism and the CPC are painted in his own colors. Moreover, the people identify with him. Even at the worst moments when the sacrifices demanded have been too heavy, defections were not serious. Only in Nazi Germany has the personal element accounted for so much. It is a factor, however, that may cause difficulties in the future. Castro's charisma has stunted the growth of the institutions and without him the institutions may not be able to generate the regimentation, control, and mobilization that is needed.

The institutions of the revolution are not yet firmly established in Cuba. *Fidelismo,* the attachment to the founder and leader whose word is final and whose presence is felt in every aspect of social, economic, and political life, continues to be critical to the organization of the regime. And the question is: How can the charisma of Fidel Castro be routinized without destroying it? Even now, the major link between the regime and the masses remains the leader, and not until he dies will we know whether the institutional links that have been put into place will prove to be effective instruments of command, mobilization, and support.

Conclusion

The contours of communist totalitarianism in Poland, Yugoslavia, China and Cuba indicate that there is a great distance between the totalitarian model and reality. In China the prerequisites for totalitarian control —

the control of societal forces, especially in the economy, through centralized institutions and a rigidly adhered to and enforced ideology — has not been achieved. Yugoslavia seems to be in the process of pluralization. The various competing centers, which stem from the nationalities, have also let the organization of the economy become decentralized into separate, autonomous units. In Poland a powerful Catholic culture identified with nationalism seems to be thwarting the Communist party and the army. In Cuba the communist regime seems solidly entrenched, but we will not know how well institutionalized the regime is until after the death of Castro. In the cases we surveyed, and in some we have not, we find that nationalisms, disagreements on modernization policies, powerful social forces like the Catholic church, and leadership conflicts can undermine totalitarianism.

But what about the Soviet Union? It is not only the prototype but also the oldest and most modernized totalitarian regime with well-established institutions. Yet, as we noted in Chapter 7, it too faces a number of potential crises. The Soviet economy lags behind those in Western Europe, and the dream of catching up or surpassing the capitalist world is far from materializing. Technological underdevelopment in the face of international competition is weakening the power base of the Soviet leadership both in the world at large and at home. The leadership will also have to face ethnic claims and demands, not unlike those of Yugoslavia, and must manage to reconcile them. Further, there is the problem of interest groups who want to partake in policy making and not have it imposed on them. Finally, the ideology itself — Marxism — may have to go through reconsideration, as in China, in order to allow for new market mechanisms so that consumer demands can be satisfied. The Soviet leadership may decide to give more room to private incentives and the market, as Lenin did in 1921. It may even borrow from the reforms that were undertaken for this purpose in Hungary and elsewhere. Is Soviet totalitarianism capable of these reforms? And if they are undertaken, will they not seriously qualify the totalitarian model we drew? In other words, the ultimate goal of totalitarianism, which is to permit the political leadership to control every aspect and manifestation of individual and societal life and establish unity out of diversity, remains elusive in virtually all totalitarian regimes.

Bibliography

The Chinese Communist Regime

Barnett, A. Doak. *Communist China: The Early Years, 1949–1955*. New York: Praeger, 1964.

Pye, Lucian. *China: An Introduction*, 3rd ed. Boston: Little, Brown, 1984.

Schram, Stuart. *Mao Tse Tung*. London: Penguin, 1979.

Selden, Mark, and Vitor Lippit (eds.). *The Transition to Socialism in China.* Armonk, New York: M. E. Sharpe, 1982. (Especially the essay by Edward Friedman: "Maoism, Titoism, Stalinism. . . .")
Townsend, James R. *Politics in China,* 2nd ed. Boston: Little, Brown, 1982.

Yugoslavia

Burg, Steven. *Conflict and Cohesion in Socialist Yugoslavia: Political Decision-Making Since 1966.* Princeton, N.J.: Princeton University Press, 1983.
Cohen, L. S., and J. P. Shapiro. *Communist Systems in Cooperative Perspective.* New York: Anchor Doubleday, 1974.
Denitch, Bogdan. *The Legitimization of Revolution: The Yugoslav Case.* New Haven: Yale University Press, 1976.
Horton, John H. *Yugoslavia.* Calif.: American Bibliographical Center/Clio Press, 1977.
Horvat, Branko. *The Yugoslav Economic System.* New York: International Arts & Sciences Press, 1976.
Johnson, Chalmers (ed.). *Change in Communist Systems.* Stanford, Calif.: Stanford University Press, 1970.
Nyrop, Richard F. *Yugoslavia, A Country Study.* Washington, D.C.: Government Printing Office, 1982.
Sirc, Lyubo. *The Yugoslav Economy under Self-Management.* London: Macmillan, 1979.
Stankovic, Slobodan. *The End of the Tito Era; Yugoslavia's Dilemma.* Stanford, Calif.: Hoover International Studies, 1981.

Cuba

Carmelo, Mesa-Lago. *Cuba in the 1970s.* University of New Mexico Press, 1978.
Dominguez, Jorge I. *Cuba: Order and Revolution.* Cambridge: Harvard University Press, 1978.
Draper, Theodore. *Castroism: Theory and Practice.* New York: Praeger, 1965.
Fagen, Richard. *The Transformation of Political Culture in Cuba.* Calif.: Stanford University Press, 1969.
Gonzales, Edward. *Cuba under Castro: The Limits of Charisma.* Boston: Houghton Mifflin, 1974.

9 Authoritarian Regimes

Introduction

The essence of authoritarianism is absolute and unchallengeable power. It is the oldest form of government, dating back to ancient tyrants and despots and the Roman Empire. "What pleases the Prince has the force of law" was the famous maxim that consecrated the power of the Roman emperor. It grew and blossomed in the Western monarchies of France, England, and Spain, where the monarchs claimed absolute power and prerogative and ruled by hereditary and divine right. Machiavelli, in *The Prince,* drew widely from the experiences of the Italian cities to give us his profile of unfettered princely rule and the many instrumentalities available for imposing it. In Eastern Europe and especially in Russia and the Ottoman Empire the power of the tsar or the sultan remained absolute until the end of the nineteenth century. Similarly, until the end of World War II, all the colonial peoples were ruled by their colonial masters at home.

Authoritarianism still remains widespread and is very much alive today. At least half of the political regimes in the world are authoritarian (see Appendix A), and they come in many varieties. Some are personal dynastic types, such as Saudi Arabia; others are single-party regimes or outright personal tyrannies. Some may be termed "statist" and "bureaucratic." The majority of authoritarian regimes, however, are military dictatorships or, as they are more generously called, "military regimes."

Background Factors

Before we examine the various types of authoritarianism, let us briefly discuss some of the background factors — social, economic, and political — that give rise to authoritarian regimes.

Formation of a Nation-State

Since the formation of a nation-state requires unity, it adversely affects some groups: ethnic, regional, economic, tribal, or religious. Naturally such groups balk and refuse to give their allegiance and support to the newly formed state. To quell such dissidences and ensure unity, centralized control and repressive mechanisms have to be fashioned — in other words, authoritarian governance. There are, however, some notable exceptions, especially Switzerland and the United States.

External reasons also reinforce the need of authoritarianism. A new state is always fragile. Those in control are not quite sure of their own position vis-à-vis other states, especially when they perceive other states as potentially inimical. They therefore try to strengthen their control through the use of authoritarian practices.

The formation of a nation-state also requires a period of consolidation. During this time the leadership tries to develop institutions of command and support, such as a state bureaucracy or the single-party or a military dictatorship. Efforts are made frequently to legitimize the authoritarian polity with the promulgation of constitutional documents and popular referenda.

The Survival of the State: Salus Populi Suprema Lex Esto

This Latin maxim can be paraphrased to mean "The security [or safety] of the people [or of the state or of the nation-state] is the supreme law." It represents one of the most common explanations of and justifications for authoritarianism. Security may be needed because of danger that may come from within or from outside. Usually it is needed because of internal strife, such as when opinion is highly polarized between antagonistic factions or fragmented among many; or when a small but extremely committed minority tries to subvert the existing legal order — a revolutionary party, for instance, committed to the violent overthrow of the state. Similarly, threats from outside require swift measures and tight discipline.

To meet situations of crisis, all political regimes, including democratic ones, provide for authoritarian devices. In the Roman Republic, constitutional provisions existed for what may be called a "temporary dictatorship": when there was a grave crisis, the institutions were set aside and a temporary dictator stepped in with full powers but with the understanding that within a given period of time he would step down and out. We have noted similar crisis arrangements in contemporary democracies. Article 16 of the French constitution of the Fifth Republic gives the president ample powers to deal with a crisis; the president of the United States, as a commander-in-chief, can invoke sweeping powers. Lincoln blockaded the southern ports at the outset of the Civil War, and hundreds of thousands of Japanese-Americans found themselves in concentration camps after the Japanese attack on Pearl Harbor. In almost all contemporary regimes there are special provisions for the exercise of emergency power.

The availability of these emergency powers justifies authoritarianism, at least implicitly. They are designed to give the government the means to act "quickly," "effectively," "for the public interest," and to "save the nation" — something that by implication democratic governments cannot do. In the United States, Congress gave President Roosevelt sweeping powers during the Great Depression. "When the house is on fire, we call the fire department," said a congressman. He was speaking the same language that the Romans spoke when they would invite an illustrious figure to become a temporary dictator and put their affairs in order. The salvation of the state is the supreme law but the maxim, if carried too far (and it often is), may bring about the end of democratic government. And the danger is ever-present.

The Political Culture

The political culture — the manner in which people in a society perceive the state and their own role in it — is of great significance in assessing the origins and prospects of authoritarianism.

In most of the world the political patterns and values developed in Western Europe cannot be easily duplicated:

Separation between church and state.
Autonomous and spontaneous formation of interests and associations claiming independence vis-à-vis the state.
The growth of law both as a limitation on state power and also as a standard for the resolution of individual and group conflicts.
The development of individual entrepreneurship and liberal capitalism.
The growth of tolerance for different points of view and respect for individual freedoms.

When these values prevail, it is exceedingly difficult for a political elite to assume infallibility and impose orthodoxy, concentrate absolute power in its own hands, and cram the richness and multiplicity of social life and individual endeavors into one mold. But there is no reason to expect or to assume that these values, which became institutionalized in Western Europe and Britain over a period of centuries, can develop quickly elsewhere or, for that matter, develop at all.

Authoritarianism has developed in countries where these values are absent. More particularly:

1. In countries where there is a highly unbalanced relationship between the civil society and the state. In some cases (including Southern Mediterranean Europe) the state and its agencies overpower the civil society by playing a dominant role in the allocation of services, jobs, and benefits. In contrast, the civil society is correspondingly weak and unorganized, often consisting of large numbers of isolated individuals.
2. Where the middle classes remain weak and are unable to form associational representative parties or networks that limit the state. Liberalism and its political institutions, never having gained roots, are not valued in these societies.
3. In countries where there is a latent or inherent tendency toward statism or, to put the same idea negatively, where restraints against the state are few and weak. The state tends to incorporate rather than to represent interests, to formulate the public interest rather than synthesize it from among a number of conflicting demands and interests. The holders of coercive power — the military or bureaucrats — govern through "imperative coordination."

One of the most important landmarks to watch for in assessing the prospects of authoritarianism is power sharing. Where societal groups, through the available political instrumentalities (elections, political parties, political organizations), or through extrapolitical or parapolitical activities (interest groups, trade unions, cooperatives, lobbying, joint deliberations in economic and managerial decisions, issue-oriented organizations, demonstrations, marches, the media) begin to acquire influence and power in decision making, the prospects for authoritarianism are poor and democracy may develop. In contrast, when the ruling classes refuse to compromise and share power they will invariably resort to authoritarian solutions.

Modernization

The argument is often made that authoritarian regimes emerge at a time of rapid economic modernization. Modernization unsettles the traditional patterns of economic and social life, causes population movements, brings massive waves of immigrants from the countryside into the towns, and heightens the expectations and demands of the people. It is a process that intensifies social strife and authoritarian governance is often needed to quell it.

The opposite argument, however, is also made. Authoritarianism comes about in order to bring about modernization. A new political elite emerges and seeks to establish a new social and economic order. Authoritarianism offers the most effective political formula for countering the traditional social and economic and political elites that oppose change. Besides the Third World countries, some of the Latin American regimes, military or not, are also committed to modernization and growth. The sweeping economic reforms in the Soviet Union under Stalin in the 1930s were clearly designed to industrialize the country as fast as possible and accounted greatly for the tightening of authoritarian controls.

To summarize, authoritarianism seems to be latent in all political societies. Under certain circumstances, it can surface almost anywhere. It usually springs into being when severe internal strife or foreign danger requires leadership and concentration of power in the hand of one person (like the Roman temporary dictator). It has been most prevalent in societies that undergo rapid modernization or where some elite groups advocate modernization but other groups resist it; where a political culture that defines the relationship between citizen and the state has not generated genuine participatory linkages and individual and associational rights.

The Authoritarian Profile

Authoritarian regimes have a number of common traits. By emphasizing their characteristics we can develop a profile of authoritarianism.

1. The weight of the military is overwhelming.[1]
2. Popular participation is usually low.
3. Civil and particularly political rights do not exist or are very seriously qualified.[2] Occasionally there are elections, referendums, and plebiscites that, by huge majorities, declare support to those in power. But representative institutions, where they do exist, are only rubber stamps to endorse decisions already made by the leadership.
4. There is usually no political ideology that mobilizes the people.
5. While trying to subordinate societal and interest groups, authoritarian regimes do not undertake an extensive penetration and restructuring of the society. The governing elite often consists of a coalition of different elite groups. There is an oligarchy — an open or tacit alliance among the different elites that enables them to defend their interests and perpetuate their rule.[3]

1. The point is repeatedly made by Amos Perlmutter in *Modern Authoritarianism* (New Haven: Yale University Press, 1983).
2. Using the civil rights and political rights index ranging from a high score of 1 to the lowest possible of 7, authoritarian regimes are bunched together between 6 and 7. They include Yemen, Uganda, North Korea, Guinea, Central African Republic, Iraq, Iran, Syria, Mali, Chad, Burundi, Chile, Somalia, Ethiopia, Libya, Congo, Zaire, Saudi Arabia, Oman, Niger, Ecuador, Nigeria (since 1984), Mauritania, Jordan, Haiti, Guinea-Bissau, Gabon, Algeria, and Lagos. A second group, consisting of Tunisia, the United Arab Emirates, Zimbabwe, the Philippines, Uruguay, Paraguay, Rwandam Ivory Coast, Burma, South Korea, Togo, and Sudan, fall between 5 and 6. Authoritarian regimes placed in a third tier with a score of 5–6 consist of Upper Volta, Bolivia, Bangledesh, Bahrain, Liberia, Madagascar, Cameroon, Kenya, Peru, Brazil, Tawain, Egypt, Pakistan, Zambia, Indonesia, Nepal, Quatar, and Sierra Leone. See C. C. Taylor and D. A. Jodich, *World Handbook of Political and Social Indicators* (New Haven: Yale University Press, 1983.)
3. See Chapter 1.

With these common traits in mind, it is time now to give an overview of the most prevalent forms of authoritarianism.

Authoritarian Regimes: Major Types

In discussing the most prevalent authoritarian forms, we will use the basic criteria suggested earlier: the organization of the structure of command, the organization of supports and consent, and the organization and configuration of interests and rights. But for each regime specific historical circumstances, particular events, the restraints imposed by economic conditions, the configurations of the societal forces, the imprint of the individual leaders, and the international environment trace a particular profile and account for particular differences. I suggest the four following major authoritarian types (see Table 9-1):

1. Tyrannies
2. Dynastic regimes
3. Military regimes
4. Single-party regimes

Tyrannies

Regardless of how or why tyrants acquire power, they wield it personally and absolutely. Aristotle gave us what is probably the best portrait of a tyrant, and the ancient Greeks were just as familiar with tyranny as we are with military dictatorship. The tyrant seized political power pretty much as a modern-day gangster seizes a household or even a whole community. But his rulership (in those days it had to be a "he") was coterminus with the power he could muster to keep the household, village, small city, city-state, or even a whole people or many peoples under subjection and in his service. The purpose of rulership was selfish: to extract as much as possible for personal enjoyment and ego glorification. Dionysius (the tyrant of Syracuse, 432–367 B.C.), Aristotle tells us, "in the space of five years collected all the private property of his subjects into his own coffers."

In a few lines, Aristotle gives us the characteristics of tyranny that political scientists have been rediscovering ever since. A tyrant, once in power, will

> . . . keep down those who are of an aspiring disposition, . . . take out those who will not submit, . . . allow no public meals, no clubs, no education, nothing at all, but . . . guard against everything that gives rise to high spirits or mutual confidence; he [will not] suffer the learned meetings of those who have leisure to hold conversations with each other; he [will] en-

TABLE 9-1 Major Forms of Authoritarianism

	STRUCTURE OF COMMAND	ORGANIZATION OF SUPPORTS AND CONSENT	ORGANIZATION OF INTERESTS	RIGHTS
Tyranny	Absolute, personal	Coercion and complicity	Subordination, extortion	None
Dynastic monarchy	Absolute, personal and familial, autocratic	Traditional values, deference	Subordination	Prescriptive (some civil rights but no political rights)
Military regime Direct	Absolute, personal or collegial (junta),	Coercion	Subordination and varying degrees of freedoms	None
Indirect Control Arbitration Veto	Military and civilian officers, indirect controls, arbitration and veto	Coercion or manipulation, limited representation	Corporatism	Uncertain
Single party	Leader and party leadership	Some mobilization and participation	Some penetration and reorganiza-tion, controls	Uncertain

> deavor by every means possible to keep all people strangers to each other; he [will] oblige everyone to appear in public and the aliens to live near the city gate; . . . he [will] engage his subjects at war that they be employed and continually depend upon their general . . . and he [will] keep his subjects very poor.[4]

In summary, Aristotle sets forth three rules for a "successful" tyranny:

1. Keep the citizenry in abject disposition.
2. Do not allow them to have confidence in each other.
3. Keep them in a state of complete powerlessness.

Since tyrannies are intensely personal regimes, they are not easily amenable to institutionalization. As a result, their major pitfall lies in the organization of power. No tyrant by himself can be strong enough to keep all others under subjection. He has to organize a guard and the only way he can gain and hold its loyalty is to share some of the spoils, — goods and services — with its members. And once a guard is organized the tyrant becomes beholden to it.[5] He has to create a rudimentary set of rules and procedures for the distribution of benefits to his associates, which limits his own power. He also has to delegate some of his power to his associates and then remain in constant fear that such delegation will spawn subordinate power fiefs from which a conspiracy against him may be organized. But if the power of the tyrant lasts and if his guard controls the means of coercion, tyranny represents the most "successful" (as well as extreme) form of authoritarianism. It is a regime in which power has no restraints, can be exercised arbitrarily and even whimsically, subordinates every interest and every individual, relies on intimidation and fear, and allows no political freedoms or civil rights. The individual is less than a subject; he is literally a slave. His life and possessions are completely at the mercy of his master.

Modern tyrannies have organizations that are also far more complex than the classic prototype. The instruments of coercion are carefully developed, through the police and the army, to include prevention, repression, surveillance, and intimidation. But whatever the whims of the tyrant, services have to be performed: transportation, public health, training of the young, and, above all, domestic and national security. Without them his power may become nil. In some cases, such as Trujillo in the Dominican Republic or Somoza in Nicaragua, the army was but an

4. Aristotle, *Politics,* Book V, chapter IX (Everyman Edition) London, J. M. Dent Ltd., 1941. Aristotle defines tyranny as the regime "where a single person governs men, who are all his peers and superiors, without any form of responsibility and with a view to his own advantage rather than that of his subjects."
5. Robert Jackson and Carl Rosberg, in a discussion of some contemporary tyrannies in Africa, point out that "the key to tyranny is the relations between the tyrant and his mercenaries without whom tyranny is impossible." In *Personal Rule in Black Africa: Princes, Autocrats, Prophets, Tyrants* (Berkeley: University of California Press, 1982, p. 235).

extension of his personal guard, a private gendarmerie. In other cases, his guard consists of relatives or, more likely, associates who owe him allegiance. The tyrant is thus flanked by indispensable organizations including of course the army, the police, and the secret services, all of whom begin to develop their own practices and acquire a certain autonomy.

Tyrannies do not manage to structure and institutionalize supports. Instead they organize coercion.

CONTEMPORARY TYRANNIES: THE CASE OF THE DOMINICAN REPUBLIC (1930–1961)

Both in Latin America and, since World War II in Africa, a number of tyrannies developed — Batista in Cuba, Somoza in Nicaragua, "Papa Doc" Duvalier in Haiti, Emperor Bokassa in Central Africa, Idi Amin Dada in Uganda — but perhaps none have come so close to the Aristotelian model as the regime of "General" Trujillo in the Dominican Republic (1930–1961).

"Trujillo's was a highly personal dictatorship in which power was not shared even among a small clique, but was concentrated in the hands of one man."[6] Trujillo's career began in the ranks of the armed forces, which were established and trained by the United States during their long occupation of the island from 1916 to 1926. He gradually rose to the highest posts and reached a position that gave him control over appointments and assignments. But he did not take power by a military coup. He was "elected" president in 1930. It was a campaign in which his squads terrorized the countryside and forced the liberals to withdraw.

Once in office he organized his own personal government. The military remained the pillar of his regime, and they grew in numbers and waxed in wealth. At the very top of the officers' hierarchy were the tyrant's cronies but, as with Dionysius, Trujillo suspected them. They were shifted from post to post, special police organizations spied on them, and some disappeared. Since the governmental structure was highly centralized in the hands of Trujillo, all local autonomies were abolished and the bureaucracy grew. Unlike many tyrants, Trujillo established a party, the Dominican Party, forcing almost everybody to "belong." It was primarily an instrument of propaganda, which organized demonstrations, festivals,

6. Howard Wiarda, *Dictatorship and Development: The Method of Control in Trujillo's Dominican Republic* (Gainesville, Fla.: University of Florida Press, 1968, p. 26). I am greatly indebted to the author for the sketch I give here, although I tend to emphasize the tyrannical aspects of Trujillo's regime rather than development.

holidays, and special events to bring out the people. At election time, the party was expected to bring out the vote, one way or another. The police also grew in numbers and its presence was felt everywhere. After Trujillo's enemies had been silenced, especially among the traditional elites, potential enemies were sought out, such as those who refused to show their outright support, remained passive, or "talked with strangers." The police utilized all instruments of intimidation and terror including torture, and thousands lost their lives. Professional associations were destroyed and, in some cases, new ones were established by Trujillo.

Yet what was perhaps the most singular trait in Trujillo's tyranny was his overwhelming control of the small island's economy. Like Dionysius he amassed enormous personal wealth at the expense of his subjects, gradually dispossessed them of their property, and became the biggest capitalist on the island. He owned the two newspapers; controlled the national bank; was the biggest owner of sugar plantations; the biggest importer and exporter; the owner of the greatest part of the island's arable land; the owner of the shipyards, the dockyards, and two shipping lines; the major manufacturer of cigarettes; the biggest cattle rancher and cattle raiser; the sole distributor of pasteurized milk; the biggest meat producer and exporter; and last but not least the owner of gambling casinos and whorehouses. It was difficult to distinguish the economy from Trujillo. Some 50 percent of the gainfully employed worked for him, and their livelihood depended on his will as expressed in the form of laws that he himself drew up.

While the control of the economy was a device to acquire greater wealth for himself, his family members, and some of his immediate councilors and friends, it was also the surest instrument of political domination. Trujillo used his wealth and control over the economy to increase his power, and the citizenry was reduced to a state of abject dependency. In sum, "The state functioned as the legal servant of Trujillo's agricultural, industrial and commercial enterprises, the armed forces as its security guards, the national territory as its field of operation and exploration and the populace as its labor force, producer and consumer."[7]

There was one center of power, or at least of potential opposition, that Trujillo did not try to invade, restructure, or reduce: the Catholic church. There was no need to. The Church remained his staunchest ally in return for the many benefits and privileges he bestowed upon it. New churches were built, and special benefits and subsidies were provided

7. Wiarda, op. cit., p. 81.

for the Church and the churchmen. Above all, a Concordat was signed between the state (i.e., Trujillo) and the Church, which declared that the Catholic religion was to be the religion of the state. Only religious marriages were recognized, divorce remained outlawed, the Church was given the freedom to establish schools and, needless to say, there was no interference with ceremonies and rituals. The Church had indeed reached a position "of splendor," according to one cleric. Being rich and apparently autonomous, it lavished praise on its benefactor. It was only in the last years of Trujillo's reign that frictions developed and then the Church used its autonomy to criticize.

Although overtly Trujillo's control was total and absolute, it never became totalitarian in substance or intent. First, the ideology was kept to the level of rationalization and justification for the rule of the tyrant: it was used to extol order and obedience. Second, the ideology was used to idolize the leader rather than to mobilize the public. Fear rather than involvement characterized the public's behavior, and the majority of the people, mostly peasantry, remained atomized and apathetic. The organizations that Trujillo had set up, including the army and the police, were devoid of strong ideological attachments, or even loyalties, to Trujillo. What bound them together was no purpose other than self-interest in its most naked form. It led to corruption and the never-ending effort to satisfy an increasing number of material wants. Trujillo's wealth simply whetted the appetites of his subordinates, and economic resources were drained away from the people to satisfy the interests of the tyrant and his ruling entourage.

Trujillo met the fate that he feared, the fate that tyrants who are unable to translate their power into authority usually meet. He was assassinated. But even before his demise, the regime that he had put together began to unravel. The army, the police, the party, the middle classes, and foreign powers, including the United States and the Organization of American States, turned against him. The Church too began to reconsider its unholy alliance with the tyrant. The instruments of intimidation and control that Trujillo had set up, each operating independently of the others to carry out his will, now began to move independently of each other, and against him. It is irrelevant from where the shot that killed him came.

Dynastic Regimes

There are few dynastic monarchies in our days (Saudi Arabia, some of the Emirate states, the Sultanate of Brunei that became the 169th independent state on January 1, 1984). What distinguishes them from all other monarchies (in Britain or Scandinavia, for instance) is that the monarchs, or members of the royal family, actually govern. What distinguishes them from tyrannies is that they come to power and use it according to certain well-established rules. Power is generally shared by the king's family (as is wealth). It is a "familial" as well as patrimonial form of government. For example, the Sultan of Brunei, after acquiring independence for his tiny sultanate in the northern part of Borneo, appointed various members of his family to various governmental posts. His father became Secretary of Defense, his brother took care of foreign affairs, etc. The same is of course true in Saudia Arabia. The wealth of the kingdom is indistinguishable from the personal wealth of the monarch; he can dispose of it at will. But unlike tyrants, dynastic monarchs do not have to take it by force. It is theirs by divine law, custom, and inheritance.

In contrast to tyrannies, the power of the king is tempered by immemorial customs, conventions, understandings, and religious canons, which establish the subjection of the people to the monarch but also put restraints on arbitrary rule. The prescription against the use of alcohol must apply to all alike; the subjection of women should permit no exceptions; the lack of political rights applies to all. Subjection therefore does not result from the overt application of force — it is simply internalized by custom and tradition. Considerable discretion, however, exists for the king when his will is contradicted or when there appears to be a beginning of political dissidence. Punishment and sanctions then fit not so much the crime as the political gravity of a crime as assessed by the king.

The most conspicuous characteristic of absolutist dynastic regimes is the lack of participation and representative institutions.[8] There are no political parties or a single party, no associations dealing with political or related issues, no free press, and no free speech. The individuals and associational groups are subjects; they accept and acquiesce to the powers above. Contemporary dynastic monarchies, however, do enjoy two major sources of support and consent. The first is custom and tradition, which have been maintained in a world of change. The citizen knows that kings had commanded in the past and according to tradition they should command now. Every effort is made to insulate the people from new ideas from abroad that may undermine their loyalties. Besides insulation, some of the dynastic kingdoms have availed themselves of what no absolutist regime had possessed in the past: wealth in the form of oil. The per capita income in Saudi Arabia, the Gulf Emirates, and the newly established Sultanate of Brunei averages about $20,000. The wealth has been used to provide free services in the areas of health, selective (mostly technical) education, retirement benefits, transportation, and leisure and entertainment on a scale unknown to other parts of the world. Hence

8. Morocco is an exception. Some forms of a parliamentary government have been put in place but the king actually manipulates the legislature and controls decisions.

traditional obedience becomes reinforced by complacency, even satisfaction.

Most of the dynastic kingdoms that exist represent a peculiar combination of traditionalism and wealth.[9] As long as a fair balance is maintained between wealth that can be distributed and traditionalism that nurtures deference and as long as there are no international incidents to upset it, these regimes survive. But a change in the traditional values or a sudden fall in income may very well destroy the source that gives dynastic rulers their supports.

Military Regimes

A great deal of attention has been paid recently to various forms of military intervention and military regimes.[10] Armies that intervene and states in which army intervention occurs are often called "praetorian" armies and "praetorian" states.[11] The latter, as Amos Perlmutter defines them, are states "in which the army has the potential to dominate the political system."[12] However, to the "potential" (which exists with all armies) one must also add the "disposition" to dominate, which is not present everywhere.

Making a survey of praetorian armies, states, coups d'état, and military regimes since the end of World War II is recounting the experience of almost two-thirds of the nation-states of our world. It is a survey that will have to be rewritten and brought up to date every year as military dictatorships constantly give place to civilian rule and vice versa. In 1982–1984, for instance, there were three shifts from civilian governance to military rule in Nigeria, Guinea, and Poland. There were four from military to civilian government in Argentina, Brazil, Turkey, and Uruguay. In the next few years many more shifts are likely to occur.

Samuel Finer counted eighty-eight military coups in fifty-two countries between 1958 and 1969.[13] According to Eric Nordlinger, it was only in Costa Rica and Mexico that the soldiers have not intervened in Latin America during the last forty-five years. "Between 1945 and 1976, soldiers carried out successful coups in half of the eighteen Asian states. By 1976 the soldiers had made at least one successful or unsuccessful attempt to seize power in two-thirds of the Middle Eastern and North

9. Not Nepal or Morocco, however, where there is no oil.
10. See Eric Nordlinger, *Soldiers and Politics: Military Coups and Governments* (Englewood Cliffs, N.J.: Prentice-Hall, 1977); Amos Perlmutter, *Egypt—A Praetorian State* (New Brunswick, N.J.: Transaction Books, 1974); Abraham Lowenthal (ed.), *Armies and Politics in Latin America* (New York: Holmes and Meier, 1976); Amos Perlmutter (ed.), *The Military and Politics in Modern Times,* (New Haven, Conn.: Yale University Press, 1977).
11. The Roman emperors established a special bodyguard, known as the praetorian guard, a personal army to protect the emperor and carry out his orders. It eventually became a powerful instrument that made and unmade emperors. It became a political force and was used as such, and it had a highly destabilizing influence over the course of the Roman Empire.
12. Amos Perlmutter, op cit., p. 4.
13. Samuel H. Finaer: *Comparative Politics* (London: Penguin, 1970).

TABLE 9-2 Military Regimes in Tropical Africa, 1970–1984

COUNTRY	YEAR OF MILITARY COUPS	PRESENT STATUS
Burundi	Nov. 2, 1976	Military
Central African Republic	Sept. 20, 1979;	Military
	Sept. 1, 1981	Military
Chad	Apr. 13, 1981	Military
Ethiopia	Sept. 12, 1974	Military
Ghana	Jan. 13, 1972;	Military
	July 5, 1978;	Military
	June 4, 1979;	Military
	Dec. 31, 1983	Military
Guinea Bissau	Nov. 15, 1980	Military
Liberia	April 12, 1980	Military
Malagasy	Oct. 14, 1972	Military
Mauritania	July 10, 1978	Military
Niger	Apr. 15, 1974	Military
Nigeria	July 29, 1975;	Military
	Dec. 1983	Military
Rwanda	July 15, 1973	Military
Sudan	July 19, 1971;	Military
	July 22, 1971	Military
Uganda	Jan. 25, 1971;	?
	1980	?
Upper Volta	Feb. 8, 1974;	Military
	Nov. 24, 1980;	Military
	Nov. 7, 1982;	Military
	1983	Military
Guinea	April 4, 1984	Military

Compiled from: Africa Research Bulletin, Exeter, England, African Research Limited, *Africa Today,* 1981.
C. Cook and D. Killingray, *African Political Facts Since 1945,* London, African Publishing Co., 1978.
Robert Jackson and Carl Rosberg, *Personal Rule in Black Africa,* Berkeley, University of California Press, 1982.

African states. They established military regimes in Egypt, Syria, Iraq, the Sudan, Libya, and Algeria. . . . By 1976 coups had occurred in more than half of the African countries, and in that year the military occupied the seat of government in half of them." Nordlinger concludes that the study of military authoritarian governments "is the study of one of the most common, and thus characteristic, aspects of non-Western politics."[14] In fact the most common form of contemporary authoritarianism is military government (see Table 9–2 and Appendix).

Why Do Armies Intervene? If we can give the reasons why armies have *not* intervened in some countries, we might generalize more easily about the reasons why they do so often in so many others.

14. Eric Nordlinger, op. cit., p. 6.

There seem to be two major reasons why the armed forces do *not* intervene:

1. A strong and genuine affinity between the officer corps, the governing elite, and the public at large about the political norms, values, and institutions of the political regime. The acceptance of civilian rule and its institutions is internalized in the officer corps. Army intervention is considered improper and unacceptable by everybody concerned: the government, the people, and, most importantly, the officers themselves.
2. Civilian governance has developed roots that are so deep and legitimized that the prospects of a successful army intervention appear very dim even to those among the military who may entertain the thought of a military takeover.

It is for these reasons that old political societies are relatively immune to military coups, while the new political regimes, especially in the Third World countries, are not valued by the majority of the people; the institutions cannot compromise conflicts and translate interests and demands into policy; and the linkages and participatory mechanisms between those in the command structure and the people are inadequate. There is a pervasive crisis of legitimacy.

Special Circumstances A number of special circumstances, especially in Third World countries, trigger military intervention:

1. *Crisis:* There is a breakdown in the orderly process of community life in a locality, region, or the whole nation. Such a breakdown can be caused by an earthquake, civil disobedience, famine, or of course the threat of an enemy attack.

2. *The distribution of goods:* The army is a corporate entity entitled to privileges, rewards, and special attention. Even in democratic regimes the proposition that the army is neutral and will stay so is based on the assumption that it receives proper and often privileged consideration. In societies that are poor, however, resources are scarce to begin with and there are just not enough spoils to distribute to the military. The result is an unhappy army, which can very quickly develop a disposition to intervene.

3. *Counterrevolution:* In many cases the military intervene to protect the existing social and economic status quo and relatedly their own interests. Social protests, revolutionary ideologies, and movements inspired by Marxism endanger the governing elite, and any threats to the oligarchy spell danger to the army as well.

4. *The military savior:* In times of war, the military hero may find it easy to impose his own (and authoritarian) rule. The Roman generals fresh from victory vied with each other to become emperors. Napoleon actually did become an emperor. Although Nasser lost the Seven-Day War in 1973 his military exploits became legendary. Had the British been

forced to relinquish their control of the Falkland Islands, General Galtieri, the then president of Argentina and his military junta would have gained fame and supports instead of having to face a court martial. However, the times of the military hero seem to be gone. Today, few generals, whether from small or big countries, can lead their armies to military victory and return in triumph to impose their rule.

5. *Breakdown in succession:* Armies intervene when there are no clear and legitimized procedures to replace a ruler after his death. No head of government in an independent African state has ever given place to an opposition leader through elections.[15] Even where elections do take place, the results are frequently contested and the army intervenes. Only when there is a single party strong enough to arrange for succession is army intervention unlikely.

6. *Military aid:* While societal background factors and the lack of legitimacy play a critical role in the emergence of military rule, several international developments after World War II have also played a part. Massive military aid was given to the new nations by the United States, the Soviet Union, France, and Britain. This turn of events strengthened the position of the military and gave them the resources to influence and determine policies. With massive foreign aid, the army quickly became the dominant organization in most of the new nations.

With military aid went the training of cadres and officers both abroad and at home. They were trained at staff colleges and training schools by Soviet, French, or American instructors. The officer corps became increasingly professional since they had learned new and specialized techniques and skills. As a result, they were recruited for administrative and government positions where their job was to modernize other sectors of the society and the economy. As a modernizing agency, the army and its officers became increasingly impatient with traditional political elites. Quite often their desire to modernize prompted them to intervene.

Forms of Military Rule An army dictatorship can assume a variety of forms. As Eric Nordlinger points out, "Many [military] coups entail immediate and fundamental changes in regime structure. . . . [The officers] establish an authoritarian regime that is closed to popular participation and competition. In doing so, they destroy or alter those structural features of the previous regimes that do not accord with their own preferences."[16] Every time the army intervenes and assumes political power, it restructures the government. There are therefore different forms of praetorianism, each of which has its own special characteristics and does its own restructuring. Nordlinger identified three forms: "guardians," "moderators," and "rulers."[17] Amos Perlmutter suggests

15. According to Richard Sklar, Mauritania is the only exception.
16. Eric Nordlinger, op. cit., p. 7.
17. *Ibid.*, p. 11.

two: "guardians" and "rulers."[18] I also suggest two: direct and indirect military governance.

Direct Military Rule With direct military rule the entire army from generals down to the noncommissioned officers takes over the civilian government. Orders and decisions from the top are passed down the line for implementation and execution through the chain of command. The army in effect becomes the government. Civilian officials are often dismissed and many civilian institutions are dismantled or superseded by military ones. There is naturally an internal functional division in military governance. A collegial body usually called a "junta" (the top military officers) make the major political decisions. There is an officers' cabinet, high-ranking officers who occupy ministerial positions. There is also an executive branch staffed by middle-rank officers who implement the orders, while actual management and administration are entrusted to the lower echelons and the NCOs (noncommissioned officers).

This is the purest form of military governance, "the ideal type," which can be found virtually nowhere. Turkey between 1980 and 1983, Greece between 1967 and 1974, Chile since 1973 and Nigeria in 1984 came the closest. In reality, even when there is direct military governance, civilians are also involved. The civil service and local administrations continue to be manned by civilians. Though military courts assume and exercise ultimate jurisdiction, the civilian courts are allowed to administer at least civil justice, leaving the military to deal with the penal code. Civilian experts are asked to participate and deliberate with the military at the highest levels in the cabinet. Also, if the regime that was replaced by the military had a civilian as chief of state, a president or a hereditary monarch, the military may sometimes be inclined to keep him in office, as long as he remains pliant. The military junta in Greece (1967–1974) allowed the king to keep his throne until his opposition and his aborted military countercoup brought about his removal. In Latin America or Africa, where the office of a civilian president is often constitutionally powerful, military intervention is frequently followed by the dismissal or the arrest or sometimes the assassination of a civilian president, and a military leader takes over.

This is briefly the organization of the command structure in a military regime. The generals leave their barracks to become statesmen. But in so doing, they imbue the regime with their own alleged virtues: organization, hierarchy, command and obedience, discipline, punctuality, and efficiency. Even after leaving their barracks, they long for the simple world of the garrison and try to transform the regime into a garrison-state. They eliminate participatory mechanisms such as legislatures, parties, and political associations; they do away with competitive politics and all instrumentalities of representation in order to reduce complex issues into

18. Amos Perlmutter, op. cit., p. 4.

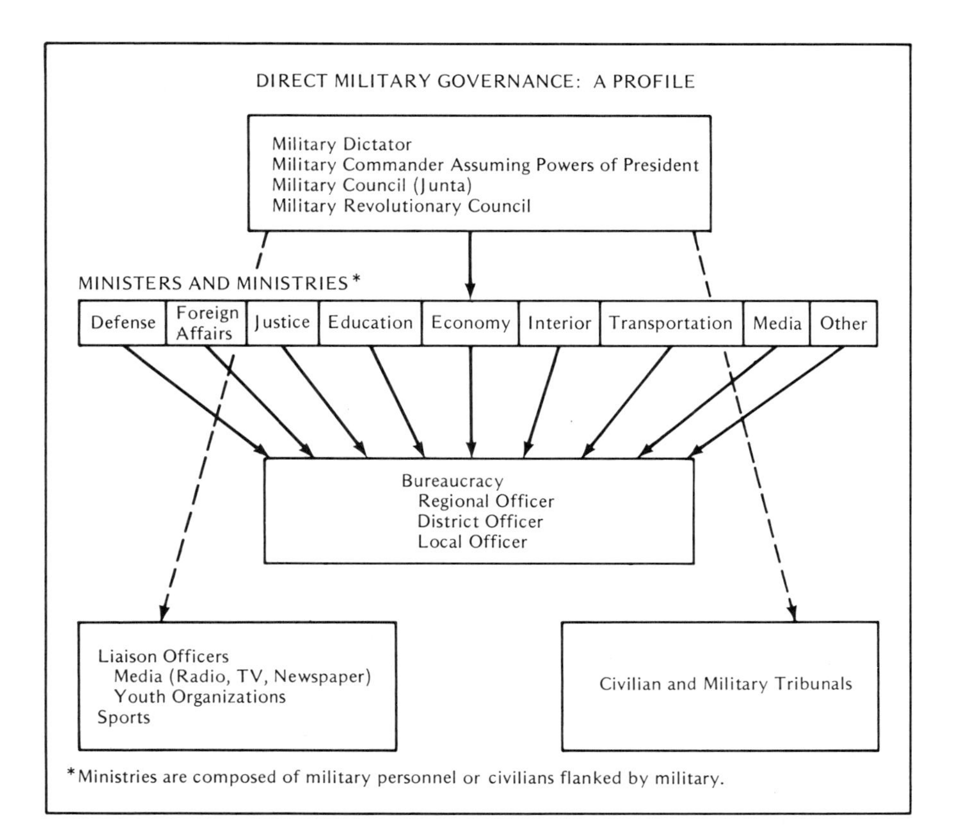

one authoritative and enforceable order. As General Pinochet of Chile said in an interview "Everything is either black or white."[19]

Naturally the major pillar of military rulership is force. Without any limits on its scope and use, military regimes not only resort to it but rely on it to keep the citizenry submissive. The military and the civilian police coordinate their efforts and special sections are set up to seek and destroy dissidence. Suspects are forced into exile or sent to concentration camps, special prisons, or deserted islands. Preventive measures are taken in the form of arrests or summary executions. Deviation from military commands is treasonous and dealt with accordingly. The rule of the military remains true to the military logic that prevails in the barracks: disagreement is rooted out and any form of disobedience is severely punished. The end purpose is to promote instant obedience or at least to prevent any overt disobedience.

Indirect Military Rule Indirect military rule differs from direct military rule in that no matter how much they are manipulated and controlled

19. *The New York Times*, August 6, 1984.

the political institutions and the civilian officials do exist. Even if only a facade, civilian government retains a degree of legitimacy. There are also some civil and political rights as well as some political participation, representation, and even competition no matter how narrowly circumscribed. After October 1983 Turkey moved away from direct military rulership to a regime where the army remains the controlling force, but elections took place and a civilian government took office. Brazil and Argentina have been moving in the same direction and it appears that the civilian government is gaining a genuine degree of autonomy in both countries.

There are three different manifestations of indirect military rule: army control, army arbitration, and army veto.

1. *Army control:* The army remains in the barracks but the civilians constantly contact the commanding generals for instructions. Usually the instructions concern foreign policy and defense, but today it is becoming more and more common to address domestic matters such as social and economic problems or conflicts. The civilians are often but a facade and provide the army with a scapegoat for its errors or failures. Thus, the army can escape any attacks on its honor, its reputation, or its efficiency. The civilians take the blame, the army the praise. Several Latin American governments operate in this manner, and such regimes may be called "cryptomilitary." This is still the case in Turkey and Thailand.

2. *Arbitration:* Again the army remains in the barracks while civilian officeholders take their own initiatives in policy making and policy formulation. Political parties develop their programs and debate them; there is representative government and competitive politics. But with conflicts or disputes that invariably pit not only political parties and leaders but also separate units of the command structure (e.g., a monarch and his parliament, a president of a republic and his prime minister, a prime minister and his parliament) against each other, the army intervenes to resolve the problem and endorses one policy or one civilian leader or one party over the other.[20] Army arbitration, frequently transformed into direct rule, has been typical not only in Latin American and some African democracies but also in a communist totalitarian regime like Poland. Army arbitration to settle a government succession crisis has been common in virtually all authoritarian regimes and some believe that it plays an important role even in the Soviet Union. An effort was made to exercise it in France in 1958 when the French generals in Algeria tried to intervene in the formation of a civilian government.

3. *Army veto:* The army veto is a far cry from direct military rulership. Civilian government and representative institutions are in full operation. Competitive politics in the form of parties and open (and often free) elections take place and civil rights exist. There are certain policy matters,

20. It was succintly put by an Uruguayan civilian leader on the eve of the first election in that country since 1974: "The military are going back to the barracks," he said, "but whether they stay there will depend on how we civilians run our democracy" (reported in the *Boston Globe*, Nov. 25, 1984).

however, for which the consent of the army is needed. The army can veto decisions made by the civilian authorities. When the specifics of the veto power are clearly known and accepted in advance, the army assumes an independent role.

In conclusion, we should note that it is not always easy to identify the varieties and variations of indirect military rule. There are many shades and degrees of indirect rule: it can range from support for a given government, to military intervention in selected policy areas, to selective military arbitration only when the civilian political leaders and the interests they speak for seem to be deadlocked, to the open preferences given by the military for some political parties and leaders as opposed to others. All these hybrid arrangements, however, correspond to various degrees of authoritarianism. As we move from direct to indirect military rulership we also move from strict authoritarianism to varying degrees of controlled pluralism where there are representative and party institutions, political participation, competitive elections, and political and civil rights. The army becomes one of the players. But its weight is ever-present even if not always seen, and, in the last analysis, the parameters of political freedom and competition are set by the army.

Cryptomilitary Democracies Indirect military control ranging from arbitration to veto is prevalent in some self-styled democratic regimes where (1) there is a constitution that formally enumerates individual rights and freedoms, (2) elections are held, and (3) the command structure is in the hands of civilians. In reality, however, these regimes operate *under* the military who can impose their policy preferences, block decisions made on foreign or domestic matters, directly influence elections, and impose their candidates in one way or another. In some such regimes the military gives direct support to political parties, as in Turkey in the election of 1983 and in the 1985 presidential election in Brazil. Frequently, if they fail to sway the electorate, they may ignore its verdict.

In cryptomilitary regimes it is not always easy to tell where the military intervention ends and the democratic practices and institutions begin. They are a mix and it is difficult to sort out the military from the democratic parts. In countries with a long history of military intervention, the viability of democracy is always assessed in terms of the army's disposition. In many Latin American republics — Argentina, Brazil, Peru, Bolivia, Uruguay, Guatemala, Colombia, and others — a democratic facade often hides the reality of indirect military rule. The military, even when in their barracks, continue to cast their long shadow.

MILITARY RULERS: GREECE (1967–1974) AND CHILE (1973–?): — A SKETCH

In two countries with quite different historical, cultural, and political traditions, a military authoritarian regime emerged practically within the same decade: in Greece in 1967, which lasted for seven years and in Chile in 1973, which is still going strong (but for how long remains uncertain). Yet despite the many background differences, the two regimes show striking similarities both in their organization and their rationale:

1. In both countries the military came to power by a coup d'état. The regimes were organized by the military and, though in different degrees and ways, were run by the military. In Greece it was the colonels who organized their coup d'état, while in Chile it was the top military officers. In both, a small group of officers — a junta — took charge of the affairs of state. The coups were aimed against a democratic regime in which left-wing forces, socialists, and communists or, at least in the case of Greece, liberal centrists had gained or seemed to have gained a strong position. Both the Greek and the Chilean military claimed to act in order to preempt a revolution from the left.
2. Once in power, the two regimes allowed for military-civilian cooperation. Although civilians worked side by side with the military in the ministries and the administration, the major policy decisions were made by the junta.
3. Both regimes turned against the country's political leaders, even conservative ones, who were exiled or fled, put under house arrest, or detained in special detention camps, and some disappeared.
4. All political parties were dissolved.
5. Civil rights were abolished, although restrictions were turned on and off, as the occasion demanded.
6. The police and secret services were expanded in order to intimidate and ferret out opposition.
7. The future of the leader was guaranteed through constitutional devices. Pinochet in Chile may yet stay in office until 1989 and thereafter, if reelected.
8. The formation of new associations and groups were prohibited unless they were controlled by the junta. Both regimes favored an atomization of the society and remained hostile to associational freedoms or corporatist arrangements. They promoted individualism, as long as the individuals remained politically docile and did not form a threatening bloc. However, they did not object to economic freedoms and in fact encouraged them.
9. The major purpose of their rule was the preservation of internal order, but in Chile emphasis was also placed on economic restructuring and reorganization. The people could and were encouraged to pursue their tasks and interests in the economy, family life, and entertainment.

However, these pursuits were always under the watchful eye of the military. The distinction between the public and the private domains was clearly drawn, and the latter was encouraged as long as it did not intrude into matters of state.

10. Any ideological positions or movements linked to ideology were eschewed. Christian and religious values were stressed and anticommunism (as defined by the military) remained the major ideological commitment.
11. Both military regimes were remarkably similar in their proximate and ultimate ends: to cure society of Marxism and instill national unity. Pinochet spoke of "guided" or "protected" democracy. The Greek colonels referred to the country as a patient on the operating table, and they promised to provide the surgical cure. The leaders claimed to be democrats. They promised that when they had ultimately restored true democracy, they would withdraw and return to the barracks.
12. Foreign agents, communists, and radicals were blamed for whatever opposition they encountered. (The junta in Chile continues to encounter it.) Both regimes claimed to speak for the people and to be committed to their welfare and happiness. They both showed the same puritanical characteristics: a commitment to simple Christian values. (Needless to say, there has always been a great deal of corruption and graft among many of the top military leaders.)
13. Neither Pinochet nor the top military leaders in Greece (who are now in jail) were charismatic figures or great orators, seeking followers and organizing demonstrations in their support. They were apolitical figures, in essence military men who only "reluctantly" assumed the burdens of the state. From beginning to the end, their virtues remained military virtues.
14. The military junta considered its role to be essentially a duty, best done in cooperation with their military fellow officers. Their reference group was always the military with whom they had shared and risked their lives, broken their bread, and drank their wine. Nonetheless, there was a clear affinity between the generals and the technocrats who shared the same devotion to organization, hierarchy, and discipline.

In two different corners of the world the Greek and Chilean military regimes appear singularly alike. Soldiers of the world, you don't have to unite. You are all alike!

BRAZIL: A PARAMILITARY REGIME?

Brazil is not a case where civilian and military institutions can be compartmentalized. The military and its institutions and the state and its institutions live together or at least have lived together in relative harmony: the military permeates the society and the state, the state and the society embrace the military. It is now more than 100 years that the military in Brazil have occupied a dominant position in both the society and the political system.

The military officers are a part of the ruling elite. They engage in business, banking, industrial, and commercial interests. Others have foreign economic interests, American and multinational, and still others are in the bureaucracy. The army is bound by a common ideology that is widely shared by most of the elites: (1) belief in private property and private enterprise, including the sanctity of contracts and profits; (2) a claim that the authority of the military should not be questioned; and (3) the need to avoid sudden political or social changes that may endanger the position of the elites (including the army).

In 1949 the Superior War College was founded for training not only military but also civilian, cadres — training that went beyond military matters. It also included social and political issues and the development of an ideology. (Between 1950 and 1967 about 50 percent of all graduates were civilian.) The training in the Superior War College stresses nationalism, the rule of the expert in social, political, and economic planning, anticommunism, and a strong central government.

The substance of the army's ideology remains developmentalist but paternalistic. Its major goal is to achieve modernization while averting the direct participation and support of the people in the selection of leaders and policies. As long as the populist forces, the workers and the peasantry, can be contained, the elites can govern, and the army makes sure that they are contained and controlled. Populism has occasionally reared its head in the person of a leader who goes over the head of the elite to appeal to the masses. This is the worst possible enemy of elite rule and hence whenever it comes close to surfacing, the army intervenes.

The army has developed many mechanisms of direct and indirect control that have been institutionalized in the Brazilian political system. First, quite a few of the top army generals have managed to become president. All the presidents between 1964 and 1984 were generals. Second, with control of the presidency, whose powers are far broader than those of an American president, the military can make key governmental appointments in the cabinet and the top echelons of the bureaucracy. Third, the military have often founded and used political parties to ensure the election of loyalists to the congress, which is usually a rubber stamp representative assembly. They have created a political-military complex. Although they are sometimes unable to control an election, they can restructure the constitution to accommodate their control. For example, to thwart President Goulart in 1963, whom the army did not trust, special provisions were introduced giving more power to the congress. The army continues to oppose the direct election of the president by the people. Instead they favor an indirect election by a congress in order to avoid the populist trait of a direct election by the people. If all these measures fail, the ultimate mechanism employed by the military has been the coup d'état — the *golpe.*

A coup d'état is often painless and almost unnoticed. It is merely a change from informal controls by the army to the assumption of formal control. However, with a coup d'état the army becomes highly visible and there may be an adverse reaction that jeopardizes its position and legitimacy. The army governed between 1964 and 1984, but Brazil entered a period of civilian government with the election of a civilian president in 1985. For how long, it remains to be seen.

In brief, the role of the army, especially in the last forty-five years, has been to monitor conflicts, to keep them within controllable bounds, and to promote and at times to impose compromises. The army sets the parameters of disagreements, determines the ones that are permissible, and steps in to suppress others. In this sense it is the arbiter of the regime — the balance wheel — but it also turns the wheel that shapes the political conduct of many of the actors.

Today the army and the elites it shields face powerful internal pressures from the peasantry and the workers, who have demanded urban and social services such as housing, education, health, transportation, employment and employment benefits, old age pensions, and insurance. There are also grievances stemming from chronic inflation. All of these factors have played a part in the demands for democratization, freedom for the political parties, and free and direct elections of the president. But the army is keeping a watchful eye over its newly established civilian president. They accept reforms, yet never allow them to go so far as to endanger the elites in power. Although its future is uncertain, Brazil remains under indirect military rule.

Single-Party Authoritarian Regimes

Similar structures often play different roles and perform different functions — a problem that has always made institutional comparisons difficult. This is particularly true with single-party systems in authoritarian regimes — military or civilian — such as those in Syria, Iraq, Tunisia, Tanzania, Egypt, Kenya, and even in Mexico, where the rule of a dominant (not single) party has been institutionalized.[21] What are the characteristics of the single-party authoritarian regimes?

Characteristics

Single parties in authoritarian regimes display different characteristics from those we found in totalitarian regimes.

First, the single party is only *one* of the organizations the regime establishes or allows in order to maintain its rule and gain supports. It vies with other organizations; notably, the army, the churches, the bureaucracy, the state, and professional groups. It is, at best, just one of the many pillars on which the regime rests. This was the case in Franco's Spain, where the single party — *Falange* — was in constant rivalry with other major organizations like the Catholic church, the army, and the bureaucracy. It never gained a dominant position. Similarly, the parties formed by dictators like Trujillo (in the Dominican Republic) or Stroessner (in Paraguay) did no more than provide instruments to regiment the population, and dispense patronage.

Second, the single party is in a constant state of flux — it goes through a period of ebb and flow. As membership increases, front organizations develop, and the leadership seeks supports. Sometimes the party seems to be on the verge of becoming a dominant political force, subordinating all others. At other times the same party seems to atrophy: membership declines; the state agencies gain ascendancy; the army or other groups overshadow it. Thus Franco occasionally had to use the *Falange* as a counterveiling force against the Catholic church, the army, business groups, or the bureaucracy, because the circumstances were always changing. In Egypt, Nasser frequently had to strengthen the Arab Socialist Union against the armed forces.

Third, in many authoritarian regimes the single party has shown clear signs of erosion and decline. All societies that go through rapid and radical changes because of powerful radical movements led by the military or by a charismatic leader tend to revert to "normalcy." The emphasis gradually shifts to performance and efficiency, to the satisfaction of everyday needs, to obedience and compliance.

In virtually the whole of Africa the party, after a period of flow, has been in decline. Henry Bienen had this to say about African political parties:

21. The most comprehensive comparative overview is Samuel H. Huntington and Clement Moore (eds.) *Authoritarian Politics in Modern Societies* (New York: Basic Books, 1970).

> . . . as the victorious parties formed governments, they lost functional relevance and coherence. The growth of state agencies proceeded, and party functions atrophied. The party became largely an agency of the government bureaucracy or, at the expense of its rank and file, in certain cases it became a mere extension of the personality of a strong president or prime minister. No matter what roles parties have been assigned, almost everywhere in tropical Africa — whether in single party, multi-party, or non-party states — they perform few.[22]

To summarize, single parties in authoritarian regimes tend to be at best agencies of support for the government. They provide only limited channels of popular participation; they are manipulated by the power-holders — frequently the military — to provide a counterveiling force against other groups or potential centers of power; after a period of flow, usually associated with a mobilizing phase to achieve national independence, there is an ebb; ideology and mobilization wane; recruitment for the government and the bureaucracy drain the party cadres; the military step in; and the party is relegated to an adjunct position.

In general, single parties in authoritarian regimes have failed to institutionalize themselves in contrast to single parties in totalitarian regimes. The latter have a strong mobilizing ideology and infuse it into the mass organizations they create while at the same time proceeding to subordinate all competing elite groups, including the army.

Bibliography

Bienen, Henry. *Kenya: The Parties of Participation and Control.* Princeton, N.J.: Princeton University Press, 1974.

———. *Tanzania: Party Transformation and Economic Development.* Princeton, N.J.: Princeton University Press, 1970.

——— (ed.). *The Military Intervenes: Case Studies in Political Development.* New York: Russell Sage Foundation, 1968.

——— (ed.). *The Military and Modernization.* New York: Lieber-Atherton Press, 1971.

Bill, James A., and Carl Leiden. *Politics in the Middle East,* 2d ed. Boston: Little, Brown, 1984.

Booth, John A. *The End of the Beginning: The Nicaraguan Revolution.* Colorado: Westview Press, 1982.

Clements, Frank. *Saudi Arabia.* Calif.: American Bibliographical Center/Clio Press, 1979.

Clogg, Richard, and George Yannopoulos (eds.). *Greece Under Military Rule.* New York: Basic Books, 1972.

22. Henry Bienen, "One Party Systems in Africa," in Huntington and Moore, op. cit., pp. 99–100.

Crasweller, Robert D. *Trujillo: The Life and Times of a Caribbean Dictator.* New York: Macmillan, 1966.

Devlin, John F. *Syria: Modern State in an Ancient Land.* Colorado: Westview Press, 1983.

Dickenson, John P. *Brazil.* Colorado: Westview Press, 1978.

Elliott, David L. *Thailand: Origins of Military Rule.* London: Zeal Press, 1980.

Feit, Edward. *The Armed Bureaucrats: Military-Administrative Regimes and Political Development.* Boston: Houghton Mifflin, 1973.

Findlay, Allan M., Anne M. Findlay, and Richard Lawless. *Tunisia.* Calif.: American Bibliographical Center/Clio Press, 1982.

Finer, Sam E. *The Man on Horseback: The Role of the Military in Politics.* New York: Praeger, 1962.

Flynn, Peter. *Brazil: A Political Analysis.* Colorado: Westview Press, 1978.

Huntington, Samuel, and Clement Moore (eds.). *Authoritarian Politics in Modern Society.* New York: Basic Books, 1970.

Jackson, Robert A., and Carl Rosberg. *Personal Rule in Black Africa: Princes, Autocrats, Prophets, Tyrants.* Berkeley: University of California, 1982.

Janowitz, Morris. *On Military Intervention.* Rotterdam University Press, 1971.

Lord Kinross. *Ataturk: A Biography of Mustafa Kemal, Father of Modern Turkey.* New York: William Morris and Co., 1965.

LaPalombara, Joseph, and M. Weiner (eds.). *Political Parties and Political Development.* Princeton, N.J.: Princeton University Press, 1966.

Lasswell, Harold, and Daniel Lerner (eds.). *World Revolutionary Elites: Studies in Coercive Ideological Movements.* Boston: M.I.T. Press, 1966.

Latin American Studies Association Forum, vol. XV, no. 2, "Pinochet in Chile," pp. 11–15 and "The Political Crisis of the Pinochet Regime," by Arturo Velenzuela, pp. 17–20.

Linz, Juan. "Totalitarianism and Authoritarianism," in *Handbook of Political Science,* vol. 3. Reading, Mass.: Addison-Wesley, 1975.

Lipset, S. M., and A. Solar (eds.). *Elites in Latin America.* Oxford University Press, 1973.

Lowenthal, Abraham F. (ed.). *Armies and Politics in Latin America.* New York: Holmes and Meier Publications, 1976.

Needler, Martin C. *Political Systems in Latin America.* New York: Reinholt and Co., 1970.

Nordlinger, Eric. *Soldiers in Politics: Military Coups and Government.* Englewood Cliffs, N.J.: Prentice-Hall, 1977.

Payne, Stanley. *The Falange: A History of Spanish Fascism.* Calif.: Stanford University Press, 1961.

Perlmutter, Amos. *Egypt: The Praetorian State.* New Brunswick, N.J.: Transaction Books, 1974.

———. *The Military and Politics in Modern Times.* New Haven: Yale University Press, 1977.

———. *Modern Authoritarianism: A Comparative Institutional Analysis.* New Haven: Yale University Press, 1981.

Shaw, John A., and David E. Long. *Saudi Arabia's Modernization: The Impact of Change on Stability.* New York: Praeger, 1982.

Stepen, Alfred (ed.). *Authoritarian Brazil: Origins, Policies and Future.* New Haven: Yale University Press, 1973.

Strauss, Leo. *On Tyranny.* Ithaca: Cornell University Press, 1975.

Wesson, Robert G. *Brazil in Transition.* New York: Praeger, 1983.

Wiarda, Howard. *Dictatorship and Development: The Methods of Control in Trujillo's Dominican Republic.* Gainesville: University of Florida, 1968.

Wiarda, Howard, and Harvey Kline. *Latin American Politics and Development,* 2d ed. Boulder, Colo.: Westview Press, 1985.

Wittfogel, Karl. *A Comparative Study of Total Power.* New Haven: Yale University Press, 1957.

Zinn, Ricardo. *Argentina: A Nation at the Crossroads of Myth and Reality.* New York: R. Speller, 1979.

10 Authoritarian Regimes: Flux and Consolidation

Introduction

There is a great deal of internal change and transformation in authoritarian regimes, and these shifts affect the institutional arrangements and structures. Guinea became a military dictatorship in 1984 while Argentina suddenly joined the democracies in 1983. Ethiopia by the end of 1984 emerged as a single-party communist regime. Brazil returned to a civilian president in 1984 after twenty years of military rule. There are also basic and fundamental changes that modify the very nature of the regime. In the 1970s the authoritarian regimes collapsed in Spain, Portugal, and Greece and many claim that military dictatorships are giving way to democracy in a number of Latin American countries.

Today authoritarian regimes are exposed to two competing ideologies: democracy (including democratic socialism) and revolutionary communism. There is no necessary reason, however, to expect that these regimes will move toward either the model of democracy or totalitarian communism. Nor is there any reason to assume that having moved in one or the other direction they may not revert to authoritarianism again. But there is every reason to seriously entertain the proposition that authoritarian regimes may develop original and lasting forms of governance that are neither democratic nor totalitarian.

We will review change and transformation in modern authoritarian regimes in terms of five major structural variables:

REGIME FLUX IN AUTHORITARIAN REGIMES (1983-1985)

Guinea—From single-party to military dictatorship
Argentina—From military to beginnings of representative democracy
Brazil—Democratic opening with elections of a civilian president
Egypt—Elections in which opposition gained 15-20 percent of the vote
Philippines—Elections with opposition gaining over 40 percent of the vote
Turkey—From military dictatorship to civilian governance
Ethiopia—From military dictatorship to single-party communist regime (with preponderant military presence in the Politburo)
Uruguay—Elections for civilian leadership after twelve years of military rule

1. The political party (or parties): What roles do they play and how do their roles change?
2. Governing elites: Are they open or closed?
3. Ideology: What kind and what function does it perform?
4. Capabilities: How able are they to govern? What kind of institutions of governance do they develop?
5. Interests: How are they organized and structured?

The Political Party[1]

Structural changes in authoritarian regimes should be studied in terms of the nonparty, single-party, and multiparty continuum. Although there are no parties in dynastic monarchies or direct military governments, many authoritarian regimes have, as mentioned, a single party and some, especially in cryptomilitary democracies, even more than one. The following patterns may be envisaged in the relationships between governments and parties:

There may be a recurrent alternation of party governance and military dictatorship. Turkey is a good illustration.

The single party may gradually develop into a mass party allowing for the participation and the representation, *on a selective basis*, of a variety of constituencies and interests. Thus, the party incorporates segments of the population from which it draws support and to which it provides services. It becomes not only a link between societal forces and the government but also a bulwark against those interests and segments of the population that remain excluded. This may well be the case with the single party in Mexico. Such parties usually are a mix of representation and participation on the one hand and exclusion and imposition on the other.

There may be a gradual emergence of a genuine two-party or a multiparty system, with genuine political competition and open elec-

1. Joseph La Polombara and Myron Wiener, *Political Parties and Political Development* (Princeton, N.J.: Princeton University Press, 1967).

tions. In this case an authoritarian regime undergoes a transformation in the direction of a democracy. However, a long time is required if the transformation is to be real, that is, legitimized. It is doubtful that even countries like Spain, Portugal, or Greece, where authoritarianism broke down in the early seventies, fully qualify as yet. Most Latin American countries, other than Costa Rica, and virtually all African regimes do not qualify despite the occasional emergence of party politics and open elections.

Under certain circumstances, a single party may broaden its appeal and membership, selectively incorporate a number of interests, professions, and social groups, and become increasingly representative. If so, it can gain a genuine degree of autonomy and develop mechanisms for internal democracy and freedom of debate. It may become an independent political force rather than an instrument of the authoritarian leadership — military or not. One might argue that such may be the case in Brazil or Tunisia. However, as we noted, such a development is carefully monitored by the military for fear that the single party will thwart their power. A single party is also feared by civilian leaders, who are afraid that the party will become strong enough to control them and even replace them.

Finally, a single party, inspired by a nationalist, independentist, and radical ideology, may move in the direction of a totalitarian regime. This kind of shift can occur when the leadership espouses Marxism-Leninism or scientific socialism, as in Mozambique or Angola, in Ethiopia, and perhaps in Nicaragua. Thus authoritarian regimes can be transformed into totalitarian ones.

Parties spell uncertainty and instability for all authoritarian regimes. While the party is needed to provide supports, it also elicits participation and carries the seeds of popular mobilization that may challenge the authoritarian rulers. Military governance is constantly facing this problem. In Turkey and in much of Latin America political parties have refused to keep their differences within the confines set by the authoritarian leadership, military or civilian. Some of them became agencies of popular mobilization that confront the authoritarian regime. Single parties in many authoritarian regimes like Paraguay, Indonesia, South Korea, or Taiwan remain, therefore, under tight control. They are agencies of imposition and regimentation; they are not permitted to encourage participation.

Governing Elites: Open or Closed?

The social composition of the governing elite, its ideology, and its ability or inability to coopt new groups are important factors in studying the internal transformation of authoritarian regimes. Past forms of authoritarianism relied on the status quo groups that resist change and popular participation. The leadership, comprised of the military, the landowners, the powerful trading and business groups, and the foreign economic interests, organized against the peasantry, the intelligentsia, the workers, and the lower middle classes. The political leadership, always in close cooperation with the military (when the military were not in power), came from among retired army officers, wealthy businessmen, and sons of the upper bourgeoisie and landowners. Since education was available to very few, it was only the sons of the privileged groups who were prepared for public office. The elites remained exclusive, avoiding as much as possible any infiltration from outside and drawing supports and sustenance from their own groups. Popular supports and involvements were not solicited, because authoritarianism rested on a closed oligarchy.

Internal transformation of authoritarianism, often referred to as "new authoritarianism," comes about because of: (1) the weakening of the established oligarchies, (2) factional disputes within the elite groups, (3) the need to expand the role of government in social and economic areas and in so doing to recruit and coopt new groups, and (4) the need to meet the challenge of an aroused political consciousness that would spur the heretofore excluded groups to organize and eventually become a force to be reckoned with. Most of these changes are the ones that are associated with the process of modernization.

Modernization precipitates the formation of new socioeconomic and professional groups while old ones are undermined; new professional skills develop and new elites emerge as the status quo groups weaken; old values and beliefs disappear and new ones develop. In an often quoted sentence, Karl Deutsch has described the destabilizing effects of modernization as a process in which "major clusters of old social, economic and psychological commitments are eroded or broken and people become available for new patterns of socialization and behavior."[2] Mancour Olson gives a more detailed account of the major instabilities that accompany rapid economic growth.

> It disrupts traditional social groupings; it undermines social ties; increases mobility of persons — both geographically and socially; produces a rapid increase in literacy and education, and increases sharply the aspirations and expectations of a great number — often beyond the level of possible satisfaction and creates the conditions for organization and participation through which wants, demands and expectations are voiced.[3]

In the last several decades the transformation of the elites has been a major characteristic of many authoritarian regimes. The traditional elites are giving place to new elites: managers, skilled professionals, bureau-

2. Karl W. Deutsch, "Social Mobilization and Political Development," *American Political Science Review*, vol. 55, no. 3 (September 1961), pp. 494–502.
3. Mancour Olson, Jr., "Rapid Growth as a Destabilizing Force," *The Journal of Economic History*, vol. 3, no. 4 (December 1963), pp. 529–552.

crats, and technocrats. As noted, many military regimes have espoused modernization and development. Moreover, these new groups demand to be taken seriously — they want participation in the decision-making process.

The following hypotheses regarding change can be envisaged:

1. The established elite refuses to share power with the newcomers and may succeed in maintaining its authoritarian rule. This is the case today with dynastic monarchies and some military dictatorships.
2. Authoritarian regimes, however, may be unable or unwilling to make the proper concession and to allow reforms. An authoritarian regime is then confronted with the prospect of revolution. It happened with the tsar of Russia and is continuously occurring in many Latin American authoritarian regimes. The mass of people — the peasantry, the marginals, the poor — demand participation, rapid socio-economic changes, and reforms in their favor. Nicaragua, El Salvador, Guatemala, and maybe Chile are cases in point.
3. In some authoritarian regimes the established elite may avoid confrontation by gradually allowing an increasing degree of power sharing.

Ideology

Authoritarian regimes either do not have an ideology or are unable to link their political organization to an ideology and give it vitality and supports. Their most representative ideologies have been nationalism, order, professionalism, or modernization. Except for nationalism, they are not "ideas that grip the masses," as Marx characterized an ideology; they do not mobilize the people.

There are two types of authoritarianism, however, that project a transformist, even a radical and revolutionary, ideology. One is found in some military dictatorships when the military abandon the emphasis on order and become advocates of drastic change. The other is the emergence of a charismatic leader, civilian or military, who goes over the head of the established elites and appeals directly to the masses to exploit dissatisfactions and weld them into a powerful protest movement against the establishment. We refer to the first as "military transformism" and the second as "populism."

Military Transformism Transformist military authoritarianism will emerge when the army becomes politicized and infused with a modernizing and transformist ideology and assumes direct rule in order to transform the society accordingly. Transformist movements within armies have surfaced in a number of instances, as, for example, in Turkey in 1923–1924. In the years immediately following World War II there were transformist movements in Egypt in the 1950s, in Portugal in 1973, in Burma in 1962, in Indonesia after 1965, and in Peru in 1968.

In all these cases army officers appeared as the main source and actors of societal and political reconstruction. Their goals were comprehensive and had far-reaching implications for both the social structure and the political regime. In Portugal, a professional army that not only espoused but actually introduced socialist reforms in industry, banking, and agriculture turned against the establishment and formed close ties with the Communist party. In Egypt, after World War II, it was the army officers who led the drive for political and social reform — for socialism — against the corrupt king and his associates and against foreign domination. The Turkish army, on the other hand, under the leadership of Kemal Ataturk (1923–1938) intervened in the name of nationalism and political and economic liberalism. It brought about a vast societal transformation. It Westernized a semifeudal society by reforming the government, the civil service, education, family life, the alphabet, and the legal code. In essence, the army initiated a revolution to bring about liberal political and economic order in one of the most backward and corrupt dynastic regimes. It destroyed both the dynasty and its religious base.

Populism Populism is above all a movement that appeals to and arouses the poor and the downtrodden — the masses — in the name of justice and economic equality. It is transformist and revolutionary in its origins. It is directed against the political, social, and economic status quo. It is intensely nationalistic and invariably addressed against foreign powers that weigh heavily upon the fortunes, or rather the misfortunes, of the country: Yankee imperialism, the multinationals, the international banks, etc. It promises liberation from those responsible for the country's plight. Many so-called socialist parties in Africa and elsewhere have in reality been populist movements promising justice, independence, and an equitable distribution of wealth.

Populist movements usually arise because of a charismatic leader: Nasser in Egypt, Qaddaffi in Libya, Peron in Argentina, Castro in Cuba, Khomeini in Iran, Bourguiba in Tunisia, and there were, of course, a great many populist traits with the Nazis and Hitler in Germany. Attachment to the leader and the mass following he generates are substitutes for political organization and political parties. Charismatic leaders organize their following into a movement or a rally or a union through which they attempt to permeate and mobilize the society. Populist movements are prevalent in societies that display the following characteristics:

1. A fluid and changing class structure. Generally the peasantry begins to wane in favor of the urban classes. Populism attracts those who move from the village or country life to the urban centers.
2. An unorganized working class and a weak middle class.

3. Low levels of political participation and regime legitimacy.
4. A strong nationalist movement.
5. An economy emerging from a state of semicolonialism or dependency.
6. A surplus of intelligentsia, surplus being defined in terms of functionality rather than numbers, i.e., the availability of legitimized and renumerated roles within a system.

Both military transformism and populism, because of the mass appeal they project and the mass support they elicit, resemble totalitarian movements. In some cases, they may move in the direction of totalitarianism — the movement becomes a single party and may espouse communism — as in the case of Fidel Castro.

POPULISM IN ACTION: A FOOTNOTE ON IRAN

Like other populist movements, the Iranian revolution was directed against the establishment. It reasserted the old values of Islam. It wanted to cleanse the society from Western influences. As an egalitarian movement, it promised to penalize the rich and make resources available to the poor. It was also intensely communitarian. It wanted to reestablish the brotherhood of Moslems, with a particular appeal to the Shiite Moslems not only in Iran but in other countries as well. The makers and ultimately the custodians of the revolution were the clergy and their religious leader, the Ayatollah Khomeini. He assumed power after the fall (and departure) of the Shah and the collapse of the army that had supported him.

Almost seven years after his triumph the eighty-five-year-old spiritual leader appears to be in control of the Islamic Republic he has founded. The Shiite Moslem clergymen control an overwhelming majority in Parliament through their single party, the Islamic Republican party. They spearhead and guide a vast network of clergymen who exercise direct influence and control over the local mosques — approximately 15,000. The mosque has become for all practical purposes the equivalent of the Communist party cell or the various Nazi or Fascist local party organizations. In the name of religion, the clergy carries out political propaganda and performs political roles. They act as if they were grand juries, deciding on whom to prosecute and very often deciding the reasons; they distribute benefits and favors; they hand out ration cards for scarce goods. They are the building blocks of Khomeini's political power.

The clergy has recruited and organized a paramilitary force, the Revolutionary Guards, about 150,000 strong. They are the eyes and ears of the clergy, the dogs that sniff out treason, and silence opposition. Whenever the spiritual arm of the clergy cannot assure conformity, the secular arm they forged is called upon to enforce it through intimidation and assassination. The party and the Revolutionary Guards permeate the society. They control family life, impose religious conformity, appeal to the young to join the army for both material and heavenly rewards, and punish those who fail to volunteer. They also deal out swift justice to anyone who violates religious taboos.

Over and above the party, the mosques, the Revolutionary Guards, and the Parliament, there are three institutions that stand supreme. The first is the Supreme Religious Guide — the Ayatollah himself. His power, aside from the popularity his stand against the Shah brought him, derives from the belief that he speaks for the hidden imam, who disappeared in 874 A.D., but who is expected to return and establish a perfect society. Until he does, Khomeini apparently speaks for him. The second is the Assembly of Experts (eighty-three clergymen), which was established in 1983 and which will decide Khomeini's succession by designating either one person or a collegial body of three, four, or five top religious leaders — all ayatollahs. The third is the Council of Guardians, a very small group of clerics (with scholarly reputations) who go over legislation, government decrees, and orders to check their conformity with the religious faith. They are, in a sense, the highest court.

Religion, even if it promises heaven, is not adequate to mobilize people for long. But nationalism and a war against Iraq that began in 1981 have provided a source of constant mobilization in which secular, religious, and national traditional values are mixed. In the process, all potential sources of opposition to the regime have been gradually wiped out. Western liberals were exiled, and members of the Communist party, now dissolved, were shown the way to jail. University students who failed to conform had to seek refuge abroad, since the universities came under the control of the clergy after having been closed down altogether. The army has been purged of all potentially pro-American officers and new recruits or properly certified converts have ascended to positions of command. The people who sought asylum and exile elsewhere, notably in France, have been victims of terrorism and assassination. The arm of the Ayatollah is at times long and spans even the Atlantic Ocean.

Thus Iran, in the name of religious fundamentalism, nationalism, and anti-Westernism, has become a totalitarian regime, and the analogies to the Nazis are striking. It is a regime that constantly evokes traditional values and is addressed to the vindication of past values. With the Nazis, it was the resurrection of the Teutonic virtues; with the Iranian revolutionary clergy, the redemption that the Ayatollah will bring about. It is a regime that is profoundly anti-Western, eschewing the concepts of enlightenment, rationality, science, and the institutions and practices of liberalism. The Nazis likewise turned against the same values from which they promised to liberate us. It is a regime where the charisma of one man anoints him with leadership and authority to command without any limitations. In the case of Iran it is a power that is legitimized in religious terms, in terms of the Ayatollah's link with the imam who disappeared. It is a regime that is dedicated to the elimination of all infidels, especially the state of Israel. It is also a regime that, after unifying the society around the basic myths it proposes, now wants to impose its ideology and political practices abroad — among fellow countrymen and particularly the Shiite Moslems who are spread throughout the region. In this sense, it is dedicated to Islamism just as nazism was committed to pan-Germanism and beyond to the rule of the Aryan race. In terms of charismatic leadership, the organization of the single party, the conformity the regime has attempted to exact, the religious mythology that it has elevated into an official ideology, and the mobilization and use of force, Iran is truly totalitarian. But it is far from being communist!

The economic structure of the society has not been seriously tampered with. The big landowners retain their land, and many clerics have joined their ranks. The foundations of private property remain unchallenged. (The redistribution of land appears to be contrary to the teachings of the prophet!) The mosques and the clergymen have gained new endowments and wealth. Merchants, tradesmen, small manufacturers, artisans, and farmers operate through the market for profit. The middle classes, no matter how politically unreliable, have kept their possessions and their income (as long as they conform). The ranks that support the leader-prophet are predominantly the small bourgeoisie and the small farmers; again the similarities to the support the Nazis received is remarkable. The dominant political class consists of the religious leaders, the party they have established, and the Revolutionary Guards they have trained. The masses provide supports: they join the army and sacrifice their lives for the elusive life they will gain in the hereafter.

While the contours of the Iranian revolutionary regime are fairly clear, one should not conclude from this sketch that it has gained stability and legitimacy. It faces three fundamental problems: First the problem of succession. There is no guarantee that the council of eighty-three clerics will reach agreement. If not, the ruling group at the top will split. The second problem is whether the present leadership can satisfy the lower-middle-class groups and the farmers who provide it with supports. Promises made are hard to fulfill in the deteriorating economic situation caused in part by the war with Iraq. Nationalism and religious fanaticism can provide for mobilization and supports for only a given period of time, but soon concern with material satisfactions will take precedence. Like so many other populist regimes, Iran may also turn to instruments of coercion, including the use of the army. Third, there is the problem of the war with Iraq. It has been going on for five years with no end in sight, and the very prolongation of the war is likely to produce increasing discontent. On the other hand, a defeat may well taint the image of the Supreme Spiritual Guide and give other powerful ayatollahs or the military the opportunity to seek supreme authority.

While the contours of the regime are easy to draw, the substance of power and authority and the continuation of supports, i.e., its legitimization, are more difficult to define or take for granted. Populist revolutionary regimes do not develop solid institutions and are inherently unstable. They live short and intensive lives. It may be so with Iran.

Capabilities

Authoritarian regimes have been generally considered to be fragile in that they are unable to cope with adversity, to resolve internal conflicts, to respond to interests and demands, and to ensure succession of the leadership in governance — in other words, unable to institutionalize themselves.[4] They often collapse when faced with military defeat or civil disobedience. Military adversities haunted the Roman emperors and dashed the hopes of many kings and dictators in the Balkans and Latin America. Napoleon the Third packed his bags in 1870 when part of the French army surrendered at Sedan; the Shah of Iran saw his power and his army wither away. In Greece in 1974 the army dictatorship collapsed overnight when Turkey invaded Cyprus. Defeat in the Falklands brought about the beginning of the end of the military junta in Argentina.

4. Juan Linz, "Totalitarianism and Authoritarianism," in *Handbook of Political Science*, vol. III, *op. cit.*

Most contemporary authoritarian regimes, however, seem to have strengthened their governing capabilities greatly and may not be as fragile as thought. Some of the reasons given are the following:

Strengthening of the decision-making institutions: The top executive structure in many authoritarian regimes has undergone drastic reforms. Professionalism and merit have replaced clientelism and nepotism. Bureaucratic structures have replaced the personalistic and familial ones, while graft and patronage have given place to broader social and collectivist considerations. The combination of military-civilian governance provides for a mix between the military organization and civilian expertise and thereby enhance performance.

Succession: When the military constitute a homogeneous corporate body that provides for collegiality, or when the single party is cohesive, stability has been great. Many military revolutionary councils and military juntas have managed to provide for succession. In twenty years of military rule five generals assumed the position of the presidency in Brazil between 1964 and 1983. In Mexico the strength of the political party has made it possible for the presidency to change peacefully every six years since 1940. The military in Egypt alone and in combination with the party, the Arab Socialist Union, managed a smooth transition from Nasser to Sadat and when the latter was assassinated to Moubarak. After the death of Colonel Boumedienne in Algeria there was a smooth transition to President Chadli. Military defeats did not bring down the authoritarian regimes in the Middle East, and the inconclusive war between Iraq and Iran, over a period of several years, has not yet adversely affected those in power. Table 10-1 attests to the remarkable durability of authoritarian regimes and leaders.

TABLE 10-1 Durability of Some Authoritarian Leaders and Regimes

Franco (Spain)	1935–1973
Salazar (Portugal)	1927–1965
Alfredo Stroessner (Paraguay)	1954–
Bourguiba (Tunisia)	1958–
Ne Win (Burma)	1962–
Argentina (military junta)	1966–1973; 1976–1983
Brazil (military junta)	1964–1984
Sekou Tourè (Guinea)	1958–1984
Houphouet-Boigny (Ivory Coast)	1962–
Qaddaffi (Libya)	1969–
Trujillo (Dominican Republic)	1930–1961
Guatemala (military control)	1954–
Mexico (IRP — single party)	1940–
El Salvador (military)	1932–1983 (?)
Algeria (military and party)	1964–
Uruguay (military rule)	1974–1985 (?)

Communication: In addition to the single party, where it exists, new mechanisms of communication and support have been developed. In Mexico the party encompasses a variety of societal groups. In some African regimes that claim to have developed a guided democracy, the party continues to provide for some participation and recruitment. In other authoritarian regimes new forms of consultation between interests and the bureaucracy have been developed in the name of corporatism. In general, executive and bureaucratic structures have been sensitive, even if for limited constituencies, to claims, demands, and grievances.

Recruitment and cooptation: The formation of new elites, the expansion of governmental functions, the professionalization of the bureaucracy, the growth of new political careers, all associated with modernization, have provided for broader and expanding avenues of recruitment and rewards. The political base of an authoritarian regime is thus widened as new groups are coopted into it.

Ideology and participation: Efforts to develop an ideology — modernization, self-reliance, communitarianism — that is suitable to the culture, experience, and circumstances of a country adds another dimension and provides the elusive link in the institutionalization of authoritarian rule. The authoritarian leadership begins to perceive the whole polity in terms of common values and thus begins to gain legitimacy.

The Organization of Interests: Authoritarian Corporatism

For all governments, the yardstick of performance is the accomplishment of trivial pursuits, not necessarily the realization of exalted ends. Transportation; the running of schools, clinics, and hospitals; the satisfaction of minimal demands for food, clothing, housing; the preservation of order and health down to the collection of garbage — these are the things that governments are judged by. Authoritarian regimes must provide them if they are to survive. Considerations of stability, consolidation, and administration invariably gain the upper hand even if revolutionary and ideological pledges have to be set aside. What is important is what can be accomplished rather than the setting forth of unrealizable ideological goals: the political party or movement is replaced by the bureaucratic state, and the political leaders give way to administrators and experts. Bureaucratic/statist/authoritarian regimes emphasize administration above all. The relationship between the governors and the governed becomes in effect a relationship between the administrators and the administered with emphasis at least in theory, on efficiency, performance, and service.[5]

5. For a full account, see Guillermo A. O'Donnell, "Tensions in the Bureaucratic Authoritarian State," in David Collier (ed.), *The New Authoritarianism in Latin America* (Princeton, N.J.: Princeton University Press, 1979), pp. 285–318.

Corporatism, which we discussed in Chapter 5, has been used by authoritative regimes as a device both to establish political control and to secure some participation and supports. The state organizes certain interests and associations, allows them representation, and gives them policy-making power on matters that concern them. Interests are functionally organized into corporations, in terms of particular economic activities and operations that bring individuals and groups together: agriculture, industry, trade, banking, transportation, etc. Thus, hundreds of corporations can be established, representing and encompassing not only economic but also social, professional, and cultural activities. Members elect their representatives who in turn elect a national council to deliberate and decide on matters like production, wages, prices, investment, etc.

In some authoritarian regimes the whole edifice is integrated under the state, which is the ultimate arbiter of the decisions made as well as the ultimate guarantor of the corporatist organization of the society. As the ultimate arbiter, the state can intervene to settle unresolved disputes and also harmonize and control various economic activities. In some cases, the state may control the various socioeconomic sectors by using a single party, such as the Institutional Revolutionary Party of Mexico.

The corporatist structure thus provides for an orderly and well-controlled integration and participation of various interests in policy making. It allows an authoritarian state to broaden its supports by structuring the participation of new interests into the corporatist network — for instance, incorporating the leaders of trade unions, professional organizations, liberal professions, agricultural interests, merchants, etc.

The two most comprehensive institutionalizations of authoritarian corporatism have taken place in Portugal under the state and the bureaucracy between 1932 and 1974 and in Mexico since 1937 under the political party.

STATE CORPORATISM: THE CASE OF PORTUGAL

The most thoroughgoing corporatist authoritarian regime was that of Portugal in the years roughly between 1933 and 1974. The constitution that came into effect in 1934 proclaimed Portugal to be "a republican and corporative state." And as Professor Howard J. Wiarda points out in his excellent book on the subject,[6] it was a corporatism that provided political integra-

6. Howard J. Wiarda, *Corporatism and Development: The Portuguese Experience* (Amherst: University of Massachusetts Press, 1977). This is an excellent study of the institutions of a corporatist state, but there is little convincing evidence of development. I am indebted to the author for the sketchy account I give here.

tion and control together with some degree of participation and some social services.

The republican institutions consisted of a National Assembly with very limited, if any, powers. It was elected every four years but there was only one slate of candidates in the elections, and it was handpicked by the top leadership: the prime minister and the Council of Ministers. There was a president of the republic, a military man, and although a figurehead he maintained links with the army. Below them there were the various units of local government; provinces, districts, municipalities, parishes, with the corresponding councils whose officials were appointed from the top.

Supports for the regime and the leadership were provided by a number of organizations, all of them established by the prime minister and the Council of Ministers. There was the National Union, which was a movement rather than a party. It had no strong, other than corporatist, political ideology, and its membership was small even though it was open to all. It comprised local bosses, bureaucrats, and notables rather than activists and ideologues and provided a network of contacts between the population or at least some segments of the population and the government. It dispensed favors and served, but only marginally, as an agency of recruitment into leadership positions. The National Union operated as an agency of the state — it was a state party — to carry the message of the leadership, disseminate the policy cues, and knit together the various interests and groups.

Below the single and official party, there were the usual popular organizations that authoritarian regimes often organize from above: the National Front of Joy and Work, which provided entertainment and festivities to occupy the leisure time of the populace; the Portuguese Youth, fashioned along lines similar to the Italian youth organizations but with far less bellicose labels and rhetoric; the Society for the Defense of the Family and the Foundation of the Mothers for Christian Education, both organizations strongly influenced, if not controlled, by the Catholic church; and the Portuguese Legion, a paramilitary organization that preached warlike virtues in close cooperation with military officers and veterans. Under the prime minister, all of these political formations served the double function of indoctrination and prevention: to bring people into accepting the regime and to make sure that others would not be tempted to oppose it.

Side-by-side with this political structure there was the corporatist one. It took a long time for corporatist institutions to develop, but when they finally did in the mid-fifties, they provided for a comprehensive organization and participation of many societal interests.

Corporations were formed for various groups representing people active in similar economic activities or in similar economic situations: workers, managers, owners, technicians, etc. There were corporations for cereals and cattle, wines, fisheries, mines, mineral waters, chemicals, electricity, banking, transportations, printing, building and building materials, credit, insurance, tourism, etc. There were of course corporations representing loftier pursuits — religious organizations, science and letters, local administration, the civil service, welfare, etc.

The corporatist structure involved at least five layers. There were (1) the primary units: the *sindicatos* (trade unions), the *casas do povo* (community centers), *pescadores* (fishermen unions), the *gremios* (guilds for small merchant artisans, shopkeepers, etc.), and the *orders* for lawyers, doctors, engineers, and other liberal professions as well as representatives of family associations. They selected (2) intermediary organizations: the unions and federations at regional and district levels that in turn elected their representatives in the corporations to which they belonged. The corporations (3), more than one hundred, elected their representative in the (4) corporative chamber, a second legislative chamber side by side with the National Assembly. This representative edifice was topped by (5) an Undersecretariat at first and later a Ministry of Corporations operating under the Council of Ministers and the prime minister.

What did the corporation actually do?

> *Politically* they would serve to represent their constituent interests; they were given the task of defending the common interests of their representative branches vis-à-vis the government; they were to assist in the negotiations of collective contracts; they would develop social services and insurance and assistance programs; and they were to lay down disciplinary rules for the self-regulation of their respective branches. [However], *in fact*, the corporations always exercised but very limited functions and most of those were of interest to the employers rather than the workers.[7]

Strikes were outlawed; the by-laws of all primary units and corporations had to be approved by the Ministry of Cor-

7. Wiarda, ibid., p. 203.

porations; all units were to subordinate their interests to the common good as defined by the state; all elections of corporate officers had to be approved by the state; and the *sindicatos* were not allowed to affiliate with international labor organizations. Finally, let us remember that behind the government — indeed a part of it — was the army, appropriately named the "balance wheel" of the regime, and the secret police. The usual armor of an authoritarian regime was in place.

Corporatism, as a scheme of interest organizations and representation, had its indispensable ally and guardian in the state and its power. Decisions in effect were made by the prime minister, the Council of Ministers, and the bureaucracy. Inputs came from the corporations and debates often resulted in some modifications or ministerial measures by the corporative chamber. But the state and the bureaucracy invariably had the last word. In fact, in the 1960s the corporations began to be viewed as social services rather than as deliberative and decision-making agencies. They increasingly became ancillary service agencies, and part of the authoritarian apparatus.

The most important function of the corporations was defensive and preemptive rather than participatory. To participate in the corporatist institutions, one had to belong to primary groups whose constitution and composition were under the control of the state. One could not simply form a *sindicato* or a *casa do povo* and become entitled to representation. Hence a given part of the population remained excluded from the organs that provided for interest representation. Characteristically enough, this was the case with the peasantry, the unemployed (and unemployment of 10–15 percent was chronic in Portugal), the marginals, and the poor. In the last analysis corporatism became an instrument of control and domination by the privileged groups. The demands and interests of the workers, the peasantry, and the poor remained excluded.

THE SINGLE PARTY AND CORPORATISM: MEXICO[8]

In Mexico political representation is virtually in the hands of a single party — the Institutional Party of the Revolution (PRI).[9] It is often referred to as the dominant party because other and smaller parties have been tolerated and are allowed to participate in elections. But their combined strength has never ex-

8. On Mexican corporatism and the role of the party, see David Levy and Gabriel Szekely, *Mexico: Paradoxes of Society and Change* (Boulder, Colo.: Westview Press, 1983).
9. PRI is the Mexican acronym for the *Partido Revolucionario Institucional*.

ceeded (and is never allowed to exceed) 20–25 percent of the electorate. For the last forty years the PRI has controlled the election of the national legislature and the nomination and election of the president, the state governors, and state legislatures. It has an official membership of over 7 million, which makes it the third largest party in the world after China and the Soviet Union. However, all members, like the workers in the British Labour party, are affiliated members. They are members by virtue of their membership in other organizations.

Affiliation with the PRI is structured by socioeconomic sectors. There are three sectors; the agrarian sector, the labor sector, and a third called the "popular" sector. The agrarian sector includes the *Confederacion Nacional Campesina* with over 2 and a half million members; the labor sector includes industrial workers of many unions (railroad workers, mining and metal workers, telephone workers, motion picture workers etc..) and has a total membership of about 2 million. Then there is a hodgepodge of civil service unions, teachers, cooperatives, small farm owners, small merchants, professionals, intellectuals, artisans, women's organizations, youth organizations, and some independent organizations grouped together in the popular sector, with a total membership of a little over 2 million.

Only some 2 and a half million wage earners are affiliated with the PRI, and more than half of them are skilled or semiskilled workers. Only a little over 2.5 million peasants and farmers are affiliated. The majority of workers and peasants are thus excluded. As for the popular sector, it represents primarily middle-class groups. The Catholic church, the military, and the business groups (in industry, banking, and trade) are *not* incorporated into the party. They act independently of the party and they can provide a counterveiling force just as the party may be used to counter them. In Mexican corporatism, therefore, all interests are not incorporated — they do not operate under the same umbrella. Some are free to operate on their own; others, notably the majority of the laborers and the peasants, have no representation at all. While it is important to keep in mind the interests that are included in the party, it is even more significant to realize that many are excluded.

What is the reason for this organization of the party? In 1929, the original purpose was to bring local and provincial notables — *the caciques* — into one organization that would provide a forum for reconciliation of regional and local conflicts and a better organized channel for dispensing patronage. Under President Cardenas (1934–1940), however, the party assumed a truly revolutionary posture. It wanted to break down the control of the local bosses and open the party to the people, especially the peasants and the workers. The party was to become the vehicle of mass participation and an instrument of supports for a program of genuine land distribution and economic reforms. The aim was to reach far down into the masses, energize them with a revolutionary, socialist, and democratic ideology and mobilize them into a participatory organization that would thwart the business community and the landowners and neutralize the Church and the army. In the Institutional Party of the Revolution the emphasis was put more on "revolution" than on "institutional." It was geared to confrontational and ideological politics.

Gradually the phenomenon we observed with most other single-party authoritarian regimes also took place in Mexico: the party provided for recruitment and participation of new groups, including some of the skilled workers, professionals, and technical personnel. They were used to promote economic and social modernization and to supply the cadres for the state and the bureaucracy whose functions continued to expand. Modernization, however, to be politically attractive, required some redistribution of wealth and privileges to the new groups and the people at large. When this took place — and the Mexican economy showed sizable gains between 1945 and 1970 — the revolution and its heirs began to face a challenge from those whose expectations had been aroused and to whom the benefits of modernization and economic growth had not been extended. The elites in the party began to defend their interests and to emphasize consolidation. Thus the party became increasingly elitist and defensive. It became an instrument of exclusion.

Instead of promoting participation, the party began to freeze it. However, as the citizenship's awareness with political problems increases, the party may be unable to contain renewed claims for participation and for economic and social reforms. The PRI will then have to either support increasingly authoritarian and repressive policies by the president and the bureaucracy in order to maintain the privileges and status of its members or else allow the formation of competing parties that may pose a threat. Repression will necessitate the use of the military; open competition may lead to instability. A third alternative is to open the party to the excluded groups but that may incur the hostility of the army, the business groups, big landowners, and of course international (i.e., American), economic and financial interests — which is no negligible factor!

In substance, therefore, the Mexican PRI, as in other authoritarian regimes, provides for integration and cooptation of only some interests and groups and only limited participation. Too much participation would democratize and possibly destabilize the regime. Like many other authoritarian regimes, the Mexican one seems to be caught between regime stability and consolidation on the one hand and the demands for radical economic and social changes on the other. Whether the corporatist organization of the party will be able to reconcile the two remains to be seen.

Conclusion

The overview of authoritarian regimes we gave suggest some generalizations:

1. Not only do regimes cover the political map of the world but authoritarianism, despite many changes in form, has displayed a remarkable durability. Most of the new nations have lived under authoritarian regimes ever since they gained independence — in virtually all of Africa, most of Asia except India, and in the Middle East, except Israel, and in Latin America it has been endemic. We can therefore no longer view authoritarianism as transitional or episodic.
2. Authoritarianism cannot be viewed simply as a "reaction" by the elites in power against new demands and movements for reform that endanger their positions and privileges. Modern authoritarianism is associated with the emergence of new elites and the displacement of old ones; with new techniques of governance; with modernization and change (at times even with a transformist ideology); and with nation building, consensus building, and even with a degree of popular involvement and participation. It has shown great versatility.
3. Almost all contemporary authoritarian regimes are going through a period of change. First, many share a modernizing outlook both with regard to the economy and to the building of an efficient administrative organization. Second, even in countries where military governance has lasted for a long time (Brazil, Argentina, Egypt, Algeria, Turkey, Paraguay, Peru, and most of Africa), many military regimes have been forced to use new organizations — to provide for participation and supports. Contrary to its own logic and despite the risks, military governance has had to expand its base of political power. Authoritarian leaders and the instruments they fashion in order to govern become, in the phrase of Amos Perlmutter, an "*authoritative* political elite" that seeks a degree of legitimacy.[10]

10. Amos Permutter, *Modern Authoritarianism* (New Haven, Conn.: Yale University Press, 1981), p. 176.

4. In all authoritarian regimes participation continues to be contrived and manipulated. Consent is often the product of intimidation and coercion. Representation is at best selective. The state or the party acts like an umbrella that shelters (and gives some power) to some but denies it to others.
5. Authoritarian regimes undergo constant change and transformation. They may move in the direction of democracy or totalitarianism or they may develop and consolidate their own political forms of governance and management. Democracy is certainly a possibility — it is clearly evident in the political vocabulary being used almost everywhere (it is increasingly democratic). There is also a growing political awareness of the poor and the underprivileged; an increasing interest of some of the more traditional elites, especially the Catholic church, in improving living conditions and protecting freedoms; and a growing concern about world public opinion on the issue of human rights. But there is no reason to assume, as so many did a century ago, that we are necessarily moving in the direction of democracy now any more than in the past. In all likelihood authoritarian regimes — military, single-party, and corporatist — will persist for a long time to come.

Bibliography

Canovan, Margaret. *Populism.* New York: Harcourt Brace Jovanovich, 1981.

Coe, Michael D. *Mexico.* 2d ed. New York: Praeger, 1977.

Collier, David (ed.). *The New Authoritarianism in Latin America.* Princeton, N.J.: Princeton University Press, 1979. See especially Collier, "Nerves of the Bureaucratic-Authoritarian Model," pp. 19–32; Guillermo A. O'Donnell, "Tensions in the Bureaucratic Authoritarian State and the Question of Democracy," pp. 285–318; and Collier, "The Bureaucratic-Authoritarian Model: Synthesis and Priorities for Future Research," pp. 319–362.

Elbow, Martin I. *French Corporalist Theory 1781–1948.* New York: Columbia University Press, 1953.

Gonzales, Casanova. *Democracy in Mexico.* New York: Oxford University Press, 1970.

Hodges, Donald C., and Ross Gandy. *Mexico 1910–1982: Reform or Revolution?* Westport, Conn.: L. Hill, 1983.

Kay, Hugh. *Salazar and Modern Portugal.* New York: E. P. Dutton, 1970.

Levy, Daniel, and Gabriel Szekely. *Mexico: Paradoxes of Stability and Change.* Boulder, Colo.: Westview, 1983.

Lowenthal, Abraham (ed.). *The Peruvian Experiment: Continuity and Change under Military Rule.* Princeton, N.J.: Princeton University Press, 1976.

O'Donnell, Guillermo A. *Modernization and Bureaucratic Authoritarianism: Studies in South American Politics.* Berkeley: Institute of International Studies, University of California, 1973.

Paxton, Robert O. *Vichy France: Old Guard and New Order, 1940–1944.* New York: Columbia University Press, 1972.

Perlmutter, Amos, *Modern Authoritarianism.* New Haven, Conn.: Yale University Press, 1981.

Schoultz, Lars. *The Populist Challenge: Argentine Electoral Behavior in the Postwar Era.* Chapel Hill: University of North Carolina Press, 1983.

Stein, Steve. *Populism in Peru.* Madison: University of Wisconsin Press, 1980.

Stepan, Alfred. *The State and Society: Peru in Comparative Perspective.* Princeton, N.J.: Princeton University Press, 1978.

Wiarda, Howard J. *Corporatism and Development: The Portuguese Experience.* Amherst: University of Massachusetts Press, 1977.

———. *Corporatism and National Development in Latin America.* Boulder, Colo.: Westview, 1981.

11 Epilogue: The Evaluation of Regimes

We have given a survey of a number of political regimes under the threefold typology of democratic, totalitarian, and authoritarian. This has been a book about institutions and structures, about the anatomy of political regimes: the skeleton, the bones, and the muscles. We can no longer evade the question of performance.

"For forms of government . . . let fools contest," wrote the eighteenth century English poet, Alexander Pope, "whate'er is best administered is best." There are at least two levels at which regime performance can be measured and evaluated. The first is functional. How well does a regime perform the major functions it must perform in order to survive? Does it maintain order? Can it prevent internal disruptive behavior? Has it gained enough recognition and acceptance to be legitimized? Has it developed adequate capabilities to make and implement decisions? Harry Eckstein suggested these three basic criteria — decisional efficacy, civil order, and legitimacy — to evaluate performance. He adds a forth criterion — the longevity or durability of a regime — "the persistence of a polity over time."[1] To these four criteria I will add adaptability and change, responsiveness, and penetration. Adaptability and change should measure the capability of a regime to generate reforms or to respond to institutional and socioeconomic changes, domestic or in-

1. Harry Eckstein, *The Evaluation of Political Performance: Problems and Dimensions* (Beverly Hills, Calif.: Sage Publications, 1971).

ternational. Responsiveness measures the sensitivity of the government to demands made by the citizenry, demands for participation, for freedoms, or for the allocation of services and goods. Penetration measures the extent and degree (or not) of the state's dominance and control of the societal forces, including the economy.

All these criteria can help us weigh performance but only in functional terms. They may tell us how well a given regime has functioned over time or how well it is functioning in the present. However, they tell us very little about the purpose of the regime and the values it implements. This is the second and more difficult level of analysis — the normative level — the critical evaluation of the purpose of a regime in terms of the goals it sets forth and the values it maintains.

The functional approach considers a regime to be an end in itself: "whate'er is best administered" and for the longest period of time "is best". The normative approach stipulates that the criteria of evaluation are outside of the regime and its functioning and that it is but an instrument to implement a moral and higher purpose. Functioning in itself is not enough to measure performance. Rather, the yardstick of performance lies in measuring the extent and the degree to which it conforms to generally accepted and universal values. What is the sense of knowing that trains run on time, as the Fascists proclaimed in Italy, unless we know where they take us? It could be to Shangri-La or to a concentration camp.

How do the regimes we surveyed compare at the two levels of analysis — the functional and the normative?

The Functioning of Political Regimes

We have already noted the durability of authoritarian regimes and it is equally clear that communist totalitarian regimes have also shown marked durability. The Soviet Union is now almost seventy years old, China, thirty-six, Cuba, twenty-six. In comparison to some European democracies, such as the German Weimar Republic (twelve years old), the German Federal Republic (thirty-six years old), the French Fourth and Fifth Republics (eleven and twenty-seven years, respectively), and democracies in Portugal or Spain (about ten to twelve years old), totalitarian regimes have lasted longer. As we noted, the same is true of some authoritarian regimes, for instance, Algeria (twenty-five years old) and Mexico (over forty-five years old). In fact, there is nothing to warrant the argument that democracies last longer than authoritarian/totalitarian regimes or that durability is an indication of performance (see Table 10-1 on p. 250).

Adaptability and Change

Like all other institutions, political regimes must adapt to new conditions, adjust to new constraints, and use new opportunities. It is with regard to adaptability, one might argue, that democracies function better than authoritarian/totalitarian regimes. Democracies have the institutional framework for changes that sometimes amount to a revolutionary reallocation of powers and services. The statement that in democracies "people agree on how to disagree" makes the point. In democracies people agree on translating their disagreements into policies and one side (the majority) wins over the other (the minority). When the lines are not clearly drawn, there are incremental changes and compromises. Thus, as we argued in this book, there is room not only for adjustment and compromise but also for change and experimentation. Democracy provides for changes *in* the polity, not *about* the polity, changes in the constitution, not about the basic rules of the constitution. The history of democracies shows this quite conclusively. England, the Scandinavian countries, the United States have made vast changes (in political participation, voting rights, the powers of the directly elected legislative assemblies, the role of political parties, the allocation of powers between the central government and the states in federal systems or between the central government and local units) without changing the regime. Even more significantly, basic structural changes have been made on economic and societal policies. The nationalization of industries in France, England, and elsewhere, the development of the welfare state, economic planning, the enormous expansion of education and health care — they all took place in democratic regimes or, to put it negatively, they did not necessitate a change of regime.

Can totalitarian and authoritarian regimes make similar changes? Let us hypothetically take the case of an authoritarian regime that allows for free elections and introduces reforms consistent with the criteria of a democracy that we discussed in Chapter 2. Such reforms would be just as basic as the adoption of universal manhood suffrage was in most of the European democracies in the nineteenth century. Or let us take the case of a single-party communist regime that allows many candidates to run at election time and also allows them to unite into national party organizations to advocate their views on policy issues. Could the regime undertake such reforms and remain totalitarian? Or, if one wishes to be even more speculative, can a totalitarian communist regime permit individual and entrepreneurial economic freedoms and initiatives, even limited ones, as easily as democracies did exactly the opposite by nationalizing ownership and many economic and industrial activities? The answer is that of course it could. But not without a fundamental change in the regime. If authoritarian/totalitarian regimes brought about such reforms, they would lose their characteristics; they would move in the direction of democracy.

Democracies, we argued, are adaptable to new conditions and circumstances. Totalitarian/authoritarian regimes, both because of the homogeneity and cohesiveness of the elite and the concentration of political powers, are less responsive to new circumstances and less adaptable. The official ideology in all totalitarian regimes (especially communist ones) may be so rigid and one-sided as to fail to consider new demands and to face new circumstances, both at home and abroad. Change may incite people to ask questions about the ideology and may threaten the power of the political elite. In terms of openness to change, experimentation, modification of power relations, and governmental structures, democracies perform better.

Legitimization

As we noted, legitimization comprises the processes that link the command structure (those who make decisions) with the people at large. We emphasized that the major criterion of legitimization is consent: the acceptance by the governed of the authority of those who govern. We discussed the processes of legitimization in terms of participation, socialization, representation, the political parties, and elections. We found that in totalitarian regimes the emphasis is on mobilization. The single party and the official ideology are the mobilizing forces. Authoritarian regimes, on the other hand, rely heavily on administrative and coercive mechanisms to ensure obedience rather than to inculcate consent. As a result, legitimization is warped in authoritarian regimes because consent and supports are uncertain. They cannot easily meet crises; their emphasis on maintaining order is so great that they allow for no alternative but complete disorder, such as acts of violence and antiregime uprisings.

We have argued that consent in democratic regimes, whatever the strength of the socializing ideology, is relatively open and spontaneous. Obedience to those who issue orders stems from participation, elections, representation, and ultimately rules that make the officials responsible to the electorate. In a sense, consent and supports to the regime is, to use a famous expression, a "daily plebiscite." In totalitarian regimes, legitimization is also the product of a socializing ideology. At times it can generate supports far more powerful than can be found in any democracy, as, for example, in Nazi Germany. But without open procedures for registering acceptance, one can never be sure how strong the supports are at any given time and how much consent there is for the regime or its policies. In contrast, in democracies supports are constantly tested (and are testable). The opposition to the war in Vietnam by Americans or in Algeria by the French, to nuclear weapons, to energy and environmental policies proves the point. But we have no way of testing legitimacy in totalitarian and authoritarian regimes except when they collapse. If they do not, compliance should not be presumed to indicate acceptance and legitimacy.

Civil Order

If a political regime is to maintain order, it cannot allow potential or actual organized violence by dissenting groups. Disruptive acts undermine the performance of a regime and conversely their absence indicates a high level of performance. Which of the regimes surveyed — democratic, totalitarian, or authoritarian — perform better in maintaining order?

It is very difficult to answer the question. On its face and in terms of the empirical data, totalitarian and authoritarian regimes perform far better than democracies in maintaining order. We do not read about strikes in Egypt and Algeria. Even in Chile demonstrations are quickly silenced. Except for Poland, there have been very few organized and collective acts of violence in communist regimes. In contrast, even though peaceful demonstrations are allowed in democracies, collective resorts to violence are only too frequent. From the French farmers who throw their produce on the highways to protest low subsidies, to the bombing of abortion clinics in the United States, to say nothing of the violence that can erupt from strikes, acts of violence are commonplace in democratic regimes. Authoritarian/totalitarian regimes seem to bask in the serenity of an orderly society while democracies seem to be constantly on the brink of anarchy. Again, the question: Which perform best?

If we view violence only in terms of private persons or groups pitted against public authorities, then there is hardly any question that totalitarian/authoritarian regimes experience little or no violence. They perform well. However, this assessment changes rapidly if we also define violence as the use of organized force by the public authorities *against* private persons and groups. Such a definition would have to consider (1) the costs incurred by a regime to repress activities against it, (2) the preemptive methods used to prevent violence from surfacing, and (3) the physical repressive measures taken against overt opposition and the sanctions used against its perpetrators. If we view violence in these terms, then we may conclude that totalitarian/authoritarian regimes may be but an organized form of public violence against the individuals and associations that comprise the society in which the regime has established itself. The extent, the degree, the persistence, and the comprehensiveness of repression is much greater, on any scale of measurement, than the acts of organized violence against public authorities in a democracy. Harry Eckstein makes the point forcefully. "But the persistent coercive repression of large social collectivities surely denotes political failure of some sort; if it is reasonable to expect polities to reduce private conflict, it is also reasonable to expect them not merely to displace it onto the public level."[2]

Undoubtedly there is far more organized and collective violence in democracies — by private groups against other private groups, by private groups against the public authorities — than in authoritarian or totalitarian regimes. But there is equally hardly any doubt that there is far more public violence in the form of coercive and repressive practices by the state and its agencies against individuals and groups in totalitarian and authoritarian regimes than in democracies. It is because of this that in authoritarian or totalitarian regimes' violence against those in command is and can only be a revolution (Locke defined a revolution as a war waged

2. Eckstein, op. cit., p. 37.

against those who begin it first). Violence in democracies, on the other hand, has limited ends and often brings about changes that ultimately are translated into public policy, but it does not topple the regime. Paradoxically enough, totalitarian/authoritarian regimes allow no disorder other than a revolution; democracies allow disorders but make revolution superfluous.

Decision Making and the Command Structure

It is incumbent upon the command structure of all political regimes to make decisions.

The critical variable to decisional efficacy is the elite. The more homogeneous and united it is, the greater the efficacy of decision making. The second significant variable relates to the organization of the governing elite, to the structure of command. The greater the concentration of power and the fewer the limitations, again the greater the efficacy. Caligula could make his horse a consul; Stalin could make a number of the historical figures of the Russian Revolution "unpersons"; Hitler replaced the political elites. Those in command can and do make decisions, irrespective of their wisdom, and they can see to it that they are carried out. Cohesiveness of the elite (as long as it lasts) and concentration of power give an edge to authoritarian/totalitarian regimes vis-à-vis democracies.

How do different regimes respond to serious crises or challenges? It is difficult to answer. No two crises are exactly the same. Even if a crisis is met, there is no proof that it was successfully met because of the decisions made by the governing elite, and there is no guarantee that these decisions will not be the source of more severe crises in the future. We really have no way to differentiate democratic/authoritarian/totalitarian regimes. Faced with a crisis, authoritarian regimes are more likely to collapse, i.e., not to meet the challenge, than totalitarian or democratic regimes, simply because they have not managed to establish and gain supports. But even this generalization begs adequate empirical evidence. We simply do not have an adequate comparative and historical evidence of how different regimes face crisis situations.

Responsiveness

In our introductory chapter we set forth a theory about regimes according to which demands and supports relate directly to decisions. The model suggests that as demands are satisfied through appropriate governmental responses, especially in the allocation of services and goods, the performance of the regime will be high and vice-versa. This is true, however, only if we state it negatively. Regimes that fail to respond over a long period of time begin to perform badly. Only in this sense can it be argued that authoritarian/totalitarian regimes may not perform as well as democracies. By failing to adapt and to respond, they lose supports. By failing to provide adequate mechanisms to gauge demands, they may respond the wrong way. However, democracies, if they respond to all demands, may become victims of their responsiveness in a number of ways. By trying to satisfy all demands, they may satisfy none. By putting the emphasis on responding to individual and group claims, they may lose sight of priorities and objective requirements (defense, for instance) that may incapacitate the regime as a whole in times of crisis. Also, excessive responsiveness may act as an accelerator and provoke more and more demands that may drown the governmental machinery and paralyze the decision makers. This is, at least according to some authors, one of the major reasons for crisis in many democratic regimes. They claim that excessive responsiveness to rising expectations has produced new demands that may not be met, thus causing a crisis and nonperformance.[3]

Penetration

Another consideration in assessing performance is the degree and the extent to which the command structure and the governing elite penetrate the societal forces, the degree to which the government reaches down and out to reshape them and to keep them under its constant supervision and control so that they will stay in step with its policies. Regimes that have strong penetration perform better than in democracies where the societal forces maintain their autonomy and where various groups can go their own way. This is particularly relevant in controlling the economy, either through nationalizations, direct or indirect planning, or outright state management. The economy follows the government and the government faces no hindrances from independent units in the making of decisions, i.e., in performance. In this sense totalitarian communist governments, and also a great number of authoritarian ones, can be expected to perform better than democracies, where not only are cultural and religious associations immune to governmental penetration but also the economy and key industrial decisions about production, prices, interests, etc. are in the hands of autonomous units.

But penetration is only a prima facie argument for performance. The very burden of control and the very scope of penetration may jeopardize, rather than enhance, performance. Penetration leaves no safety valves for spontaneous activity, incentives, and experimentation; it makes little room for the many small mistakes inherent in many decisions. The Ford Motor Company could produce the famous Edsel car that proved to be a huge loss, but Ford and the economy as a whole survived it. The American farmers suffer when they produce more than what the market consumes (some of them may go bankrupt), and service industries, small entrepreneurs, and manufacturers face and suffer a high bankruptcy rate, but the economy as a whole may survive and even prosper. Can state-run

3. Samuel H. Huntington, et al., *The Crisis of Democracy* (New York: New York University Press, 1979).

EVALUATION OF PERFORMANCE

	Totalitarian	Authoritarian	Democratic
Durability	X	/	X
Legitimacy	X	/	+ — X
Civil Order	+	+	X —
Decision Making	+	+	/
Adaptability	/	/	+
Responsiveness	/	—	+
Penetration	+	/	—

\+ High
X Relatively High
/ Relatively Low
— Low

industries and state-administered economic activities make the same mistakes without suffering in terms of performance? This is not meant as an argument for free enterprise and the market economy. It is only meant to indicate that total penetration of the society may bring about severe crises in performance. Every mistake becomes a political mistake.

In fact, excessive penetration may become just as debilitating to performance as excessive responsiveness. In the first case the state absorbs the society but may be unable to digest it. It may be unable to bring together the various societal forces under a common policy formula. In the second case the societal forces drown the state with their demands, making it in turn impossible for the state to provide a satisfactory policy formula.

Both democracies and totalitarian/authoritarian regimes face the same prospects of decisional inefficacy but for different reasons. The first because they attempt to command the social structure, the second because they are unable to resist it.

The criteria we have just discussed provide us with the major yardsticks for evaluation of the performance of various political regimes. It is a difficult undertaking because we cannot easily find comparable data in time or space. Case studies might prove to be illuminating: for example, response by different regimes to the Great Depression of 1929; response to a threat of war and, in case of war, to defeat; the handling of crisis situations such as severe environmental problems, rapid inflation, or a shift in foreign alliances; crises of authority associated with withdrawal of supports; crises generated by increased demands and expectations; crises associated with demand for autonomy or independence of ethnic or other minorities in a multiethnic regime; and elite crisis, notably how it faces the demands of nonelite groups to share power. Unfortunately, no such case studies have been undertaken, and all we can offer (see chart on p. 268) is an overview of performance in terms of the general categories we listed. It is meant to be only suggestive.

Challenges and Transformations

A number of interacting processes affect all political regimes in varying degrees, and they account for transformations. Sometimes they are only incremental changes such as in the organization and distribution of political roles and powers and the allocation of goods and services, but sometimes they are so radical that they cause a change in the political regime itself.

International politics — how various political regimes interact with one another — is a source of transformation and yet also a major constraint to change. Nobody can discuss communist totalitarian regimes without considering their relations with the Soviet Union. In a number of cases alliances with the Soviet Union (willed or imposed) account for serious restraints to internal changes, as the case of Poland shows. In other Eastern European countries changes have been only incremental, and mostly in the direction of the market economy and flexible mechanisms that allow some individual initiatives. No changes have been made in the single-party rule or with regard to individual freedoms. Since authoritarian and military regimes supported by the Soviet Union tend to tilt toward communist single-party totalitarianism, all that is required to strengthen the single party is an infusion of communist ideology. Ethiopia has moved in this direction and other African regimes are tilting the same way.

Democratic regimes, including the United States, have not managed to impart their ideology and institutions to many of their allies. Democracy, as opposed to single-party totalitarianism, is far more difficult to export and to institutionalize. Also modernizing societies remain highly unstable and prone to statist solutions, as we pointed out. Economic and military aid given by the United States or Western democracies, notably France, often result in military rule.

Over and beyond the dominant role played by the United States and the Soviet Union, there are other forces that influence all political regimes. One is ideology — the spread of new political ideas that focus on human rights and freedoms. Regimes that fail to pay at least lip service to these ideas face many constraints in their relations with other political regimes as well as at home. South Africa is a clear case in point. Regimes that pay only lip service to new ideologies face constant criticism. Chile, Poland, Iran, Turkey, Israel, South Korea, the Philippines, France (in some of its remaining overseas possessions), Argentina, Brazil, Vietnam, the Soviet Union, and the United States are constantly exposed to criticism of their military interventions, treatment of minorities, unwillingness to make concessions to demands for autonomy and independence, waging war, or using military power. There seems to be a world opinion that is constantly monitoring the behavior of political regimes and trying to influence them. No political regime is an island unto itself.

There are also international economic forces, which are just as significant as the role ideas play. The distance between the advanced industrialized nations and backward or developing ones, and the economic inequalities between them, give to the advanced countries a leverage that can be used to shape not only their societies but the structure of their political regime as well. Military and economic power combined puts many of the new nations in a state of tutelage. Their political development often depends on the will of the wealthier nations. The modernization of their economies and their societies depends increasingly on the availability of capital, which is available only in the wealthy democracies and the Soviet Union (especially the former). The wealthier nations, therefore, can impose both economic and political conditions; the poor nations, whichever their political regimes, operate under constraint.

Beyond considerations of dependency, however, there are considerations of economic interdependence among all nations. Economic interdependencies and common markets regulate forms and patterns of economic interaction: trade, technology and technology transfers, prices of raw materials and finished goods, regularized exchanges at agreed prices, and trade relations in specific products. Authoritarian, totalitarian, and democratic regimes find themselves in constant interaction under a common umbrella of rules, regulations, and agreements that influence their behavior toward one another and often determine domestic policies.

Convergences

Authoritarian, democratic, and communist totalitarian regimes show some interesting similarities with regard to the organization of the command structure.

The growth of the executive and the civil service: In all of them the executive branch has grown in numbers and expanded the scope of its powers. We mentioned the ascendancy of the presidency and the cabinet in both presidential and parliamentary regimes. Initiative for policy making comes from the executive leadership, and delegation of powers by the legislature to the executive has been the rule in most democratic regimes. Similarly, the role of the bureaucracy, which is to implement decisions or to participate very closely in decision making, has been strengthened in most democratic regimes. The bureaucracy as an organization has grown along almost identical lines in all industrialized societies, democratic or not. There is little to separate the roles and functions of a Soviet administrator from his or her counterpart in the United States or in Brazil. They all operate under generally accepted rules, are subject to hierarchical responsibility, and are linked together under the same general precepts that guide superior-inferior relations in a bureaucratic organization.

Effacement of the legislature: As we noted, there has been a decline in the role of the legislature in all regimes, including democracies. Laws are increasingly initiated or made by the executive, the budget is prepared by the executive, and the control of the army and foreign policy is left in the hands of the executive. Even when they meet frequently, as they do in democratic regimes, the legislatures have declined as law-making and deliberative bodies. The major differences among authoritarian, totalitarian, and democratic regimes lies in the nature and the scope of debate. Legislatures continue to be powerful political debating societies (forums or arenas) in democracies (see Chapter 3), but they do not play the same role in authoritarian or in communist totalitarian regimes.

The welfare state: The role of the state in economic and welfare matters has increased everywhere. The differences between communist and democratic regimes is only one of degree. In industrialized democratic societies, for example France, over half of all industrial production is owned and managed by the state. In Italy and England the proportion is smaller. In democracies where the state has not undertaken massive nationalization, subsidies, indirect incentives, tax arrangements, supports for imports and exports, and public investment policies account for the expansion of the role of the state. A characteristic trend in democratic regimes has been the growth of social services — what we called the welfare state. Almost all democratic regimes give their citizens an appreciable part of the gross national product in the form of social services: health care, pensions, social security, education, transportation, family income and maintenance, unemployment benefits, and job retraining. As we noted, democracies have emphasized economic rights during the last half century. They are coming closer and closer to the professed goals of socialist regimes.[4]

The military: In all political regimes that we surveyed the role and the influence of the military have grown. Military dictatorships, direct or indirect, are the most blatant forms of military rule. But the military presence has also grown in other societies, including democracies. The military have resources and influence that no other group — labor, the churches, the academic community, industrial associations — possesses. Given the new technological requirements of defense, there has naturally been a close cooperation between industry and the military. The so-called military-industrial complex is not a phenomenon unique to the United States. It is quite prevalent in the Soviet Union and France and may again become quite visible in Japan and Germany. All over the world

4. Alexander J. Groth and Larry L. Wade (eds.). *Comparative Resource Allocation, Politics, Performance and Policy Priorities,* vol. 13, Sage Yearbooks in Politics and Public Policy (Beverly Hills, Calif.: Sage Publications, 1984).

military demands and needs are absorbing more and more of the national income.

Political parties: The political parties, whether under single-, two-, or multiparty systems, are in decline. As we noted, in many of the new nations and notably all over Africa the single party has atrophied. In communist regimes there are cases where the party has become either pluralized and therefore unable to mobilize and govern, as in Yugoslavia, or downright impotent, as in Poland where the army has become the major organ of governance. In the Soviet Union there are indications that the CPSU can no longer play the same mobilizing role. Its ideology seems to be waning and the problems facing the country can no longer be resolved through mass mobilization. As we noted, the problems have become increasingly administrative and technical with regard to the economy in general and agriculture in particular. But the same decline of the political party has been noticeable in most Western democracies. As with authoritarian and totalitarian regimes, democracies also seem to be in search of new ways to maintain participation and supports, ways that will bypass the political party.

In sum, confronted with the similar tasks of governance — maintaining some kind of order, resolving conflicts, and making difficult economic choices, especially on income redistribution and the production of goods and services — most industrially advanced societies develop similar mechanisms of regulation and control. There is a convergence in the structural organization of the modern state whatever the regime might be. But such a convergence does not hide the differences, which in the last analysis, are of critical importance.

Divergences

The major differences between democratic and other regimes (authoritarian or totalitarian) lie in the manner in which the relationship between society and state is structured. In communist nations, the effort continues to be to absorb the societal forces into the state and make them conform. In democracies, whatever the extent and degree of state intervention in economic and social matters, the emphasis continues to be on the separateness between the state and society. For this fundamental proposition major divergences follow.

- — If society is separate from the state, so are the individuals who comprise it.
- — Associations formed by the individuals are separate too.
- — The state and its agencies are beholden to the society for supports and ultimately responsible to it.

There are some significant institutional trends in contemporary democracies that buttress the societal forces and strengthen their autonomy vis-à-vis the state.

Decentralization: Decentralization of decision making has been noticeable not only in federal regimes but also in many unitary democracies such as England and especially, in the last few years, in France. Emphasis is put on local and regional autonomy. Local voters are allowed to make decisions on the basis of local considerations.

Functional federalism: In regimes where nationalizations of the economy — in industry, transportation, and communications — have taken place there is a functional federalism, which amounts to the devolution of powers to run and manage those activities. There is a great deal of independence from the central government. Decisions usually involve the participation of all those who work in a given enterprise and those who use its services. Functional federalism is of particular significance in broadcasting and television where every effort is made (not always satisfactorily) to detach these services from governmental controls. Special consultative and advisory bodies, often set up by the legislature, participate in decision making.

Participation: Participation is the key word today in most democracies: participation of citizens by locality, region, state service agencies, and public enterprises. Advisory and representative bodies consisting of workers, managers, clerical personnel, and users of services all share in decisions. In this way societal interests maintain their integrity and separatedness and are allowed their freedom and their say in the making of decisions.

The Judiciary: A typical trend in all democracies has been the strengthening of the judiciary to impose limitations on the state and its agencies, especially in the realm of civil and political rights. The French constitutional council has assumed greater powers vis-à-vis the executive branch and has rendered a number of decisions favoring the independence of the legislative assemblies and protecting individual freedoms, including freedom of the press. Human rights in Western Europe have found additional protection with the European Court to which all individuals, irrespective of their nationality, can appeal, sometimes against their own governments. By limiting the state, the courts maintain the safeguards that democracy provides to individuals and to the many economic, cultural, political, and religious associations.

Cultural freedoms: Autonomy and independence of action are of critical importance in cultural activities, even when the associations that perform them are directly subsidized by the state. This is notably the case with universities, schools, athletic associations, and religious organizations, especially churches. In some democracies their freedom is preserved in the name of a wall that separates them from the state (e.g., the separation between church and state in the United States) and precludes any direct or indirect state aid. In most other democracies, however, freedom is maintained even though the state provides the financial means for the existence of a church or a parochial school. In France indirect aid to the Catholic schools is plentiful but state intervention in the hiring of teachers and the selection of the curriculum is not permitted. As for universities, there is a long tradition that considers the university as an independent entity, even though virtually all universities in democracies are supported by public funds. Religion, culture, and education are, according to democratic theory, the mainsprings of individual freedoms, innovation, and participation. They continue to be safeguarded.

Self-management: With regard to the economy and industrial production, democracies (even when the state has nationalized certain sectors) allow, in the name of self-management, autonomy and freedom for those in charge to act, make decisions, and produce. The profit motive to be sure is qualified, at times seriously, but there is remuneration in the form of bonuses, special privileges, and services. Thus individual effort is encouraged in pretty much the same way as with salaried and executive personnel in big corporations in a capitalistic society. In other words, the autonomy of economic organizations is encouraged and strengthened so as to remain relatively free.

In sum, in all democracies institutional trends continue to show a marked concern for the maintenance of pluralism — the institutionalization of societal forces so that they continue to remain beyond the control of the state. Even where the state has become the major agency of production, distribution of goods, communication, transportation, and education, every effort is made to divest it *from* direct management and administration. Thus the convergence we noted between authoritarian/totalitarian and democratic regimes with regard to the command structure is offset by the differences democratic regimes show in their continuing concern with individual and associational freedoms and with the decision-making autonomy of various societal sectors, which are organized independently of the state, even when subsidized by the state. Among the most important of these freedoms is that of being allowed to oppose the government in office or setting up associations and political parties to oppose it.

Common Challenges

There are a number of common challenges that have not been surmounted by the regimes we have studied.

Peace: No political regime has as yet managed to produce a formula for peace. Big wars seem to have been avoided since World War II but little ones have mushroomed in every corner of the world, and no regime has advanced a formula for international cooperation and disarmament.

Population: The only regime that has dealt directly, and it appears successfully, with the population explosion is China. In almost all others, though in varying degrees, the growth of population remains unchecked and unplanned, putting heavy burdens on fragile national economies and the international economy as a whole.

Environment: There is no indication that any of the contemporary regimes have managed to cope with environmental waste. There have been efforts in some Scandinavian countries, in the European Common Market (but very minor ones), and in Canada (to a degree), but neither the United States nor the Soviet Union has allowed industrial considerations or defense expenditures to yield to environmental concerns. Relatedly, none of the major powers seems to have come to grips with the problems of nuclear waste.

Equitable allocations of resources: Neither democracies, nor totalitarian communist regimes, nor authoritarian ones have managed to provide for a more equitable distribution of resources in their own societies, let alone the distribution of resources in the world. Not only is our world one where there are two parts — the rich and the poor nations — but it is also one where within every regime there are "two nations" — the rich (the few) and the poor (the many). Both communist regimes and some democracies have tried to bridge the gap, but the gap continues to yawn wide.

Special Challenges

The special problems individual regimes face often mirror their special characteristics.

Freedoms and information: In the communist regimes, specifically in the Soviet Union and Eastern Europe, there are problems concerning individual freedoms such as religious and political. In the Eastern European countries, there are demands for domestic freedom and national independence. For how long can a governing elite in an age of satellite communications and video cassettes manage to inhibit the free flow of information? The more it attempts to do so, the higher the cost to the society as a whole and the weaker its legitimacy.

Economic freedoms: There is also a demand for greater economic freedoms in communist regimes, including the Soviet Union. At present such demands concern only economic efficiency and productivity, and they may be implemented, within limits, under the existing political order. But the quest for economic freedoms and economic initiatives may spill over and beyond economic considerations and combine with the demands for political and individual freedoms. At this point the fate of communist regimes will depend very much (aside from international considerations) on the attitudes of the Soviet elite. While, it remains united, it can enforce its policy. However, divisions may lead to conflicts in which either one faction will gain the upper hand and impose authoritarian controls (a return to Stalinism) or the competing factions will learn to live side by side and compromise their interests in a regime that will gradually become pluralized.

Crisis of authority: Democratic regimes face a crisis of authority and participation, a crisis produced by the openess of their political structures and institutions and by the wealth some of them have generated. Rapid economic growth has whetted the appetites of many (and also aroused their sense of justice). The principal source of crisis is the demand of the relatively poor to occupy important political roles, exercise power, and make decisions. As a result, participation and mobilization have increased and spilled over the traditional mechanisms through which they manifested themselves — they bypassed the parties, the trade unions, and the local and national agencies including the representative assemblies. In most industrialized democracies there has been a crisis of authority that has been exacerbated by the ongoing economic crisis. Will democratic regimes be capable of facing the challenge and refashioning their political institutions to provide for greater participation and a more equitable distribution of resources?

Crisis of authoritarian regimes: Authoritarian regimes are in a triple bind. They face problems of legitimization, the equitable distribution and allocation of resources, and those arising from demands for political and individual freedoms, including freedom of information and communication. The continuation of authoritarian forms is consistent, or could be made consistent, with a better and more equitable distribution of resources. Legitimization, however, requires (in the greater number of cases) new participatory mechanisms through the party or the introduction of corporatist practices, which to a certain extent can be reconciled within the authoritarian model, as the case of Mexico shows. As we pointed out, the political party may provide for some degree of participation and legitimization along corporatist lines. Authoritarian regimes, at least some of them, attempt to do so. It is the problem of freedoms — individual and political — that is the most urgent, especially the demands of excluded groups to enter the political process and play political roles, that is, to share political power and share in policy making. In this regard, the crisis of authoritarianism is endemic, and the inability to provide for participatory mechanisms may provoke mass insurrectional movements that are difficult to contain.

A Concluding Note

As political regimes in our world today attempt to find the proper means of interaction among themselves — to reshape an international order — they are all faced by common and special problems and they will have to adjust to them. The magnitude of all the problems combined raises one critical question. Can they be resolved within the structure of a political regime? Many problems transcend the confines of a single country, even very large and powerful ones like the United States and the Soviet Union. Many problems are worldwide in scope and cannot be packaged in a manner that makes a single state capable of resolving any of them. Every political regime should be viewed as a building block of a larger international edifice, but unless the blocks begin to fit, the task of building a stable international political order remains beyond reach.

The Normative Question

If there are difficulties in evaluating political regimes in terms of their performance, the difficulties of judging them in normative terms are much greater. Long ago Aristotle pointed out that the purpose of a political regime was not mere material satisfaction and mere functionality. The purpose of the state was to provide for the best possible life. In other words, what is "administered best" must also be judged in terms of what *is* best. What criteria shall we use? Freedom? Equality? Abundance? Order and protection? Justice and happiness for all? Can we agree?

All regimes, even authoritarian ones, set forth normative goals to be attained in the future. Totalitarian communist regimes and democratic regimes share by and large some of the same ultimate goals: to bring about individual freedom, to give people all the opportunities to realize themselves and their talents, and to build a world of cooperation and peace. But it is not enough to set forth the goals. A regime must infuse values into its political institutions and structures, in accord with the goals. It must give them life and meaning so that the goals become *operative*.

In both democracies and communist regimes there is considerable (at times very great) disparity between ultimate goals and operative institutions and practices. Democracies have ignored the very strong linkages between equal rights and equal opportunities on the one hand and equality of living conditions and income on the other. There is still truth in the argument that in democracies many of us are free only to be homeless and hungry. But communist totalitarian regimes have blatantly ignored the links between political and individual freedoms and the material equalities to which they are committed. Without the former, there is no guarantee that material equalities (even if they exist) can be preserved. There is no assurance that equals are free to develop their talents or participate in the political process and jointly share in the formation of common goals and common pursuits. A society of equals (in the sense of material and physical increments of wealth) may consist of persons living in a permanent state of subjection. All slaves are equal to each other!

Equality and freedom continue to remain the two major values. Regimes must be evaluated in terms of the institutions and practices they establish to implement these values, and the processes set up to attain them can give us some clues that we can observe and study. Difficult as the measurements may prove to be, they at least provide a handle for assessing performance in normative terms.

Have communist regimes increased material equality for most? Compared to what? Have they enlarged the area of individual freedoms? Compared to what? If we compare the Soviet Union or China with prerevolutionary Russia or China before the communist revolution, the answer is unhesitatingly yes. If we compare them (and this applies primarily to the Soviet Union seventy years after the revolution) to their ideology — to the goals they meant to implement — the answer is no. The same answers would be given with regard to political participation, the organization of rights and consent, and associational freedoms. While for many the ultimate goal of communism remains a beacon of hope, the achievements thus far have not brought us closer to it.

What about democracies? While they too fall short of many of the pledges explicit in democratic ideology, their operative institutions and practices show important realizations both in the realm of individual and political freedoms and also in the realm of economic well-being. Power sharing has become increasingly the rule, participation has been broadened, limitations on governance ensure some degree of individual freedoms, and the welfare state has provided for a minimal economic security for most — but severe economic inequalities still continue.

Freedom and equality, both material equality and equality of opportunity; civil order and domestic tranquility in our persons and properties; and a real opportunity for all people to work and live their lives in a society that provides rewards for their respective talents — these are the conditions that make up justice. Can political regimes be compared on the scale of justice? Which regimes provide it best? What operative ideas, institutions, and practices — not simply abstract ideological propositions — implement it? Where does justice infuse the structures, the forms, and the institutions we surveyed? Without justice, what is "administered best" may be the worst. "Kingdoms without justice, how like they are to robber-bands," wrote St. Augustine. His plea continues to challenge us all.

Appendix: Political Regimes Of Major Countries

The table on p. 280 represents an effort to classify the political regimes of the major countries of our world into the three types we discussed: — democratic, totalitarian (mostly communist), and authoritarian regimes. To a degree, all classifications distort reality. Political regimes do not always fit easily into the categories we suggest. There is a "mix," particularly in authoritarian regimes where there is often a combination of military rule and the single party. Some "democracies" are in substance authoritarian regimes operating under indirect military rule. We indicate these with a question mark. We have put them in the democratic column but with a question mark, since they are cryptomilitary democracies. Of the 122 major countries (Fascist Italy and Nazi Germany are not counted) we list, sixty are authoritarian and eighteen totalitarian; we have listed thirty-nine as democratic but twelve of them are cryptomilitary democracies. We listed five as uncertain because they face internal revolutions or foreign intervention.

Democracies		Totalitarian	Authoritarian			Uncertain
Senegal (?)	Argentina (?)	**Communist (17)**	**Dynastic (11)**	**Military (41)**		Afghanistan
Mauritius	Denmark	Mozambique	Morocco			El Salvador
Israel	Finland	Angola	Bahrain	Algeria	Central African	Nicaragua
India	Turkey (?)	Cambodia	Jordan	Egypt	Republic	South Africa
Sri Lanka	Iceland	Vietnam	Kuwait	Libya	Thailand	Lebanon
Malaysia	Norway	People's Republic	Oman	Sudan	Congo	
Philippines (?)	Sweden	of China	Qatar	Benin	Gabon	**Uncertains (5)**
Japan	United Kingdom	North Korea	Saudi Arabia	Gambia	Zaire	
Canada	Austria	Mongolia	United Emirates	Ghana	Iraq	
United States	New Zealand	Poland	Nepal	Guinea	Yemen	
Costa Rica	Australia	Czechoslovakia	Brunei	Guinea-Bissau	South Yemen	
Guatemala (?)	Belgium	Hungary	Haiti	Liberia	Bangladesh	
Honduras (?)	France	Rumania		Mali	Pakistan	
Panama (?)	The Federal Republic	Bulgaria		Mauritania	Burma	
Bolivia (?)	of Germany	Albania		Nigeria	Indonesia	
Colombia (?)	Holland	Yugoslavia	**Single Party (8)**	Sierra Leone	Republic of Korea	
Brazil (?)	Spain	People's Republic	Tunisia	Togo	Guyana	
Ecquador (?)	Portugal	of Germany	Ivory Coast	Upper Volta	Paraguay	
Peru (?)	Switzerland	USSR	Kenya	Burundi	Chile	
Venezuela	Greece	Cuba	Malawi	Ethiopia	Uruguay	
			Tanzania	Malagasay	Dominican	
Democracies (27)		**Noncommunist (1)**	Zambia	Kwanda	Republic	
Cryptomilitary		Iran (1979–)	Mexico	Somalia		
democracies			Peru	Uganda	**Total 60**	
(12)				Cameroon		
		Germany (1933–1945)				
		Italy (1922–1944)				

Index